The Pursuit of Public Journalism

THEORY, PRACTICE, AND CRITICISM

Tanni Haas

Routledge
Taylor & Francis Group
New York   London

Earlier and substantially different versions of most of the chapters in this book appeared in the following scholarly journals: Chapter 2: *Journalism: Theory, Practice & Criticism*, Volume 2, 2001; Chapter 3: *Journalism & Mass Communication Quarterly*, Volume 79, 2002; Chapter 4: *Journalism: Theory, Practice & Criticism*, Volume 7, 2006; Chapter 5: *Newspaper Research Journal*, Volume 22, 2001; Chapter 6: *Journal of Development Communication*, Volume 15, 2004; Chapter 7: *Harvard International Journal of Press/Politics*, Volume 8, 2003; Chapter 8: *Journalism Studies*, Volume 6, 2005.

Routledge
Taylor & Francis Group
270 Madison Avenue
New York, NY 10016

Routledge
Taylor & Francis Group
2 Park Square
Milton Park, Abingdon
Oxon OX14 4RN

© 2007 by Taylor & Francis Group, LLC
Routledge is an imprint of Taylor & Francis Group, an Informa business

Printed in the United States of America on acid-free paper
10 9 8 7 6 5 4 3 2 1

International Standard Book Number-13: 978-0-415-97825-5 (Softcover) 978-0-415-97824-8 (Hardcover)

Library of Congress Cataloging-in-Publication Data

Haas, Tanni.
   The pursuit of public journalism : theory, practice, and criticism / Tanni Haas.
     p. cm.
   Includes bibliographical references.
   ISBN 978-0-415-97824-8 (hardback : alk. paper) -- ISBN 978-0-415-97825-5 (pbk. : alk. paper)
   1. Journalism--Social aspects. I. Title.

PN4749.H24 2007
302.23--dc22
                                                2007004039

Visit the Taylor & Francis Web site at
http://www.taylorandfrancis.com

and the Routledge Web site at
http://www.routledge.com

The Pursuit of
Public Journalism

CONTENTS

ACKNOWLEDGMENTS

This book is but a small manifestation of the blessed support that I have enjoyed over the course of my career. I could not have given shape to my vision without Linda Steiner, my colleague and friend, who has tirelessly guided me on my intellectual journey. Her belief in me and my scholarly aspirations gave me the confidence to trust myself. Tim Gura, my chair, has taught me about the pleasure of scholarship. His passion for language, ability to make the ordinary extraordinary, and brilliant humor have breathed life and laughter into my academic experience. To both of you, it is with deep gratitude that I thank you for your unwavering mentorship. I can only hope to be the kind of teacher to others that you have been to me. President Christoph Kimmich, I gratefully thank you for awarding me the gift of time and space to write. Finally, I want to thank the person closest to my heart, my beautiful son, Milan. You are my reason for being.

ONE

THE EMERGENCE OF PUBLIC JOURNALISM

The journalistic notion known as "public journalism" is a multifaceted phenomenon. It simultaneously represents, as Jay Rosen (1995, p. v), one of public journalism's founding scholarly advocates, puts it: (1) "an *argument* [italics added] about where the press should be going," (2) "a set of *practices* [italics added] that have been tried in real-life settings," and (3) "a *movement* [italics added] of people and institutions concerned about the possibilities for reform." In this introductory chapter, I provide a broad overview and discussion of public journalism as a journalistic notion. In so doing, I touch upon many of the topics that will be explored more fully in subsequent chapters. Following Rosen's tripartite distinction, I outline public journalism's basic arguments and their historical roots, describe how public journalism manifests in practice, including examining some of the earliest and most influential public journalism initiatives, and consider the individuals and institutions most responsible for the emergence and subsequent development of public journalism as a journalistic reform movement.

I begin by outlining public journalism's basic arguments, focusing particular attention on what some of its founding scholarly and journalistic advocates—notably Jay Rosen, Davis Merritt, and Arthur Charity—have said about the relationship between journalism and democracy, how journalists should conceive of the public, and what role journalists should play in public life. Next, I trace the historical roots of these arguments from the famous debate between journalist Walter Lippman and philosopher John Dewey in the 1920s, through the reports of the Hutchins Commission on Freedom of the Press in the 1940s and 1950s and several theoretical and empirical works on deliberative democracy in the 1990s, to the much-criticized 1988 U.S. presidential election. Then, I describe how public journalism manifests in practice. After a brief overview of the practice of public journalism, I examine in more detail some of the earliest and most influential public journalism initiatives, notably those by the *Charlotte* (North Carolina) *Observer*, the Columbus, Georgia, *Ledger-Enquirer*, the Norfolk *Virginian-Pilot*, the *Wichita* (Kansas) *Eagle*, and the *Wisconsin State Journal*. Following this discussion of the theory and practice of public journalism, I consider the role played by various individuals and institutions in the emergence and subsequent development of public journalism as a journalistic reform movement, including the Kettering Foundation, Knight-Ridder, the Pew Center for Civic Journalism, the Project on Public Life and the Press, and the *Public Journalism Network*. I conclude by outlining the structure and argument of subsequent chapters.

BASIC ARGUMENTS

While public journalism, as Rosen (1995) correctly notes, needs to be understood both in terms of what has been said and done in its name, its founding scholarly and journalistic advocates—Rosen included—have arguably failed to clearly articulate public journalism as a journalistic philosophy in its own right. Indeed, one of this book's central arguments is that public journalism is in need of a guiding "public philosophy." In the next chapter, I take on the challenge of developing such a public philosophy.

Despite this general lack of theoretical development and specificity, the writings of some of public journalism's founding scholarly and journalistic advocates do contain certain broad-based arguments that help distinguish public journalism from conventional, mainstream journalism. Most fundamentally, advocates argue that public journalism is based upon the underlying assumption that journalism and democracy are intrinsically linked, if not mutually dependent. While advocates acknowledge that the practice of journalism depends upon certain democratic protections, most notably freedom from government intervention, they maintain that a genuine democracy depends upon a form of journalism that is committed to promoting active citizen participation in democratic processes (see, for example, Charity, 1995; Merritt, 1998; Rosen, 1999a). Conventional, mainstream journalism's lack of commitment to such citizen participation, advocates argue, has contributed to widespread withdrawal by citizens from democratic processes, as manifested by declining voter participation in political elections and, more generally, by declining civic participation in local community affairs. It also has contributed to declining public interest in, and perceived relevance of, journalistically mediated political information, as evidenced by declining newspaper readership. Put differently, advocates perceive contemporary society as being riven by two widening, but not irreversible, gaps: between citizens and government and between news organizations and their audiences. To help alleviate, or at least reduce, those gaps, advocates argue that journalists should see their primary responsibility as one of stimulating increased civic commitment to, and active citizen participation in, democratic processes. As Glasser and Lee (2002, p. 203) put it, "Public journalism rests on the simple but apparently controversial premise that the purpose of the press is to promote and indeed improve, and not merely report on and complain about, the quality of public or civic life." Rosen (1998, p. 54) makes a similar point, arguing that journalists should "help *form* [italics added] as well as *inform* [italics added] the public."

While advocates maintain that journalism's primary responsibility is to promote active citizen participation in democratic processes, they have failed to make clear which particular form(s) of democracy journalism should help promote. In one of the only explicit, but still exceedingly vague, statements on this topic, Merritt (1998, p. 142) merely notes that public journalism "does not seek to join with or substitute itself for government....[I]t seeks to keep citizens in effective contact with the governing process." Despite this lack of theoretical specificity, the actual practice of public journalism suggests that its newsroom practitioners are committed to a form of deliberative democracy that combines features of representative and direct-participatory democracy. More specifically, newsroom practitioners appear to be committed to a form of deliberative democracy in which government officials are held accountable to the citizenry and in which the citizenry actively participates in local community affairs.

While news organizations practicing public journalism, as I will subsequently describe in more detail, have done much to challenge prevailing election reporting practices—for example, by focusing their coverage on problems of concern to voters rather than on the campaign agendas of candidates for office, soliciting voter-generated questions about what the candidates are planning to do to address those problems and publicizing candidates' responses, and organizing various voter-candidate encounters—news organizations have also done much to promote active citizen participation in local community affairs; for example, by focusing their coverage on problems of concern to local residents, elaborating on what residents themselves can do to address those problems, and sponsoring various temporary and more permanent sites for deliberation and problem-solving, including roundtable discussions, town hall meetings, and local civic organizations. In the next chapter, I return to the question of which form(s) of democracy journalism should help promote by articulating a problem-solving model for public journalism. Specifically, I argue that, rather than casting this question as a choice between representative and direct-participatory forms of democracy, journalists should carefully consider (in a contextually sensitive manner) which kinds of intervention—governmental or citizen-based—would best help address given problems under investigation.

Aside from failing to make clear which form(s) of democracy journalism should help promote, advocates have neglected to consider how journalists should conceive of public discourse. While the public journalism literature abounds with references to journalists' responsibility for facilitating public discourse, it is unclear whether journalists should conceive of public discourse as "face-to-face dialogue" and/or as "mass-mediated deliberation." Although the actual practice of public journalism, as noted above, shows that both are integral to journalists' work, advocates have not make clear what the proper relationship is between them. Again, in one of the only explicit, but still exceedingly vague, statements on this topic, Merritt (1998, p. 97) merely notes that public journalism depends upon journalists' "ability and willingness to provide relevant information and a place for that information to be discussed and turned into democratic consent." This lack of specificity also manifests itself, as I shortly discuss in more detail, in advocates' references to contrasting conceptions of public discourse found in the theoretical literature on deliberative democracy.

To help further a deliberative democracy, whether understood in representative and/or direct-participatory terms, advocates argue that journalists would need to change the ways in which they traditionally have conceived of the public and of their own role in public life. Instead of perceiving the public as "thrill-seeking spectators" (Rosen, 1996, p. 49) who only attend to the news to be entertained by the political spectacle, or even as "consumers" (Merritt, 1998, p. 140) who attend to the news to be informed about the deliberations and actions of government officials, experts, and other elite actors, journalists should perceive of the public as engaged and responsible "citizens" (Charity, 1995, p. 12) who are interested in and capable of active democratic participation. These and countless other similar statements in the public journalism literature mirror Carey's (1987, p. 14) often-cited argument that the public "will begin to reawaken when they are addressed as conversational partners and are encouraged to join the talk rather than sit passively as spectators before a discussion conducted by journalists and experts." Implicit in this argument is the claim that conventional, mainstream journalism's tendency to focus election reporting on campaign-managed events, candidates' strategies and image-management techniques, and whose-ahead-and-whose-behind horse race polls, and, more generally, scandal-ridden news coverage, positions the public as mere spectators to a political spectacle. At best, conventional, mainstream journalism's efforts to inform the public about elite deliberations and actions suggest that the democratic process is one in which the public itself need not be actively involved. While public journalism's founding scholarly and journalistic advocates have done little to theorize the nature of the public beyond arguing that journalists should perceive the public as active participants in, as opposed to passive spectators to, democratic processes, there has been some subsequent scholarly debate about whether public journalism's understanding of the public should be embedded within a communitarian or a liberal democratic framework. In the next chapter, I take issue with both of these possibilities as well as outline a third, arguably more viable, option: Habermas's (1989) proceduralist-discursive notion of the "deliberating public."

Second, and equally important, advocates argue that journalists would need to reconceive their own role in public life. Instead of perceiving themselves as disinterested (or neutral) observers who occupy a privileged position above, or detached from, citizens and their particular concerns, journalists should perceive themselves as "political actors" (Rosen, 1996, p. 22) or "fair-minded participants" (Merritt, 1998, p. 7) who care about whether public life goes well. As Rosen (1996, p. 63) puts it, "If journalists are to have any sort of critical voice or challenging role within a community, they must live in some fashion as members of that community. The force of their reporting will originate not in the distance they keep but in the connection they make to the real aspirations and daily struggles of the people they report on." Indeed, Rosen (1996, p. 6) argues that journalists should acknowledge that journalism represents a "political institution [that] has a legitimate stake in whether politics works for all or becomes the professional playground of a privileged few." Implicit in this argument is the claim that the increasing professionalization of journalism, with its virtually exclusive focus on the agendas and perspectives of elite actors, has distanced journalists from the concerns of ordinary citizens.

Ironically, despite advocates' call for journalists to acknowledge, as Rosen (1996, p. 22) puts it, that they are "political actors," advocates have spent more energy delineating what journalists should not—as opposed to should—do in the interest of remaining politically neutral. Specifically, advocates have argued, as I discuss in more detail in the next chapter, that journalists should be concerned with the processes, but not with the outcomes, of citizen deliberation; refrain from endorsing particular politicians, candidates for office, and political proposals; and avoid partnering with special interest groups that seek to further particular political interests. Taking issue with these and other stipulations, I argue that, under conditions of widespread social inequality, journalists should be concerned with whether both the processes and outcomes of citizen deliberation serve the interests of marginalized social groups; endorse politicians, candidates for office, and political proposals that would promote those interests; and partner with special interest groups that seek to further their particular interests.

HISTORICAL ROOTS

Although public journalism is a relatively recent journalistic notion, with scholarly and journalistic writings on this topic dating back to the early 1990s, its basic arguments have deep historical roots. Beginning with the famous debate between journalist Walter Lippmann and philosopher John Dewey in the 1920s, scholars trace public journalism's underpinnings to the reports of the Hutchins Commission on Freedom of the Press in the 1940s and 1950s as well as to several theoretical and empirical works on deliberative democracy in the 1990s.

Public journalism advocates' central arguments that journalists should perceive citizens as active participants in, as opposed to passive spectators to, democratic processes as well as assume a more proactive role in public life themselves can be traced back historically to the Progressive Era and, more precisely, to the 1920s debate between Walter Lippmann and John Dewey about the role and responsibility of journalism in a democratic society. In *Public Opinion* and *The Phantom Public*, Lippmann (1922, 1925) argued that the political problems of modern society are of a scale and complexity that make it impossible for citizens to participate actively in its governance. At best, citizens would be able to elect political leaders who, with the help of well-informed experts, could communicate the results of their deliberations and actions through journalists to the citizenry. Journalism's primary responsibility, Lippmann thus argued, is to translate the technical deliberations and actions of political leaders and experts into a publicly accessible language to inform, as best as possible, a citizenry incapable of governing itself.

In *The Public and Its Problems*, Dewey (1927) took issue with Lippmann's (1922, 1925) elitist (or expert-based) model of democracy by calling for a more involved citizenry via a more active role for journalism. Dewey argued that the modern means of mass communication, notably the daily newspaper, offer an unprecedented opportunity for journalists to help bring a deliberative public into being. The daily newspaper, Dewey emphasized, provided the opportunity to widen the arena of learning by educating the public about political problems, helping form the public by reporting on the connections between political decisions and their consequences, and assisting the public with acting on its understandings. Thus, Dewey concluded, modern means of mass communication offer the possibility of creating a "great community" where the public can both learn about and actively participate in democratic governance. For Dewey, as for public journalism's founding scholarly and journalistic advocates, democracy represents, as Glasser and Craft (1998, p. 207) put it, "a way of life and not merely...a form of government." (For references to the importance of Dewey's work to public journalism, see, for example, Bybee, 1999; Coleman, 1997; Perry, 2003.)

The Lippmann–Dewey debate was revived in large part by the late Professor James Carey of Columbia University, whose works, in turn, inspired some of public journalism's founding scholarly and journalistic advocates, including Professor Jay Rosen of New York University and former editor of the *Wichita Eagle* Davis Merritt. Indeed, Rosen (1999b, p. 24) has gone as far as to state that "the world's shortest definition of public journalism is actually three words: 'what Dewey meant.'" In a series of articles widely cited in the public journalism literature and circulated among its newsroom practitioners, Carey argued that, if journalists were to help stimulate citizens to participate more actively in democratic processes, they would need to move from a Lippmannesque "journalism of information" to a Deweyan "journalism of conversation" (see Carey, 1987, 1993, 1995). That is, instead of perceiving themselves as disseminators of "expert information," journalists should perceive themselves as facilitators of "public conversation."

The democratic ideals underlying Dewey's (1927) vision were brought to bear more directly on journalism in the works of the Hutchins Commission on Freedom of the Press. In its report *A Free and Responsible Press*, the Hutchins Commission (1947, pp. 21–28) concluded that journalism should: (1) "provide a truthful, comprehensive and intelligent account of the day's events in a context which gives them meaning," (2) "serve as a forum for the exchange of comment and criticism," (3) "project a representative picture of the constituent groups in society," (4) "be responsible for the presentation and clarification of the goals and values of society," and (5) "provide full access to the day's intelligence." These ideals, which subsequently were summarized by three of the Hutchins Commission's members as the "social responsibility theory" of the press in the report *Four Theories of the Press* (see Siebert, Peterson, & Schramm, 1956), can, as many scholars have noted, be seen to undergird public journalism advocates' arguments about journalists' responsibilities vis-à-vis the public (see, for example, Gunaratne, 1998; Lambeth, 1998; Delli Carpini, 2005). Aside from these early historical influences, several theoretical and empirical works on deliberative democracy published in the 1990s—notably those by James Fishkin, Daniel Yankelovitch, Richard Harwood, and Robert Putnam—have had a strong impact on public journalism's founding scholarly and journalistic advocates.

Advocates' understanding of what constitutes genuine public discourse owes much to the influence of the theoretical works of James Fishkin and Daniel Yankelovitch. In *Democracy and Deliberation*, Fishkin (1991) outlined a proposal for how a more direct-participatory form of democracy could be furthered within large-scale, complex societies. In explicit opposition to conventional public opinion polls, Fishkin advocated the development of so-called deliberative opinion polls in which statistically representative, random samples of citizens would be brought together and offered opportunities to deliberate, both in small groups and as a plenum, about given political problems over an extended period of time. Such deliberative opinion polls, which subsequently have been implemented numerous times both in the United States and abroad, would thus "provide the possibility of recreating the conditions of the face-to-face society in a manner that serves democracy in the large nation-state" (Fishkin, 1991, pp. 92–93).

In contrast to Fishkin's (1991) "dialogical" conception of public discourse, with its emphasis on facilitating actual face-to-face dialogue among groups of citizens, Yankelovitch (1991) outlined in *Coming to Public Judgment* an explicitly "deliberative" conception of public discourse. Instead of merely informing the public about given political problems, Yankelovitch argued that journalists should help form the public by guiding individual citizens through a three-step process that involves: (1) raising citizens' "awareness" that a problem exists and must be resolved; (2) helping citizens "work through" the problem by formulating choices, articulating the competing core values underlying those choices, and examining the consequences of each choice; and (3) bringing about "public judgment" as to how the problem should be resolved. Public judgment, or the point at which actual resolution of a problem occurs, thus represents "the state of highly developed public opinion that exists once people have engaged an issue, considered it from all sides, and accepted the full consequences of the choices they make" (Yankelovitch, 1991, p. 6).

While public journalism's founding scholarly and journalistic advocates cite Fishkin's (1991) and Yankelovitch's (1991) contrasting conceptions of public discourse approvingly—sometimes even within the same works (see Charity, 1995; Lambeth, 1998; Rosen, 1994)—none have elaborated on whether journalists should conceive of public discourse in dialogical and/or deliberative terms and, as previously mentioned, on what the proper relationship is between these two forms of public discourse. I return to these important questions in the next chapter where I argue that public discourse is best understood—and furthered—in terms of a dialectic interplay between "face-to-face dialogue" and "mass-mediated deliberation."

Finally, but not least importantly, public journalism advocates' emphasis on inspiring citizens to participate more actively in the civic affairs of their local communities has been animated in large part by the findings of two empirical works on deliberative democracy by Richard Harwood and Robert Putnam, respectively. In *Citizens and Politics*, Harwood (1991) found, based on focus group discussions with samples of citizens in 10 U.S. cities, that the then-prevailing assumption that citizens are not interested in politics and do not want to participate actively in public life is incorrect. Rather, Harwood found, citizens feel excluded from virtually every area of public life by a closed political system and cannot envision any meaningful political role for them. Citizens are, however, involved in the civic affairs of their local communities, but only when they believe that such involvement can bring about genuine change. Thus, Harwood concluded, journalists should reorient their news reporting from a focus on elite deliberations and actions to a focus on the problems of concern to citizens while at the same time help create spaces where citizens can deliberate about and act upon those problems themselves. Like Harwood, Putnam (1995) documented, in *Bowling Alone*, a long-term decline in civic participation in local community affairs and, more generally, that citizens have become suspicious of one another as they tend to interact less and less in public settings. To counteract the increasing disappearance of a vibrant civic and public life, Putnam called for the development of "social capital," which he defined as "features of social organization such as networks, norms, and social trust that facilitate coordination and cooperation for mutual benefit" (p. 67). (For references to the importance of Harwood's and Putnam's work to public journalism, see, for example, Charity, 1995; Rosen, 1999a; Sirianni & Friedland, 2001.)

If public journalism advocates' basic arguments, as outlined above, have deep historical roots, the most immediate context for the emergence of public journalism was the much-criticized 1988 U.S. presidential election featuring republican George Herbert Bush and democrat Michael Dukakis. Numerous observers note that this election represented an all-time low. While the news coverage focused overwhelmingly on the candidates' personalities, strategies and tactics, and whose-ahead-and-whose-behind horse race polls, the candidates themselves used simplistic image-management techniques to appeal to voters, as exemplified by television advertisements featuring Mr. Bush's visits to flag factories to show his patriotism and Mr. Dukakis climbing aboard a tank to signify his tough stance on defense policy. Following the election, scholarly and journalistic observers alike, many of whom subsequently became advocates of public journalism, called for radical changes in election reporting, notably, a move away from coverage of candidate strategies and tactics to a focus on substantive policy issues of concern to voters (see, for example, Fallows, 1996; Merritt, 1988; Rosen, 1991).

PRACTICAL MANIFESTATIONS

While much has been said (and continues to be said) in the name of public journalism, this journalistic notion is arguably defined more by how it manifests in practice. Indeed, in contrast to its founding scholarly and journalistic advocates' rather general, if not vague, pronunciations about what public journalism is and should be, its actual newsroom practitioners have engaged in a variety of practices that are clearly different from those of conventional, mainstream journalism. Here, I provide a brief overview of the practice of public journalism, followed by a more detailed description of some of the earliest and most influential public journalism initiatives.

As a domain of journalistic practice, public journalism is best understood as a series of experiments that emerged within the mainstream news media in the United States in the late 1980s and early 1990s. Since 1988, when the first public journalism initiative was launched by the Columbus, Georgia, *Ledger-Enquirer*, an initiative I describe in more detail below, more than 600 such initiatives have been carried out across the United States and abroad (see Friedland & Nichols, 2002; Mwangi, 2001). While many television and radio stations, both public and commercial, have been involved with public journalism (see Dinges, 2000; Potter & Kurpius, 2000), the vast majority of initiatives have been conducted by newspapers. Indeed, Friedland and Nichols (2002) found that more than 300 daily newspapers, or about one fifth of all daily newspapers in the United States, have been involved with one or more public journalism initiatives. Similarly, while most of these initiatives have been carried out by individual newspapers, more than 160, or about one quarter of all initiatives conducted to date, have included multiple-media partnerships between newspapers, television, and radio stations (Friedland & Nichols, 2002).

While the public journalism initiatives carried out to date exhibit a variety of characteristics, these initiatives can usefully be grouped within three overarching categories: (1) election initiatives, (2) special reporting projects, and (3) efforts to make public journalism an integral part of routine information-gathering, news-reporting, and performance-evaluation practices. During local and national elections, news organizations practicing public journalism have made efforts to focus their reporting on problems of concern to voters rather than on the campaign agendas of candidates for office. This has been accomplished by identifying voter concerns through telephone surveys, in-depth interviews, and focus group discussions; elaborating on voters' opinions and where they differ from those of candidates; soliciting voter-generated questions to the candidates and publicizing candidates' answers; facilitating actual social interaction between voters and candidates in the form of town hall meetings; and reporting back on the outcomes of such voter-candidate encounters.

Although such election initiatives represent one of the earliest and most visible manifestations of public journalism's practice, they only account for about 10% of the initiatives conducted to date (Friedland & Nichols, 2002). Indeed, the vast majority of initiatives have taken the form of special reporting projects on problems of concern to residents of given communities. Since the early 1990s, news organizations practicing public journalism have engaged in an astonishing variety of short-term and long-term reporting projects on such problems as racism, educational inequality, and poverty, among numerous others. As in the case of election initiatives, news organizations have used various information-gathering methods to identify problems of concern to local residents; reported on those problems from the perspectives of residents rather than local government officials, experts, and other elite actors; offered residents opportunities to articulate and debate their opinions; elaborated on what residents themselves can do to address given problems in practice; and helped organize sites for deliberation and problem-solving in the form of roundtable discussions, community forums, and local civic organizations.

Aside from these project-based initiatives, many news organizations have taken steps to make public journalism an integral part of their routine information-gathering, news-reporting, and performance-evaluation practices. While some news organizations have restructured their newsrooms from conventional beat systems revolving around certain institutional sources of information to include multiple geographically-based or topic-based teams focusing on specific neighborhoods or problems of concern to local residents, many more news organizations have made it a routine part of their news operations to meet up with groups of residents on a regular basis to discuss which problems they would like to see covered, report on those problems, and subsequently invite residents to evaluate their coverage.

Having outlined the practice of public journalism in broad strokes, it might be useful to consider some of the earliest and most influential public journalism initiatives. The very first initiative, as noted above, was carried out by the Columbus, Georgia, *Ledger-Enquirer* in 1988. Based on a telephone survey with local residents as well as in-depth interviews with residents, local government officials, and academic experts, the *Ledger-Enquirer* published an eight-part series called "Columbus Beyond 2000," which examined various challenges facing the city, including a faltering school system, low wages, and transportation problems. When the series failed to draw the attention of local residents, Jack Swift, the newspaper's editor at the time, took the then-unusual step of organizing a town hall meeting to discuss these and other problems of concern to residents. Three hundred residents showed up for the 6-hour meeting. Shortly thereafter, Mr. Swift helped establish a new civic organization, United Beyond 2000, to follow up on the problems discussed at the meeting. Led by a 13-member steering committee, which included Jack Swift himself, the organization was divided into various smaller task forces responsible for addressing particular problems, including employment, health care, and race relations (see, for example, Charity, 1995; Rosen, 1991; Waddell, 1997).

The *Ledger-Enquirer*'s efforts to take the problems examined beyond the news pages and into the community have, as previously mentioned, become one of the distinguishing characteristics of the practice of public journalism. Numerous other news organizations have helped establish temporary sites for citizen deliberation and problem-solving, such as roundtable discussions, community forums, and town hall meetings, or more permanent sites, such as local civic organizations. Indeed, like the "Columbus Beyond 2000" series, some of the most widely acclaimed public journalism initiatives began as relatively modest newspaper series. As I describe in more detail in chapter 5, the *Akron* (Ohio) *Beacon Journal*'s Pulitzer Prize–winning race relations project "A Question of Color" began as a series of articles whose sole aim was to examine various race-related problems confronting the city of Akron. When the first installment of the five-part series failed to draw the attention of local residents, the *Beacon Journal* decided to broaden the scope of the project by hiring two facilitators who were charged with bringing local civic organizations together to improve race relations. Subsequently, the *Beacon Journal* helped establish a new civic organization. The "Coming Together Project," which still exists today, sponsors various activities for participating member organizations, middle and high school students, and the city at large.

While the *Ledger-Enquirer*'s efforts to involve local residents more actively in community affairs were subsequently lauded by James Batten, then-CEO of its corporate owner Knight-Ridder, a major newspaper chain, who named Jack Swift 1989-1990 "Editor-of-the-Year," the "Columbus Beyond 2000" series was very controversial. Indeed, Mr. Swift was widely criticized, including among his own newsroom staff, for assuming a too-activist stance vis-à-vis the local community, notably by serving on the steering committee of United Beyond 2000. Two subsequent public journalism initiatives by the *Wichita* (Kansas) *Eagle*—the 1990 "Your Vote Counts" and the 1992 "People Project"—have had a more lasting impact on the practice of public journalism.

Following the widely criticized news coverage of the 1988 U.S. presidential election, the *Wichita Eagle* decided to take a different approach to its coverage of the 1990 gubernatorial election in Kansas. Instead of reporting the daily events along the campaign trail and what the candidates were doing to win votes, the *Eagle* decided to cover the election from the perspectives of voters. Based on a telephone survey, the *Eagle* identified 10 topics that voters would like to see covered. Each topic subsequently became the subject of an in-depth article in the Sunday edition and was regularly charted in "Where They Stand," a weekly feature that summarized the candidates' positions on the topic and that reported on what, if anything, the candidates had said about the topic during the preceding week. In 1992, the *Eagle* broadened its new approach to news coverage on aspects of public life not directly related to election reporting. Based on almost 200 in-depth interviews with local residents, the *Eagle* launched, in collaboration with two local television (KSNW-TV) and radio (KNSS Radio) stations, a 10-week-long series called "The People Project," which focused on various problems of concern to residents, including crime, education, and health care. Each problem became the subject of one or more articles that included suggestions to what local residents could do to address the problem, outlined what local residents had already done to address it, and contained comprehensive lists called "Places to Start," with the names, addresses, and telephone numbers of local civic organizations working on the problem (see, for example, Charity, 1995; Merritt, 1998; Rosen, 1996).

Like the *Wichita Eagle*, numerous other news organizations have, as previously mentioned, engaged in election initiatives and special reporting projects aimed at involving citizens more actively in given problems under examination. Indeed, as I describe in more detail in chapter 3, empirical research shows that, compared to mainstream news organizations more generally, news organizations practicing public journalism tend to carry more election-related mobilizing information, such as information on how to register to vote and where to go to cast one's ballot, as well as more information on how to become involved in local, community-based interventions, such as by including contact information for local civic organizations.

While the "People Project" was conceived and carried out as a collaboration between a newspaper, a television station, and a radio station, this was not the first public-journalism–inspired multiple-media partnership. Since 1991, a large consortium of newspapers, television, and radio stations, led by the *Wisconsin State Journal*, Wisconsin Public Television, and Wisconsin Public Radio, has been involved with a series of initiatives known collectively as the "We the People" project in Madison, Wisconsin. The "We the People" project is noteworthy not only because it represents the earliest and longest lasting of the many multiple-media partnerships that have been formed to date (it exists to this day), but also because it has reversed the roles played by citizens and elite actors in most other public journalism initiatives. Instead of encouraging citizens to take part in local, community-based interventions while relegating the development of more broad-based, systemic solutions to problems to experts, the "We the People" project has encouraged citizens to develop systemic solutions to problems themselves. Since the early 1990s, the project partners have sponsored various so-called civic exercises. These have included mock legislative panels in which local residents, either on their own or after having received testimony from state legislators, would develop detailed political proposals for reform of property taxes and the state's health care system as well as proposals on how to balance the state's budget and address the federal budget deficit. These civic exercises, which have been broadcast live on Wisconsin Public Television and accompanied by extensive coverage in the *Wisconsin State Journal* and on talk shows on Wisconsin Public Radio, have always been preceded by more extensive deliberations, up to as many as six town hall meetings, on the particular problems in question (see, for example, Friedland, 2003; Friedland, Sotirovic, & Daily, 1998; Sirianni & Friedland, 2001).

Although these civic exercises have reversed the roles played by citizens and elite actors in most other public journalism initiatives, their primary goal has been simply to teach citizens how to grapple with complex political problems. Their purpose has not been to provide input into formal political decision-making processes, but rather to help form public opinion in a more informed and deliberative manner. In chapter 6, I outline a deliberative method known as the "consensus conference model" whereby news organizations could engage citizens and experts more interactively and equitably in the search for systemic solutions to problems while at the same time involve government officials in the process of actually implementing those solutions in practice.

If the "We the People" project was the first of many public-journalism–inspired multiple-media partnerships, the *Charlotte* (North Carolina) *Observer* was the first news organization to make public journalism an integral part of its news operation. Following its widely acclaimed 1992 "Your Voice, Your Vote" election initiative, the *Observer* launched in 1994, in collaboration with a local television station (WSOC-TV) and two local radio stations (WBAV-FM and WPEG-FM), an 18-month-long special reporting project called "Taking Back Our Neighborhoods." Based on a review of local crime statistics, the *Observer* identified the 10 inner-city neighborhoods with the highest crime rates. Subsequently, the *Observer* convened neighborhood advisory panels consisting of local residents and community leaders to help guide its reporting, devoted in-depth coverage to the particular problems facing each neighborhood and the reasons for those problems, and organized town hall meetings where local residents and community leaders could discuss those problems among themselves (see, for example, Charity, 1995; Friedland, 2000; Iggers, 1998).

One of the most important structural outcomes of the "Taking Back Our Neighborhoods" initiative was the reorganization of the newsroom from a conventional beat system revolving around certain institutional sources of information to include multiple geographically-based teams focusing on specific neighborhoods. Like the *Charlotte Observer*, some news organizations have, as previously mentioned, made public journalism an integral part of their newsroom operations by reorganizing their newsrooms around geographically-based or, more commonly, topic-based teams. These include such newspapers as the Columbia, South Carolina, *State*; the *St. Louis* (Missouri) *Post-Dispatch*; and the *St. Paul* (Minnesota) *Pioneer Press*. Moreover, as I describe in more detail in chapter 7, many non-U.S. news organizations have made public journalism an integral part of their news operations, such as by establishing mobile newsrooms that travel to different cities to identify problems of concern to local residents; devoting articles, and at times entire sections, to reporting on those concerns; and meeting up with groups of local residents on a regular basis to receive feedback on coverage.

While many news organizations both in the United States and abroad have made citizen concerns the focus of their information-gathering, news-reporting, and performance-evaluation practices, few have gone as far as the Norfolk *Virginian-Pilot*. Aside from reorganizing its newsroom from a conventional beat system to include multiple topic–based teams and holding regular meetings with groups of local residents, the *Pilot* featured, from 1997 to 2001, three kinds of so-called civic life pages, titled respectively "Public Life," "Public Safety," and "Education," which appeared three times a week in the Metro section. These pages were centered around the three middle columns, which included an in-depth article on a local political problem. While the left column explained which actions local government officials had taken or were planning to take to address the problem, the right column outlined what local residents themselves could do to address the problem; for example, by including web site addresses for local civic organizations working on the problem in question and describing what local residents in other cities had done to address similar problems (see, for example, Friedland, 2003; Sirianni & Friedland, 2001; Warhover, 2000).

Like the *Virginian-Pilot*, several other news organizations have experimented with alternative ways of reporting the news. One of the most innovative initiatives is that of the *Colorado Springs Gazette*. In recent years, the *Gazette* has been shifting from conventional balanced accounts in which each article contrasts two or more conflicting perspectives to producing multiple stories on given topics, each written from the perspective of a certain key public. This experiment in "civic framing," as former editor Steven Smith calls it, was first implemented in 1996 when the *Gazette* covered an upcoming vote on a proposed increase in property taxes for local public schools. Instead of producing one major article, Mr. Smith asked two reporters to cover the same story from the perspectives of four different key publics (residents with children in public schools; teachers; students and recent graduates; and residents without children in public schools). Each article, which ran on consecutive days leading up to the vote, was prefaced by an editor's note explaining from whose perspective the article was reported (see Rosen, 1999a).

While the vast majority of the public journalism initiatives conducted to date have been local in orientation, there have been efforts to carry out initiatives of a national scope. In contrast to most local initiatives, these initiatives have been led by public radio and television. Indeed, both National Public Radio (NPR) and the Public Broadcasting Service (PBS) have been involved with public journalism. Since 1994, NPR and PBS have carried out a number of election initiatives, both on their own and as joint projects. During local and national elections, NPR and PBS, in collaboration with local newspapers as well as commercial television and radio stations, have conducted telephone surveys, in-depth interviews, and focus group discussions to identify problems of particular concern to voters; sponsored and broadcast debates where voters discussed those problems among themselves; and staged voter-candidate encounters where candidates responded to voter-generated questions (see, for example, Charity, 1995; Dinges, 2000; Sirianni & Friedland, 2001).

SOURCES OF INDIVIDUAL AND INSTITUTIONAL SUPPORT

If public journalism's early newsroom practitioners helped manifest in practice what its founding scholarly and journalistic advocates had envisioned, a number of individuals and institutions helped ensure that public journalism was going to become, as one prominent sociologist–historian puts it, "the best organized social movement inside journalism in the history of the American press" (Schudson, 1999, p. 118). Drawing on a number of scholarly sources (see Nichols, 2004; Rosen, 1999a; Sirianni & Friedland, 2001) as well as my own personal experiences, I briefly outline here the role played by various individuals and institutions in the emergence and subsequent development of public journalism as a journalistic reform movement.

The history of public journalism as a journalistic reform movement can be traced back to 1987 when James Batten, then-CEO of Knight-Ridder, instituted a company-wide initiative known as "Community Connectedness," which was aimed at strengthening the relationship between its newspapers and their local communities. When Mr. Batten, as mentioned earlier, learned of Jack Swift's efforts to involve local residents more actively in community affairs through the "Columbus Beyond 2000" initiative, he appointed him "Editor-of-the-Year," thereby indicating that those efforts were representative of what he had in mind. Indeed, many of public journalism's earliest newsroom practitioners, including the *Akron Beacon Journal*; the *Charlotte Observer*; the Columbia, South Carolina, *State*; and the *Wichita Eagle*, were and remain owned by Knight-Ridder.

At the same time as he was being lauded for his efforts, Jack Swift contacted the Kettering Foundation, a non-profit foundation working to strengthen democracy in the United States and abroad, which, in turn, brought him into contact with Professor Jay Rosen of New York University. Both Jay Rosen and the Kettering Foundation were to play key roles in the development of public journalism as a journalistic reform movement. Aside from influencing the nascent movement through his own writings, which were and remain widely circulated among public journalism's newsroom practitioners, Jay Rosen helped establish, through a grant from the John S. and James L. Knight Foundation, a non-profit organization working to promote journalistic excellence, the Project on Public Life and the Press at New York University. Led by Jay Rosen and Lisa Austin, a former journalist from the *Wichita Eagle*, the Project on Public Life and the Press, which was in operation from 1993 to 1997, documented the early experiments in public journalism and organized four yearly seminars at the American Press Institute, a journalism training and research institute, where prominent journalism scholars and practicing journalists, including the late James Carey and Davis Merritt, discussed what journalism could do to inspire more active citizen participation in democratic processes. Similarly, since the early 1990s, the Kettering Foundation has helped support public journalism by publishing books by some of its founding scholarly and journalistic advocates and by awarding resident fellowships to journalism scholars and practicing journalists from around the world interested in learning more about the movement.

In 1993, the Project on Public Life and the Press was joined by the Pew Center for Civic Journalism, funded by the Pew Charitable Trusts, a major non-profit foundation working to strengthen public life in the United States. A decade-long initiative set in motion by Ed Fouhy, a nationally renowned former CBS producer and its first president, and Jan Schaffer, a Pulitzer Prize–winning editor from the *Philadelphia Inquirer* who became president when Ed Fouhy stepped down in 1998, the Pew Center for Civic Journalism emerged as the most important institutional vehicle for the public journalism movement. From 1993 to 2003, the Pew Center for Civic Journalism supported the movement by organizing numerous workshops for editors and reporters interested in learning more about public journalism; funding more than 120 newsroom experiments in public journalism; recognizing and publicizing the most innovative of those experiments through its "James K. Batten Awards for Excellence in Civic Journalism"; engaging in extensive publication and outreach efforts, notably through its quarterly "Civic Catalyst" newsletter and various publications on the theory and practice of public journalism; sponsoring empirical research on public journalism's performance; and maintaining a comprehensive archive of newsroom experiments in public journalism submitted to it for recognition and/or advice (now housed at the Wisconsin Historical Society).

In addition to these efforts, the Pew Center for Civic Journalism complemented the work of the Project on Public Life and the Press by reaching out to commercial television and radio stations, including by funding numerous multiple-media partnerships between newspapers, television, and radio stations and by establishing contacts with and workshops for news directors, producers, and reporters at National Public Radio and the Public Broadcasting Service. Finally, but not least importantly, the Pew Center for Civic Journalism was an early supporter of the Civic Journalism Interest Group (subsequently renamed the Civic and Citizen Journalism Interest Group in 2006) of the Association for Education in Journalism and Mass Communication. This interest group, which was established in 1994, remains one of the most important sites for journalism scholars, educators, and practicing journalists to discuss the theory, practice, and teaching of public journalism.

Since the Pew Center for Civic Journalism closed down in 2003, much of its work has been continued by the *Public Journalism Network*, a global professional association of journalism scholars, educators, and practicing journalists committed to public journalism. Led by Professor Leonard Witt of Kennesaw State University in Georgia, who holds an endowed chair in public journalism, the *Public Journalism Network* cosponsors various workshops in collaboration with the Civic and Citizen Journalism Interest Group, produces publications on the theory and practice of public journalism, serves as a forum for the sharing of curricular and instructional innovations in the teaching of public journalism, and maintains a weblog with continuously updated information about public journalism initiatives around the world.

STRUCTURE OF THE BOOK

Having described public journalism's basic arguments and their historical roots, how public journalism manifests in practice, and some of the individuals and institutions responsible for the emergence and subsequent development of public journalism as a journalistic reform movement, it might be useful to briefly outline the structure and argument of subsequent chapters. In chapter 2, I articulate a guiding "public philosophy" for public journalism by addressing three fundamental questions: (1) how journalists should conceive of the public, (2) what forms of public deliberation and problem-solving journalists should help promote, and (3) how journalists, as a matter of practice, should facilitate public discourse. Drawing on Habermas's (1989) theory of the public sphere and Fraser's (1990) critique thereof, as well as the writings of various public journalism scholars, I argue, among many other issues, that journalists should conceive of citizens as members of a deliberating public committed to common deliberation, promote public deliberation and problem-solving that serves the overarching goal of reducing social inequality among dominant and subordinate social groups, and facilitate a form of public discourse that combines the strength of face-to-face dialogue and mass-mediated deliberation.

Following this broad-based, theoretical discussion of wherein the "publicness" of public journalism ought to reside, I summarize, in chapter 3, the empirical research literature on public journalism. Focusing on the three most prevalent research concerns—mainstream journalists' attitudes toward public journalism, differences in the news coverage of news organizations practicing public journalism and mainstream news organizations more generally, and the impact of public-journalism-inspired news coverage on citizens—I show that mainstream journalists are positively disposed toward many, but not all, of the practices associated with public journalism, that public-journalism–inspired news coverage differs from that of conventional, mainstream journalism in many important respects, and that such news coverage has a positive impact on the civic knowledge, attitudes, and behaviors of citizens. I also discuss methodological shortcomings in some of the studies reviewed, notably problems relating to conceptualization, measurement, and interpretation, and offer suggestions to how future research could broaden the substantive scope of inquiry. Specifically, I outline general gaps in the empirical research literature as well as more specific questions relating to how closely the practice of public journalism approximates the democratic ideals underlying my proposed public philosophy.

In chapter 4, I summarize, analyze, and respond to some of the most important criticisms that have been directed at public journalism by journalism scholars and practicing journalists by drawing on my proposed public philosophy and the empirical research literature on public journalism, as well as other relevant material. I show, among many other issues, that while critics correctly fault public journalism advocates for having ignored the potential constraints imposed by commercial media systems, news organizations practicing public journalism have been able to promote broad-based citizen participation in democratic processes, despite management's interest in catering to the demographically most attractive segments of the citizenry.

After this broad discussion of the theory, practice, and criticism of public journalism, in chapter 5 I take a closer look at how news organizations have positioned citizens and elite actors as participants in public journalism initiatives. In a detailed case study of one of the most widely acclaimed and longest-running public journalism initiatives, the *Akron Beacon Journal*'s Pulitzer Prize–winning race relations project "A Question of Color," I show, among many other issues, that the *Beacon Journal* failed to help create a genuine public sphere for citizen–elite actor deliberation by nurturing two separate spheres of argument. While the project quoted citizens' concrete experiences with racism through the recounting of personal anecdotes, the project quoted elite actors' more general reflections on the causes and consequences of various race-related social inequalities. More generally, I show that my proposed public philosophy can be applied as a normative framework by which to identify problematic aspects of given public journalism initiatives and to outline what those initiatives could have done differently and better.

In chapter 6, I continue the discussion of how news organizations could promote better deliberation between citizens and elite actors by introducing a widely applied deliberative method known as the "consensus conference model." I argue that the consensus conference model is particularly well suited for engaging citizens and experts in the search for broad-based, systemic solutions to problems while at the same time involving government officials in the process of implementing those solutions in practice.

I turn, in chapter 7, to one of the least well-known aspects of public journalism, namely its practice outside the United States. Following a broad overview of how public journalism is practiced in Africa (Malawi, Senegal, Swaziland), the Asia/Pacific Rim (Australia, Japan, New Zealand), Europe (Finland, Sweden), and South America (Argentina, Columbia, Mexico), I examine in more detail the Danish experiments with public journalism. The Danish public journalism initiatives are particularly interesting not only because they have differed the most from those in the United States, but also, and more significantly, because they have furthered important aspects of my proposed public philosophy. Specifically, I show that, in contrast to U.S. news organizations, Danish news organizations have (1) advocated their own solutions to given problems and debated those solutions with other relevant actors, (2) made consistent efforts to both highlight and address the concerns of marginalized segments of the citizenry, and (3) encouraged citizens to formulate substantive solutions to problems while using experts as citizen-advisors. I argue that, while the more activist, journalistic stance assumed by the Danish news organizations could be attributed to a more activist professional self-understanding among Danish journalists, this activism, and especially the prominent role accorded citizens vis-à-vis experts, could also be seen as a manifestation of the increasing populism of Danish news media more generally.

I conclude the book, in chapter 8, by summarizing the most recent data on the practice of public journalism as well as by discussing whether some of the newer, citizen-based venues for news reporting, deliberation, and problem-solving are furthering the democratic ideals that have animated the public journalism movement thus far and, according to my own more activist vision for the movement, ought to animate the future practice of public journalism. I show, first, that while the public journalism movement continues to attract new and committed newsroom practitioners, and news organizations more generally are taking important steps to nurture a critical public sphere "about" journalism, news organizations are presently doing more to facilitate interaction between their newsroom staff and audiences than to facilitate interaction among citizens themselves and between citizens and government officials. Simply put, of the two gaps that inspired the public journalism movement in the first place—between news organizations and their audiences and between citizens and government—news organizations are doing more to bridge the former than the latter. Moreover, I show that, while the discourse found on Internet-based media of communication such as citizen-produced weblogs and hyper-local community web sites runs counter to the public journalism movement's democratic ideals and actual accomplishment, the global *Indymedia* network represents one of the best approximations of what a genuinely public approach to journalism, organized by citizens themselves, might look like.

TWO

A PUBLIC PHILOSOPHY FOR PUBLIC JOURNALISM

While public journalism's founding scholarly and journalistic advocates, as discussed in the previous chapter, have advanced certain broad-based arguments about journalism's role and responsibility in a democratic society, public journalism still lacks what several scholars correctly refer to as a guiding "public philosophy" (in the sense of a distinctive set of foundational principles) that clearly explicates wherein the "publicness" of public journalism lies or ought to lie and why (see Andersen, Dardenne, & Killenberg, 1997; Glasser, 2000; Glasser & Craft, 1998). By a guiding public philosophy, I understand a theoretically-based account of how journalists should conceive of the public, what forms of public deliberation and problem-solving journalists should help promote, and how journalists, as a matter of practice, should facilitate public discourse. While the lack of such a public philosophy, as Glasser and Craft (1998) speculate, may account for much of public journalism's acceptance in newsrooms (practitioners have been able to define it in vague, sometimes contradictory, and at times even self-serving ways, a point I return to in chapter 4), its absence is both philosophically problematic and strategically disadvantageous. Indeed, without a public philosophy, it is difficult for public journalism advocates to properly criticize existing journalistic practices, defend their ideas for improving those practices, propose and justify new, more radical practices, address potential obstacles standing in the way of implementing those practices, and, not least importantly, avoid co-optation by purely commercial interests. To take just one of many possible examples, without a guiding public philosophy, public journalism's emphasis on addressing citizen concerns could, as Richards (2000, p. 178) correctly notes, be "used by management to justify more of the narrow market research traditionally conducted by newspaper circulation departments, [thereby becoming] just another step along the path to total commercialism." Phrased in more positive terms, ideally a coherent public philosophy should guide the adoption of specific public journalism goals that, in turn, should inspire the development of particular public journalism practices and means of assessing whether the practices applied helped further those goals.

In this chapter, I articulate such a guiding public philosophy for public journalism by drawing on Habermas's (1989) theory of the public sphere and Fraser's (1990) critique thereof, as well as the writings of various public journalism scholars. While many scholars have argued that Habermas's and Fraser's works are relevant to public journalism (see, for example, Bybee, 1999; Compton, 2000; Glasser, 1999; Glasser & Craft, 1998; Lambeth, 1998), with one scholar even going as far as to propose Habermas as public journalism's "philosophical patron saint" (see Lambeth, 1998, p. 21), none have elaborated in any detail on how their ideas could inform the theory and practice of public journalism. In the process of developing this public philosophy, I enter into important, ongoing debates among scholars sympathetic to the general spirit of public journalism, address issues that remain inadequately theorized, and broach topics that so far have not been discussed at all.

I begin by considering how journalists should conceive of the public. After having identified conceptual and practical problems with communitarian and liberal views of the public, I argue that Habermas's notion of the "deliberating public" committed to "common deliberation" would serve public journalism well. I proceed to examine several related topics, notably who should decide what the public is to deliberate about in the first place and whether journalists should conceive of public discourse in dialogical and/or deliberative terms. Then, I discuss what the actual goals of promoting public deliberation should be and which institutional arrangements would best further those goals in practice. Here, I depart from Habermas's ideal of a single, unifying public sphere in which citizens bracket social inequalities as a means to pursue consensual solutions to common problems in favor of Fraser's ideal of a public sphere composed of multiple discursive domains in which citizens thematize social inequalities as a means to articulate their particular concerns and highlight salient conflicts of interest among them. Next, I develop a problem-solving model that explicates the role ordinary citizens, experts, government officials, and journalists should play in the process of formulating and enacting solutions to given problems under investigation. I conclude by summarizing my proposed public philosophy as well as by outlining how this philosophy will guide the discussion in subsequent chapters.

THE DELIBERATING PUBLIC

The first and arguably most fundamental task is to consider how journalists should conceive of the public. While public journalism's founding scholarly and journalistic advocates, as mentioned in the previous chapter, have made little effort to theorize the nature of the public beyond arguing that journalists should conceive of citizens as active participants in, as opposed to passive spectators to, democratic processes, there has been some subsequent scholarly debate about whether public journalism's understanding of the public should be embedded within a communitarian or a liberal democratic framework. Briefly put, while some scholars argue that public journalism should be embedded within a communitarian democratic framework, which assumes that the public represents a unity of citizens who share an overarching vision of the "common good" (see Christians, 1997, 1999; Coleman, 2000a; Heikkila & Kunelius, 1996), other scholars argue that public journalism should be embedded within a liberal democratic framework, which assumes that the public represents an aggregate of citizens who share little more than a "common membership" in a given nation-state (see Barney, 1996, 1997; Hodges, 1997; Merrill, 1997, 2000).

Christians (1999, p. 67), for example, asserts that "the future of public journalism depends on the notion of the common good." He takes "community formation [as] public journalism's overriding mission" (p. 71), with news and other forms of political discourse serving as agents of community formation. Christians (1997, p. 21) even acknowledges that the focus of a communitarian approach to public journalism should not be "communal values per se, but universal ones—not the common good understood as the communal good, but common in its richest universal meaning." Similarly, Heikkila and Kunelius (1996, p. 86) argue that "if public journalism is to reach across the diversity of culture—ways of living and talking about the world—it needs to elaborate the aspects of public conduct that is not reducible to the various constituencies of people that it is talking to."

Barney (1997, p. 72), in contrast, believes that public journalism should promote "individualism—the inclination and ability of individuals to retain rights to self-determination in the face of community pressures." He criticizes the communitarian approach to public journalism for devaluing "truth in favor of community loyalty and conformity at the expense of individual moral development" (1996, p. 140). Similarly, Merrill (1997, p. 56) asserts that "the individual is prior to the community, not the other way around; individual perfection is the goal; as individuals get better, society will improve." Indeed, Merrill criticizes what he regards as public journalism's communitarian vision, including its misguided ambition to supplant liberalism with "a more collectivized, group-oriented and cooperationist theory, which will eliminate social friction and establish a kind of communitarian heaven on earth" (p. 56).

The problem, however, is that neither communitarianism nor liberalism offer democratically viable conceptions of the public. While the communitarian view of the public underestimates the existence of conflicting visions of the common good both within and beyond the local community, thereby positing a view of the public that is too strong to allow for the negotiation of mutually conflicting values among citizens, the liberal view of the public lacks a strong, shared sense of solidarity and purpose needed to undergird citizen participation in joint deliberation and problem-solving. Thus, in terms of journalistic practice, the problem with these two conceptions of the public is that, while the communitarian view of the public would require journalists to cede editorial and reportorial autonomy to dominant community values in pursuit of community consensus, the liberal view of the public defines journalists' responsibility in terms of neutral information brokerage whose sole aim, at best, is to protect individual citizens from government interference.

Given these conceptual and practical problems, I propose that public journalism be embedded instead within Habermas's (1989) proceduralist-discursive notion of the "deliberating public." Habermas assumes neither that citizens share an overarching vision of the "common good" (the communitarian view) nor that citizens merely share a "common membership" in a given nation-state (the liberal view), but rather that citizens share a commitment to engage in "common deliberation." This is indeed a reasonable assumption. Not only have more than half (58%) of the more than 600 U.S. public journalism initiatives conducted to date featured some form of news media–sponsored public deliberation (see Friedland & Nichols, 2002), empirical research shows, as I describe in more detail in the next chapter, that citizens believe sponsoring such deliberation ought to be an essential aspect of journalistic practice more generally. A genuine public comes into being, Habermas argues, when citizens subject their own opinions, and their underlying reasons for espousing those opinions, to rational–critical evaluation by others and, at the same time, subject the opinions of others, and their underlying reasons for espousing those opinions, to rational–critical evaluation. More formally, rational–critical evaluation, which Habermas also refers to as "ideal role-taking" (see Habermas, 1990) or "reciprocal perspective-taking" (see Habermas, 1993), requires citizens to take into consideration the perspectives of others by according them equal weight to their own rather than to elevate their own perspectives to an indisputable standard.

Habermas's (1989) notion of a deliberating public committed to common deliberation could be taken to imply that journalists should help create and sustain an open-ended, unbounded public sphere to which all citizens have access and in which all topics of concern to citizens and all opinions available can be articulated, deliberated, and critiqued. Indeed, it suggests that journalists should nurture what Anderson et al. (1997, p. 98) call a "conversational commons": "A site for public dialogue shared by all citizens and accessible to all citizens." The purpose of such a conversational commons should be to provide "a forum in which citizens hear each other's voices—where positions that could not or would not be explored elsewhere are advanced, argued, assessed, and acted on" (p. 98). To require journalists to help create and sustain such a public sphere (or conversational commons) does not presuppose, as some scholars claim, a "passive public" (see Coleman, 1997, 2000a; Grimes, 1999). Rather, it implies that not enough opportunities exist for citizens to come together as an active, deliberating public. Instead of assuming that a deliberating public already exists, it presupposes that journalists can help bring such a public into being. As Carey (1997, p. 12) puts it, journalism should be seen as "an instrument which both expresses the public and helps it form and find its identity." This implies that journalism should "support the maintenance of public space and public life; it must find ways in which the public can address one another, and it must enhance those qualities of discourse...that allow public space to develop and to be maintained" (pp. 12–13).

To offer citizens opportunities to engage in rational–critical evaluation, journalists would not only need to incorporate a broad and diverse spectrum of citizen voices in their reporting but also, and equally important, to highlight citizens' underlying reasons for espousing certain opinions. Indeed, without an adequate understanding of others' reasoning processes, citizens would be unable to properly evaluate the relative merit of various opinions. More broadly, journalists would need to conceive of citizens' opinions as contributions to an ever-evolving (and changing) process of public deliberation, not as competitive input designed to defeat other ones (e.g., the liberal marketplace of ideas) or, conversely, as building blocks for a higher consensus (e.g., the communitarian common good). As Anderson, Dardenne, and Killenberg (1994, p. 53) correctly note, journalists should conceive of citizens' opinions "as contingent messages contributed to the public conversation, ones that could be sharpened, or rounded, even substantially altered, and certainly explored by a variety of subsequent voices."

Moreover, to ensure that the process of public deliberation is genuinely open and inclusive, journalists would need to expose and condemn views that attempt to disqualify certain citizens from equal participation. A couple of scholars have argued that proceduralist approaches to public deliberation cannot specify what journalists should do when certain community segments (or entire communities) espouse illiberal, if not anti-democratic, values. What should journalists do, Glasser (1999, p. 9) asks, "when a community consensus calls for a book burning? What is an appropriate response...when a popular vote yields a racist mayor?" Similarly, Schudson (1999, p. 131) asks, "Is segregation okay when it has been traditional for generations? Or are anti-sodomy laws acceptable when they express dominant community values?" I would argue that proceduralists, such as Habermas, can indeed respond to such scenarios. Insofar as proceduralism implies that all citizens should enjoy equal opportunities to participate in public deliberation, journalists would be expected to expose and condemn views designed to exclude other ones. For example, journalists would be required to expose specific articulations of racism, classicism, and sexism, even if these apparently represent dominant community values. The basis for such condemnation is that racist, sexist, and classicist views, as well as other discriminatory forms, inhibit full participation in public deliberation.

The notion of the deliberating public thus helps journalists figure out to whom they should be listening (and not listening) and why, to avoid the charge of pandering. Instead of grounding their reporting in particular communities (and community values), whether conceived in territorial or symbolic terms, journalists should be committed to hearing out all citizens and providing a forum through which citizens can hear each other out and evaluate conflicting, if not competing, values and interest claims. Indeed, the notion of the deliberating public implies that grounding reporting in a single community (or a single definition of community values) is democratically unviable. This would inhibit, rather than promote, the development of an impartial vantage point from which citizens can reflectively evaluate and compare mutually conflicting interests in a rational–critical manner.

Finally, but not least importantly, to avoid situating themselves above or detached from the deliberating public, journalists should also help nurture what several scholars refer to as a critical public sphere "about" journalism (see Glasser & Bowers, 1999; Glasser & Craft, 1998). That is, journalists should disclose the assumptions and aspirations that guide their reporting, offer citizens regular opportunities to criticize and evaluate their coverage, and then respond publicly to citizens' criticisms and evaluations. The development of such a public sphere about journalism is particularly important considering that citizens are rarely invited to assess news media performance. Indeed, in the most comprehensive study of sourcing patterns in articles about news media performance conducted to date, Bishop (2001) found that citizens accounted for only 6% of sources quoted; the most commonly cited sources were former and current journalists (40%), representatives of journalism organizations (13%), and journalism educators (11%).

In sum, the notion of the deliberating public would require journalists to further a genuinely public, as opposed to a community-based, approach to journalism. The latter grounds reporting in the topics, opinions, and values presumed to characterize a particular community—an inherently problematic presumption. A public approach to journalism, in contrast, begins by engaging in conversation with all citizens, without presuming some natural, local, or transcendent consensus. Indeed, if the notion of community is useful to public journalism, it is in the sense of "a community that exists by virtue of reasoning together" (Compton, 2000, p. 459).

SETTING THE NEWS MEDIA AGENDA

If journalists are to help bring a deliberating public into being, who should decide what the public is to deliberate about in the first place? This question of who should set the news media agenda—journalists and/or citizens—has, surprising as it might seem, received little attention among public journalism's founding scholarly and journalistic advocates. Indeed, in one of the only explicit, but still exceedingly vague, statements on this topic, Rosen (1996, p. 71) merely notes that journalists should involve "citizens in shaping a news agenda."

Nevertheless, there has been some subsequent scholarly and journalistic debate on this topic. Lichtenberg (1999, p. 347) summarizes this debate by noting that, while some argue that were journalists to "allow the public to set the news agenda, they [would] cede their independence and an essential part of their role, becoming followers where they should be leaders and allowing others to usurp their autonomy, [others argue that, in reality,] journalists take too active a role: what they should do…is to let others set the news agenda and not assume this task for themselves."

Glasser (2000, p. 684), for example, argues that "by denying the press the authority to set its own agenda, public journalism substitutes the community's judgment, however defined, for the judgment of journalists; it confuses community values with good values, as though the former always implies the latter." As a result, "Public journalism deprives the press of an opportunity—and diminishes the importance of its obligation—to set forth, clearly and convincingly, its politics; to explain and defend…its values and how and where they coincide with, or depart from, what it understands to be the expressed or implied values of the community" (p. 685). "Without a fully articulated newsroom agenda," Glasser thus concludes, "journalists and the public alike are cheated out of what they need most from the press: a candid account of why some issues receive more attention than others…and why, alas, some issues receive no attention at all" (p. 685).

Schudson (1999, p. 122), in contrast, argues that "public journalism… stops short of offering a fourth model of journalism in democracy, one in which authority is vested not in the market, not in a party, and not in the journalist but in the public." Characterizing public journalism as a cautious, even conservative, reform movement in the tradition of the Progressive Era, Schudson argues that public journalism "speaks loudly of the public but addresses itself to a professional group [of journalists] without challenging that group's authority" (p. 119). To enhance the public's agenda-setting power vis-à-vis journalists, Schudson proposes a number of formal media accountability systems, including citizen media review boards, a national news council, and even publicly elected publishers and editors.

At one level, my response to the question of who should set the news media agenda is relatively straightforward: If journalists, as previously discussed, are to help create and sustain a public sphere to which all citizens have access, and in which all topics of concern to citizens can be articulated, deliberated, and critiqued, journalists would need, as Iggers (1998, p. 149) correctly notes, to engage "citizens as *active partners* [italics added] in the newsmaking process." And, indeed, this is precisely what journalists do in practice. As described in the previous chapter, news organizations practicing public journalism have applied various informal means of involving citizens in the agenda-setting process, such as by conducting in-depth interviews, focus groups, and roundtable discussions before embarking on given election initiatives or special reporting projects or by meeting with groups of citizens on a regular basis to discuss which topics they would like to see covered as part of daily news reporting. The problem, however, is that only a few news organizations have instituted more formal means of involving citizens in the agenda-setting process, notably by restructuring their newsrooms from conventional beat systems revolving around certain institutional sources of information to include multiple teams focusing on particular topics of concern to citizens. Indeed, one of the few sustained efforts to include citizens in journalistic agenda-setting, decision-making, and performance processes is that of the Mexican newspaper group *Groupo Reforma*. As I describe in more detail in chapter 7, *Groupo Reforma* has developed a comprehensive network of so-called editorial councils, which offers citizens opportunities to formally discuss with journalists which topics they would like to see covered and how they would like to see those topics reported as well as to evaluate whether coverage adequately reflected their concerns.

While I thus agree with Schudson's (1999) call for more formalized means of involving citizens in the agenda-setting process, I concur with Glasser's (2000) argument that journalists should render more explicit the particular values upon which they ultimately base the news agenda, regardless of whether they include citizens in the decision-making process or not. Indeed, without an "intelligible and defensible political agenda" (Glasser, 2000, p. 685), separate and distinguishable from those of given communities (and community values), journalists would find it difficult to maintain a critical editorial and reportorial stance vis-à-vis those communities, avoid glossing over community conflicts for fear of upsetting certain community segments, and not succumb to dominant community values. Equally important, without such a political agenda, journalists would be unable to help nurture a critical public sphere about journalism in which citizens can publicly criticize news coverage in terms of explicitly stated journalistic values and journalists can publicly respond to citizen criticism with reference to those values. Put differently, failing to acknowledge how they necessarily act as gatekeepers—selecting which topics to cover, whose opinions to include, and so on—would leave journalists unmindful of citizen criticism and external to democratic processes.

PUBLIC DISCOURSE BETWEEN DIALOGUE
AND DELIBERATION

Unlike the question of who should set the news media agenda, the notion of the deliberating public does not in and of itself imply an answer to the question of what should be regarded as genuine public discourse. Briefly put, does a deliberating public come into being only when groups of citizens engage one another in actual face-to-face "dialogue" about given topics? Or, alternatively, does a deliberating public also come into being when mass-mediated political coverage prompts individual citizens to "deliberate" (in the sense of critically reflect) about given topics, even if such deliberation does not coincide with or subsequently result in actual social interaction with others?

Glasser and Craft (1998) argue, following Thompson (1995), that the notions of "dialogue" and "deliberation" point to very different models of democracy and envisage very different roles for journalists: "The challenge for the press in a direct, participatory democracy rests on journalists' commitment not only to local associations and local dialogue, but also to preserving the identity and integrity of these local associations as their discussions feed into successively larger discussions" (pp. 212–213). Deliberative democracy, in contrast, poses different challenges for journalists: "While deliberation does not formally require journalists to accommodate an unrestricted dialogue among citizens, it does require that the day's news be written in a way that invites each citizen's considered judgment. At a minimum, this means framing topics as issues rather than as events and then soliciting debate and commentary without regard for the speaker's power or privilege in society" (p. 213).

If one examines the literature on public journalism, it becomes apparent, as mentioned in the previous chapter, that advocates are unclear about whether journalists should conceive of public discourse in dialogical and/or deliberative terms and what the proper relationship is between these two forms of public discourse. On one hand, advocates appear committed to a dialogical form of public discourse, notably by calling on journalists to sponsor Fishkin's (1991) "deliberative opinion polls" in which groups of citizens engage in face-to-face dialogue about given topics over an extended period of time. On the other hand, advocates also appear committed to a deliberative form of public discourse, notably by calling on journalists to promote Yankelovitch's (1991) notion of "public judgment"; that is, to stimulate critical reflection on given topics on the part of individual citizens.

Contrary to what Glasser and Craft (1998) appear to imply, I do not believe that journalists would need to choose between conceiving of public discourse in dialogical or deliberative terms. Indeed, I would argue that the notion of the deliberating public is best furthered in an explicitly dialectic relationship between these two forms of public discourse. While a process of mass-mediated deliberation can expose a wide audience of citizens to the opinions (and reasoning processes) of others, face-to-face dialogue can offer groups of citizens opportunities to more carefully evaluate the relative merit of others' opinions (and reasoning processes). In turn, the evaluations formed during such face-to-face encounters can be channeled back into a process of mass-mediated deliberation for the benefit of a wider audience of citizens.

The actual practice of public journalism shows that face-to-face dialogue and mass-mediated deliberation are essential, mutually supportive aspects of public discourse that can be integrated into a continuous cycle. Briefly put, news organizations practicing public journalism typically sponsor various dialogical encounters among citizens, cover those encounters for the benefit of a wider audience of citizens, and subsequently report back on the dialogical encounters among citizens that their reporting helped inspire. Indeed, there is evidence to suggest that news organizations do so in a manner that satisfies the requirements that Glasser and Craft (1998, p. 213) stipulate for genuine dialogue and deliberation to occur. While news organizations generally preserve "the identity and integrity" of citizens' dialogical encounters by retaining the to-and-fro of argument in their reporting instead of merely summarizing their outcomes in their own words, news organizations also tend to frame "topics as issues rather than as events" and to solicit "debate and commentary without regard for the speaker's power or privilege in society." Not only has the vast majority of public journalism initiatives focused on long-standing issues of concern to citizens rather than on political elections and other so-called newsworthy events (see chapter 1), those initiatives, as I describe in more detail in the next chapter, have relied more on ordinary citizens, including women and minorities, as sources of information than does mainstream journalism more generally.

THE GOALS OF PUBLIC DELIBERATION

So far, I have argued that journalists should help bring a deliberating public into being by creating and sustaining a public sphere to which all citizens have access and in which all topics of concern to citizens and all opinions available can be articulated, deliberated, and critiqued. To facilitate the emergence of such a public sphere, journalists should involve citizens in the process of setting the news media agenda as well as promote a form of public discourse that combines the strengths of face-to-face dialogue and mass-mediated deliberation. In considering what the actual goals of public deliberation should be, and which institutional arrangements would best further those goals in practice, I turn to Fraser's (1990) important critique of Habermas (1989).

To Habermas (1989), genuine public deliberation can occur only if citizens set aside social inequalities and interact, instead, as if they were social equals. Only by abstracting from social inequalities, Habermas assumes, would citizens be able to focus their deliberations on topics of common concern. Fraser (1990) takes issue with this assumption, as well as with the goal of focusing deliberations on topics of common concern to all citizens, on the grounds that such abstraction from social inequalities has always functioned to privilege the interests of dominant social groups over those of subordinate social groups by universalizing narrow group interests. Thus, instead of abstracting from (or "bracketing") social inequalities, Fraser argues that citizens should explicitly articulate (or "thematize") them.

Fraser's (1990) argument for making social inequalities visible directs attention to a question that public journalism's founding scholarly and journalistic advocates have failed to consider: What kind of public deliberation should journalists help promote, given widespread social inequality?

The problem of social inequality remains inadequately theorized, in large part, because of advocates' underlying communitarian assumption that a community represents a unified site bounded by shared values and interests. By virtue of inhabiting a certain geographical territory, citizens are assumed to confront common problems and to share an overarching vision of the common good that enables them to reach consensual solutions to those problems. Merritt (1998, p. xiii), for example, describes public life in terms of "common problems" and "common goals." Similarly, Rosen (1997, p. 20) equates positioning individuals as citizens with conceiving of them "as citizens of the whole, with shared interests." This communitarian view leads advocates to presume that citizens will be able to reach consensual solutions to common problems if only they treat one another with mutual understanding and respect. Charity (1996, p. 11), for example, assumes that "if one conversant is courteous, the other will also be courteous; they'll speak in ways that focus on solutions rather than grievances."

This view of community and of public deliberation is problematic, however, because it ignores how even the smallest of communities tend to be fragmented into multiple social groups, situated in what Fraser (1990, p. 66) calls "relations of dominance and subordination," structured (or fractured) especially by race, class, and gender. Indeed, social inequality may preclude the emergence of a shared, overarching vision of the common good. Consensus may not even be the most realistic or appropriate goal. As Hackett and Zhao (1998, p. 205; see also Compton, 2000; Howley, 2003; Pauly, 1999) correctly note, public journalism advocates "overestimate the possibility of community consensus, because [they] overlook the extent of conflicting interests and standpoints. Nor is an apparent consensus inherently desirable, if it means ratifying an unjust status quo or precluding further debate."

Instead of promoting public deliberation aimed at reaching consensual solutions to problems of presumed common concern to all citizens, I would thus encourage journalists to follow Fraser's (1990) lead and help citizens reflect on their different, and potentially conflicting, concerns. This could be accomplished by making salient social inequalities the very subject matter (or focal point) of public deliberation. That is, aside from offering citizens opportunities to reflect on one another's underlying reasons for espousing certain opinions, journalists should also offer citizens opportunities to articulate the social locations from which they view given topics and to reflect on how those social locations affect their sense of problems and solutions. Thereby, journalism could become a means through which citizens understand not only that they have different, and perhaps conflicting, interests, but also that some interests are more in need of protection and promotion than others. In short, journalists should stimulate citizens to explore the bases for differences in perspective by recovering latent conflicts of interest among different social groups.

To help citizens explore the grounds for their conflicting perspectives would require journalists to engage in serious public listening, especially listening for difference. Equally important, journalists should encourage an acknowledgment (and acknowledgment largely absent from conventional, mainstream journalism) that some social locations hinder, or even prevent, certain citizens from speaking in public, from fully participating in public deliberation. Since an emphasis on transcendent communion may itself be silencing, and may work against articulated citizen participation, journalists should help citizens consider how social inequalities may harm some citizens' abilities to participate on an equal footing. Moreover, journalists themselves must be mindful of how some citizens are silenced and actively seek out those citizens in terms, at times, in places, and on topics that would permit their participation.

This view of public deliberation does not imply that journalists should essentialize, promote divisiveness, or exaggerate the impact of minor differences. Indeed, journalists should help citizens distinguish between significant and trivial differences. Moreover, journalists should not mechanistically or reductively assume that single social identifiers determine one's perspective, but rather help articulate the interrelations between various social signifiers. That said, a sense of solidarity is more likely to emerge from mutual respect—which acknowledges difference—than from an abstract pursuit of commonality.

If journalists are to help recover latent conflicts of interest among different social groups, they should not only make salient social inequalities the very subject matter (or focal point) of public deliberation but also help citizens challenge entrenched distinctions between "topics of public interest" and "matters of private concern." To Habermas (1989), genuine public deliberation not only requires that citizens set aside social inequalities and interact, instead, as if they were social equals, but also that citizens leave behind their private identities and interests. Fraser (1990) takes issue with this latter requirement on the grounds that, like abstracting from social inequalities, such a requirement has traditionally served the interests of dominant social groups over those of subordinate social groups by rendering certain topics off-limits for public deliberation. In the absence of a priori, natural boundaries, Fraser argues, what should be regarded as topics of public interest and matters of private concern should be decided through discursive contestation rather than be determined in advance. Indeed, participatory parity in the public sphere requires opportunities for subordinate social groups to convince dominant social groups that what in the past was not considered a topic of public interest should now become so. Specifically, Fraser challenges the notion of "economic privacy" for excluding some topics from public deliberation by economizing them: "The issues in question are here cast as impersonal market imperatives or as private ownership prerogatives or as technical problems for managers and planners, all in contradistinction to public, political matters" (p. 73). Fraser criticizes the parallel notion of "domestic privacy" for shielding some topics from public deliberation by personalizing and/or familiarizing them: "It casts these as private-domestic or personal-familial matters in contradistinction to public, political matters" (p. 73).

Following Fraser (1990), I would argue that journalists should make every effort possible to keep the process of public deliberation as open and inclusive as possible. To recover latent conflicts of interest among different social groups, journalists should help subordinate social groups challenge entrenched distinctions between topics of public interest and matters of private concern by providing them with opportunities to introduce topics for deliberation that in the past were ruled off-limits, including topics relating to the workplace (e.g., "economic privacy") and the home (e.g., "domestic privacy"). More broadly, when considering how citizens' perspectives differ, journalists should work to avoid essentializing some social locations (e.g., enclaving certain topics as private and therefore unaddressable in the public sphere). Instead of taking for granted a few predetermined subject positions, journalists should offer citizens opportunities to decide for themselves which subject positions are salient in given contexts.

THE STRUCTURE OF THE PUBLIC SPHERE

The important question, then, is which institutional arrangements would best further the goal of making the process of public deliberation as open and inclusive as possible? Once again, I turn to Fraser's (1990) critique of Habermas (1989) for a viable answer. To Habermas, a focus on topics of common concern to all citizens requires the establishment of a single, unifying public sphere. The problem with this model of the public sphere, Fraser argues, is not only that it presupposes that topics of common concern exist (an inherently problematic assumption, as previously discussed), but also that it would deprive subordinate social groups of spaces for intra-group deliberation about their particular concerns outside the supervision and control of dominant social groups. Fraser thus endorses a public sphere composed of multiple discursive domains organized around distinct bases of affinity and interest, since, in socially stratified societies, "arrangements that accommodate contestation among a plurality of publics better promote the ideal of participatory parity than does a single, comprehensive, overarching public [sphere]" (p. 66).

Importantly, by endorsing a public sphere composed of multiple discursive domains, Fraser (1990) does not mean to advocate an "isolationist," as opposed to a "publicist," notion of publicness. Indeed, Fraser argues that, while such a model of the public sphere would offer subordinate social groups opportunities to invent and circulate counterdiscourses through which to formulate oppositional interpretations of their identities, needs, and interests, it also should function as a basis and training ground for agitational activities directed toward wider publics. Fraser notes that "it is precisely in the dialectic between these two functions that [the model's] emancipatory potential resides. This dialectic [would] enable [subordinate social groups] partially to offset, although not wholly to eradicate, the unjust participatory privileges enjoyed by members of dominant social groups in [socially] stratified societies" (p. 68).

Following Fraser (1990), I would encourage journalists to help nurture a public sphere composed of multiple discursive domains in which members of different social groups could articulate and deliberate about their particular concerns among themselves. Indeed, by offering separate discursive spaces for deliberation, journalists could help ensure that subordinate social groups enjoy the same opportunities as dominant social groups to participate in the process of public deliberation. Nevertheless, to retain the public sphere's publicist, as opposed to isolationist, orientation, and, as Fraser puts it, to accommodate discursive contestation among a plurality of publics, journalists should also work to bring members of different social groups together within a joint discursive space. After all, public journalism is not only about creating the conditions for genuinely open and inclusive public deliberation but also about creating the conditions for joint public problem-solving, even if citizens disagree about which problems are politically most compelling.

This model of the public sphere has practical, journalistic implications. It implies, first, that when sponsoring dialogical encounters among citizens in the form of focus groups, roundtable discussions, and the like, journalists should offer members of different social groups opportunities to deliberate among themselves before inviting all the participants to do so jointly. Second, and relatedly, journalists should help retain the distinctive character of those encounters when reporting back on them for the benefit of a wider audience of citizens. While carrying articles on given intra-group deliberations would help audiences understand how particular social locations affect certain groups' sense of problems and solutions, articles reporting back on more encompassing inter-group deliberations would help audiences compare conflicting concerns as well as identify possible points of overlap that might subsequently form the basis for joint public problem-solving.

PROMOTING PUBLIC PROBLEM-SOLVING

If public journalism is as much about promoting public problem-solving as it is about facilitating public deliberation or, as Rosen (1999b, p. 22) puts it, about helping the public "act upon, rather than just learn about, its problems," what kind of problem-solving should journalists help promote and why? To ensure that the deliberating public brought into being by journalism has more than a temporary existence, I would argue that journalists should encourage citizens to continue their deliberations—and act upon their outcomes—within the institutions of the wider civil society; that is, the multitude of civic organizations through which citizens can organize themselves for political deliberation and action. This could be accomplished by offering citizens what Lemert (1981) calls "mobilizing information," or information about how to join up with relevant civic organizations that work on given problems. And, indeed, this is precisely what journalists do in practice. As I describe in more detail in the next chapter, the empirical research literature shows that news organizations practicing public journalism carry significantly more mobilizing information than do mainstream news organizations more generally.

Indeed, while participation in news media–sponsored focus groups, roundtable discussions, and community forums can be both educational and symbolically satisfying, those venues offer no genuine substitute for sustained, public engagement with problems. As Glasser (1999, p. 11) correctly notes, such sites "create at most an ad hoc venue for discussion, a small and temporary site for a debate managed by and too often only for the press. Without the means to sustain these discussions over time and the conviction to broaden the range of topics they cover, the press cannot claim to have established much in the way of a tradition of civic participation." Iggers (1998, p. 146) agrees that citizens brought together for news media–sponsored encounters do not constitute a genuine public. Rather, they represent "a collection of strangers…who may not see each other again…and who have not had the opportunity to develop the relationships of trust and understanding that are essential to democratic cooperation."

Like the relationship between dialogical and deliberative forms of public discourse (see above), I propose that the public sphere (of journalism) and civil society (of civic organizations) be seen as standing in an explicitly dialectic and mutually supportive relationship. While civil society can offer citizens opportunities to cultivate their political identities as well as to articulate, deliberate, and act upon particular political positions that emerge, the public sphere can nurture discursive spaces in which those positions are shared and discussed among a wider audience of citizens. Indeed, by letting a wider audience of citizens evaluate the appropriateness and effectiveness of given political activities, journalism would not be reduced to the status of community booster, but rather would become a means by which citizens can debate and propose new directions for political activity. The outcomes of such citizen deliberations, in turn, can be channeled back into the institutions of civil society, thereby forming a continuous cycle.

In practice, however, journalists have exhibited more commitment to promoting a complementary relationship between dialogical and deliberative forms of public discourse than to promoting a complementary relationship between the public sphere and civil society. While news organizations practicing public journalism, as discussed in the previous chapter, commonly report back on the various citizen encounters that they help organize, they rarely report back on any subsequent political activities that their reporting help inspire. This suggests, in turn, that despite of advocates' often-voiced argument that journalism should help improve public life, the notion of public life continues to be understood in narrow, media-centric, as opposed to more expansive and inclusive, terms.

Despite my general call for journalists to encourage citizens to continue their deliberations—and act upon their outcomes—within the institutions of the wider civil society, I believe it is essential that journalists carefully consider which particular kinds of intervention would be required to adequately address given problems before they promote any public problem-solving activity. Indeed, a number of scholars have rightly taken issue with news organizations' virtually exclusive focus on local, citizen-based intervention to the detriment of other, potentially more appropriate forms of intervention, arguing that such a focus is likely to create a false sense of participatory involvement that serves entrenched elite interests (Glasser, 1999; Parisi, 1997) and/or increase public cynicism toward government and politics, the very cynicism public journalism hoped to reduce, if not eliminate (Iggers, 1998; Schudson, 1999).

Parisi (1997, p. 682), for example, argues that public journalism's "emphasis on 'personal power and responsibility' and 'solving it ourselves' merges comfortably into a political moment when the very idea of the 'public good' as addressed by large-scale social programs faces systematic challenge." Public journalism's focus on local, citizen-based intervention, Parisi emphasizes, "could be interpreted as evidence of an underlying alliance with dominant interests, and [public journalism] could thus be termed 'hegemonic'—a means of accommodating the contradictions of current news gathering without bringing about genuine change" (p. 682). Similarly, Glasser (1999, p. 10) worries that "'convening the community' might bring about only the illusion of reform" or, worse, that public journalism might become "a technique of co-optation or legitimation that creates a false sense of participatory involvement without challenging entrenched elite interests." Iggers (1998, p. 150) adds to these concerns by noting that "to encourage the public to participate in public discussion in a context where there is little prospect that the conversation will have an impact runs the risk of deepening public cynicism and disaffection." Indeed, Iggers argues that when journalists "invite the local community to 'solve it ourselves,' they risk foreclosing the possibility that the causes and solutions of a local problem needs to be understood and addressed on a larger scale" (p. 152). Similarly, Schudson (1999, p. 129) notes that, by promoting local, citizen-based intervention, "public journalism… may unintentionally reinforce the very cynicism that it sees as a symptom of contemporary decline and disillusionment."

To ensure that the public problem-solving activity promoted corresponds to the nature of given problems, I propose that journalists carefully consider two fundamental questions. First, journalists need to consider whether given problems could be adequately addressed by citizens themselves or whether those problems would require more deep-seated, systemic intervention by government officials. Second, journalists need to consider whether given problems could be adequately addressed through local intervention, whether citizen-based or governmental, or whether those problems would require intervention of a broader regional, state, national, or even international scope.

For problems potentially resolvable by citizens themselves, either within a given locality or on a broader scale, journalists should support and promote citizens' own efforts to formulate and enact concrete solutions to those problems (e.g., a "direct-participatory" form of public problem-solving). This could be accomplished by describing what citizens in other localities have done in the past and/or are presently doing to address similar problems, creating spaces for citizens to deliberate about those problems among themselves, encouraging citizens to join existing or create new (local or larger-scale) civic organizations, and publicizing citizens' applications for resources. While journalists, as previously mentioned, commonly promote local, citizen-based intervention, they rarely describe what citizens in other localities have done and/or are presently doing to address similar problems or encourage citizens to join existing (or create new) larger scale civic organizations to address those problems.

Conversely, for problems requiring more deep-seated, systemic intervention, either within a given locality or on a broader scale, journalists should encourage citizens, in consultation with experts who have particular knowledge about the problems in question, to formulate possible solutions and then to lobby relevant government officials to enact those solutions in practice (e.g., a "representative" form of public problem-solving).

This problem-solving model poses several challenges to the theory and practice of public journalism. It implies, first, that journalists would need to conceive of the public in more expansive and inclusive terms than they have done until now. Simply put, while some problems may be resolvable by citizens themselves, many other problems require collaboration between citizens, experts, and government officials to be adequately addressed. To facilitate the creation of such a "macro public," journalists would need to move beyond what several scholars correctly refer to as their apparent distrust of expertise, or the faulty belief that expert participation in problem-solving would somehow taint, if not undermine, the authentic expression of public opinion, as well as their antagonistic relationship to government, which assumes that the involvement of government officials is inadequate at best and detrimental at worst (see Iggers, 1998; Levine, 1998; Parisi, 1997; Schudson, 1999).

Second, and equally important, this problem-solving model implies that journalists would need to reconsider their own role in the process of identifying viable solutions to given problems. To appreciate why this is the case, it is useful to briefly examine how the question of the proper reach of journalistic involvement has been conceptualized. According to public journalism's founding scholarly and journalistic advocates, journalists should be involved with the "processes," but not with the "outcomes," of citizens' efforts to solve problems. Charity (1995, pp. 144–146), for example, argues that "public journalism has a golden role—an ethical line—every bit as sharp as mainstream journalism's rule, and just as easy to elaborate into a code book of professional conduct: Journalism should advocate democracy without advocating particular solutions." Merritt (1998, p. 97) agrees, arguing that journalists "must exhibit no partisan interest in the specific outcome [of citizen deliberation] other than it is arrived at under the democratic process." To

Rosen (1996, p. 13), it is essential that journalists maintain a stance of "proactive neutrality" that "prescribes no chosen solution and favors no particular party of interest."

I certainly agree that journalists should be concerned with whether citizen deliberations are conducted in a democratic manner. As previously discussed, under conditions of widespread social inequality, one of journalists' primary responsibilities should be to ensure than subordinate social groups enjoy the same opportunities as dominant social groups to articulate and deliberate about their particular concerns, including by offering members of different social groups separate discursive spaces for deliberation. But journalists' responsibilities should extend further than that. If journalists are to help ensure that the concerns of subordinate social groups are not only articulated and heard but advanced, they would also need to be concerned with whose interests the outcomes of given citizen deliberations serve. As Sirianni and Friedland (2001, p. 229) correctly note, journalists should "hold citizens themselves accountable" for the outcomes of their deliberations. Thus, if the interventions endorsed by citizens fail to advance the overarching goal of reducing social inequality or, worse, serve to strengthen such inequality by advancing the interests of dominant social groups over those of subordinate social groups, journalists should see it as their right—indeed their responsibility—to publicly say so, including by advocating their own alternative interventions and lobbying relevant government officials to enact those interventions in practice. Put differently, if journalism is indeed an important political institution, it retains the responsibility to advocate measures that correspond to given problems. The publicness of public journalism, then, extends beyond offering citizens opportunities to participate in public deliberation and problem-solving to journalists acting in what they perceive to be in the best public interest. The focus of journalists' problem-solving efforts shifts from what citizens themselves can do, or are willing to do, to address given problems to what needs to be done to solve those problems. Thus, journalists should not only help nurture a public sphere about journalism by publicly responding to citizens' criticisms in terms of explicitly stated journalistic values but also actively assert and defend those values, especially the value of social equality, when these are perceived to be threatened by interventions endorsed by citizens themselves.

More broadly, the problem with the distinction between the processes and outcomes of citizen deliberation is that it could turn public journalism into a social experiment with little substance and direction. Indeed, such a distinction betrays a disinterest in how citizens should work together and for what ends, a problem that Glasser (1999, p. 10) aptly refers to as public journalism's lack of an underlying "telos."

My call for more active, if not assertive, journalistic involvement in problem-solving also implies that journalists should not, as several advocates argue, maintain a stance of political neutrality with respect to particular politicians, candidates for office, and special interest groups to avoid, as Rosen (1999a, p. 76; see also Austin, 1997; Coleman, 2000a; Sirianni & Friedland, 2001) puts it, conflating "doing journalism" with "doing politics." Quite the contrary, I would argue that journalists should actively endorse those politicians, candidates for office, and special interest groups whose agendas would best serve the overarching goal of reducing social inequality. As Glasser (1999, p. 10; see also Nord, 2001; Pauly, 1999) correctly notes, "Public journalism's fear of political advocacy isolates the press from the very centers of power that are likely to make a difference locally, regionally, nationally, and even internationally." Thus, in addition to encouraging citizens to join local and broader-based civic organizations, journalists should, depending on the particular problems in question, also encourage citizens to join such partisan, political interest groups as political parties, trade unions, and civil rights organizations, among numerous others.

A PUBLIC PHILOSOPHY FOR PUBLIC JOURNALISM

If public journalism is to prosper as a distinct and legitimate journalistic notion in its own right, it is essential that it be embedded within a guiding public philosophy rather than remain defined by its criticisms of perceived flaws in conventional, mainstream journalism and by its own alternative practices. While a reactive approach to defining public journalism might have been necessary during the movement's early years, when advocates were vilified by critics for even tentatively distinguishing public journalism from conventional, mainstream journalism, a point I return to in chapter 4, a more proactive approach is needed if public journalism is to develop and justify its own distinctive set of goals and practices. Indeed, to assess the democratic viability of given public journalism practices, and to stipulate what could be done differently and better, requires normative standards—something to measure actual performance against.

In this chapter, I have attempted to develop such a public philosophy for public journalism. Drawing on Habermas's (1989) theory of the public sphere,

I argued that journalists' primary responsibility should be to help bring into being a deliberating public by creating and sustaining an open-ended, unbounded public sphere to which all citizens have access and in which all topics of concern to citizens and all opinions available can be articulated, deliberated, and critiqued. To help facilitate such a public sphere, journalists should share their authority with citizens by instituting various formal and informal means of involving citizens in the setting of the news media agenda as well as promote a form of public discourse that combines the strengths of face-to-face dialogue and mass-mediated deliberation.

While Habermas's (1989) work offers a useful theoretical foundation for considering how journalists should conceive of the public and of public deliberation, I turned to Fraser (1990) to discuss what the actual goals of public deliberation should be and which institutional arrangements would best further those goals. Given widespread social inequality, I argued that the notion of the deliberating public is best conceptualized—and furthered—not as a unitary phenomenon but rather as consisting of multiple social groups situated in relations of dominance and subordination. To promote participatory parity in the public sphere, and to help recover latent conflicts of interest and perspective among different social groups, journalists should help nurture a public sphere composed of multiple discursive domains in which different social groups can articulate and deliberate about their particular concerns as well as challenge entrenched distinctions between topics of public interest and matters of private concern.

Finally, I developed at model that explicates the role ordinary citizens, experts, government officials, and journalists should play in the problem-solving process. I argued that, while some problems may be potentially resolvable by citizens themselves, other problems may require that citizens collaborate with experts and government officials on the formulation and enactment of given solutions. Journalists should feel entitled to join the problem-solving process themselves by advocating particular solutions on their own when the interventions endorsed by other actors run counter to their values or, more broadly, do not help advance the overarching goal of reducing social inequality.

In subsequent chapters, I apply this public philosophy to various aspects of the theory and practice of public journalism. Without going into too much detail here, I show that this philosophy can be used to outline future avenues for empirical research on public journalism (chapter 3), respond to criticisms directed at public journalism by journalism scholars and practicing journalists (chapter 4), specify what given public journalism initiatives could have done differently and better (chapter 5), evaluate the appropriateness of widely used deliberative methods (chapter 6), examine why some news organizations have better been able than others to approximate its underlying democratic ideals (chapter 7), and assess current developments in the practice of public journalism (chapter 8).

THREE

THE EMPIRICAL RESEARCH ON PUBLIC JOURNALISM

If public journalism's founding scholarly and journalistic advocates, as discussed in previous chapters, have failed to clearly articulate public journalism as a journalistic philosophy in its own right, the public journalism movement has nevertheless inspired much evaluative research. Indeed, since the mid-1990s, when the first empirical studies of public journalism appeared, more than 70 studies have investigated the practice of public journalism in the United States and, to a lesser extent, abroad.

In this chapter, I offer a comprehensive overview and discussion of social–scientific (quantitative as well as qualitative) research on public journalism. Specifically, I focus on the three most prevalent research concerns: (1) mainstream journalists' attitudes toward public journalism, (2) differences in the news coverage of news organizations practicing public journalism and mainstream news organizations more generally, and (3) the impact of public journalism–inspired news coverage on citizens. The findings of other important, but less frequently researched, lines of inquiry will, where appropriate, be discussed in subsequent chapters.

Following a broad overview of what the empirical research literature reveals about the three topics mentioned above, I discuss methodological shortcomings in some of the studies reviewed, notably, problems relating to conceptualization, measurement, and interpretation. While these shortcomings do not raise doubts about the validity of the body of research as a whole, they do direct attention to deficiencies that future studies ought to address. Finally, I offer suggestions to how future research could broaden the substantive scope of inquiry. Here, I focus on general gaps in the empirical research literature as well as on more specific questions relating to how closely the practice of public journalism approximates the democratic ideals underlying my proposed public philosophy.

MAINSTREAM JOURNALISTS' ATTITUDES
TOWARD PUBLIC JOURNALISM

During the past decade, a number of studies have investigated mainstream journalists' attitudes toward public journalism. Contrary to what appears to be the conventional wisdom, these studies show that the majority of journalists—editors as well as rank-and-file reporters—approve of many of the practices associated with public journalism (see Arant & Meyer, 1998; Bare, 1998; Campaign Study Group, 2001; Corrigan, 1999; Dickson, Brandon, & Topping, 2001; Gade et al., 1998; Jeffres, Cutietta, Lee, & Sekerka, 1999; McDevitt, Gassaway, & Perez, 2000; Payne, 1999; Voakes, 1999; Weaver & Wilhoit, 1996; Weaver, Beam, Brownlee, Voakes, & Wilhoit, 2006). While journalists are generally favorably disposed toward public journalism, such approval has been found to be higher among journalists who work for smaller than for larger news organizations (see Arant & Meyer, 1998; Campaign Study Group, 2001; Voakes, 1999; Weaver & Wilhoit, 1996) and among journalists who work for news organizations that have been involved as opposed to not involved in actual public journalism initiatives (see Arant & Meyer, 1998; Bare, 1998; Dickson et al., 2001; Gade et al., 1998). These findings are not surprising. Although news organizations of all sizes have experimented with public journalism (see Arant & Meyer, 1998; Dickson & Topping, 2001; Friedland & Nichols, 2002), proportionally more larger than smaller news organizations have been involved with public journalism. Indeed, the most comprehensive study conducted to date found that almost three quarters (74%) of U.S. public journalism initiatives have been carried out by newspapers with a daily circulation of 250,000 or less (see Friedland & Nichols, 2002).

Despite this generally strong approval of public journalism's practices, journalists have been found to be attitudinally most comfortable with the practices that differ the least from those of conventional, mainstream journalism. In a survey of more than 1,000 U.S. newspaper journalists, Voakes (1999) found that, although the majority of respondents expressed strong approval of all four practices under investigation, they expressed significantly higher approval of the "modest" (or more conventional/less activist) practices of focusing attention on given community problems and of reporting on possible trade-offs between alternative solutions to those problems than of the "bolder" (or less conventional/more activist) practices of conducting public opinion polls to identify what citizens believe are the most important problems facing their community and of sponsoring town hall meetings to offer citizens opportunities to deliberate about and formulate possible solutions to those problems. In a study based on the same four measures of public journalism, Payne (1999) found the same pattern to hold true for journalists working at the Columbia, South Carolina, *State*, a newspaper that, as described in chapter 1, has made considerable efforts to make public journalism an integral part of its daily information-gathering and news-reporting practices.

Voakes's (1999) finding that journalists are attitudinally more comfortable with practices that resemble those of conventional, mainstream journalism has been replicated in a number of other studies, albeit with slightly different measures of what constitutes "modest" and "bolder" approaches to public journalism (see Arant & Meyer, 1998; Corrigan, 1999; Dickson et al., 2001; Jeffres et al., 1999; McDevitt et al., 2000; Weaver & Wilhoit, 1996; Weaver et al., 2006). Taken together, these studies show that journalists are more likely to agree that it is their responsibility to focus their reporting on problems of concern to citizens, incorporate citizens' views on those problems in their coverage, and provide information on local civic organizations that work on those problems than to agree that it is their responsibility to sponsor forums where citizens can deliberate about and formulate possible solutions to problems, try to help citizens reach consensus on how given problems should be resolved, and work directly with local civic organizations to help implement actual solutions to those problems.

Although journalists have been found to express strong approval of some, but not all, of public journalism's practices, research shows that journalists continue to adhere to conventional journalistic practices such as investigating government claims, providing analysis and interpretation of complex problems, and getting information to the public quickly; that is, practices that tap into what Weaver and Wilhoit (1996) call journalists' "interpretive/investigative" and "disseminator" role conceptions, respectively (see Arant & Meyer, 1998; Jeffres et al., 1999; Weaver & Wilhoit, 2006). Importantly, this pluralistic orientation to newswork also manifests itself among journalists who work for news organizations practicing public journalism. In a comparative study of 40 journalists from the *Wichita Eagle* and the traditional Mobile, Alabama, *Register*, Gade et al. (1998) found that, while 7 of the 20 respondents from the *Wichita Eagle* were attitudinally most comfortable with practices that represented a public journalism–inspired role conception, the remaining 13 respondents were attitudinally more comfortable with role conceptions that represented a blend of public journalism–inspired and conventional journalistic practices. Similarly, in a comparative study of more than 400 journalists from the *Wichita Eagle*, the traditional Raleigh, North Carolina, *News & Observer*, and what he termed the "quasi-public" *Omaha* (Nebraska) *World-Herald*, Bare (1998) found that, although the *Wichita Eagle* respondents scored highest among all the respondents on measures of "personal public journalism" (journalists' attitudes regarding their personal duty to help solve community problems) and "institutional public journalism" (journalists' attitudes regarding their news organization's duty to help solve community problems), they also scored high on measures that tapped into journalists' investigative/interpretive and disseminator role conceptions.

While only a couple of comparative studies of journalists' and citizens' attitudes toward public journalism have been conducted, the available evidence points to significant differences. In a study comparing the attitudes of 600 citizens with those of journalists from Weaver et al.'s (2006) study, Heider, McCombs, and Poindexter (2006) found that citizens were much less likely to state that it is important for journalists to act as watchdogs on government and get information to the public quickly, practices that tap into journalists' interpretive/investigative and disseminator role conceptions, respectively. More significantly, citizens were much more likely to state that it is important for journalists to sponsor community forums aimed at offering citizens opportunities to deliberate about given problems. Both citizens and journalists agreed, however, that reporting on possible solutions to problems is important. In a secondary analysis of the same data, Poindexter, Heider, and McCombs (2006) found that women, African Americans, Latinos, and poorer and less educated citizens were much more likely than men, Caucasians, Asian Americans, and wealthier and more educated citizens to state that it is important for journalists to report on possible solutions to problems. Similarly, in a study comparing the attitudes of 360 blue-collar workers with those of journalists from the Raleigh, North Carolina, *News & Observer*, Fee (2002) found that the blue-collar workers were much more likely to state that it is important for journalists to help citizens solve community problems and much less likely to state that it is important for journalists to act as watchdogs on government and provide analysis and interpretation of complex problems. These findings are indeed significant. They show not only that a disconnect exists between what citizens and journalists expect from the press but also, and equally important, that members of marginalized social groups, whether based on race, class, or gender, perceive a need for a form of journalism that is committed to help articulating and addressing their particular concerns.

PUBLIC JOURNALISM'S NEWS COVERAGE

Although mainstream journalists have been found to have a generally pluralistic orientation to newswork, as manifested by strong support for public journalism–inspired *and* conventional journalistic practices, research has uncovered a number of important differences between the news coverage of news organizations practicing public journalism and mainstream news organizations more generally. With some exceptions (see Choi, 2004; Maier & Potter, 2001; Roselle, 2003), quantitative content analyses of public journalism–inspired election initiatives, special reporting projects, and daily news coverage show that news organizations practicing public journalism (1) carry longer, more staff-written, and more locally–oriented stories (Blazier & Lemert, 2000; Kennamer & South, 2002; Loomis, 1998; McMillan, Guppy, Kunz, & Reis, 1998; Miller, 1994; Reynolds, 1997, 1999); (2) focus more attention on substantive policy issues than on isolated political events (Blazier & Lemert, 2000; Friedland & Nichols, 2002; Kennamer & South, 2002; McGregor, Comrie, & Fountaine, 1999; McGregor, Fountaine, & Comrie, 2000; McMillan et al., 1998; Meyer & Potter, 2000; Miller, 1994; Reynolds, 1997, 1999); (3) report more on possible solutions to given problems under investigation (Friedland & Nichols, 2002; McGregor et al., 1999, Moscowitz, 2002); (4) emphasize political candidates' issue positions, qualifications for office, and policy records (Evatt, 1999; Kennamer & South, 2002; McGregor et al., 1999, 2000; McMillan et al., 1998; Meyer & Potter, 2000; Miller, 1994; Reynolds, 1997, 1999); (5) deemphasize campaign-managed events and candidates' strategies and image-management techniques (Evatt, 1999; Kennamer & South, 2002; McGregor et al., 1999, 2000; Miller, 1994; Reynolds, 1997, 1999); and (6) feature less horse race coverage and who's-ahead-and-who's-behind public opinion polls (Evatt, 1999; Friedland & Nichols, 2002; Kennamer & South, 2002; McGregor et al., 2000; Meyer & Potter, 2000; Miller, 1994; Reynolds, 1997, 1999).

These apparently successful efforts to reorient news coverage along the lines recommended by public journalism's founding scholarly and journalistic advocates (see chapter 1) also manifest themselves in attempts to involve citizens more actively in democratic processes, notably through the inclusion of "mobilizing information." Compared to mainstream news organizations more generally, news organizations practicing public journalism have been found to carry more election-related mobilizing information, such as information about how to register to vote and where to go to cast one's ballot (McMillan et al., 1998; Miller, 1994), and to carry more information about how to become involved in local, citizen-based interventions, such as by including contact information for local civic organizations working on given problems under investigation (Blazier & Lemert, 2000; Moscowitz, 2002). News organizations practicing public journalism not only carry more mobilizing information, but also tend to display such information more often in visual form, including through the use of prominent graphics (Coleman, 2000b; Coleman & Wasike, 2004).

While news organizations practicing public journalism have done much to challenge prevailing news reporting conventions, the research on sourcing patterns is more mixed. On one hand, many studies have found that news organizations practicing public journalism feature more ordinary citizens (Blazier & Lemert, 2000; Friedland & Nichols, 2002; Kennamer & South, 2002; Lee, 2001; Massey, 1998; Moscowitz, 2002; Roush, 2003), including women and minorities (Ewart, 2000, 2002, 2003; Kurpius, 2002; Massey, 1999), as sources of information than do mainstream news organizations more generally. This suggests, in turn, that news organizations do indeed make efforts to provide citizens, including members of marginalized social groups, with opportunities to articulate their particular concerns in public. Yet, when it comes to the overall sourcing pattern, the results are more inconclusive. While some studies have found news organizations practicing public journalism to quote more citizens than elite actors (Blazier & Lemert, 2000; Ewart, 2000, Moscowitz, 2002), other studies have found news organizations to quote an equal number of citizens and elite actors (Friedland & Nichols, 2002; Massey, 1998, 1999; Roush, 2003) or even to quote more elite actors than citizens (Ewart, 2002, 2003; Kennamer & South, 2002; Lee, 2001; McMillan et al., 1998; Reynolds, 1997, 1999).

PUBLIC JOURNALISM'S IMPACT ON CITIZENS

The above-mentioned features of public journalism's news coverage have, with few exceptions (see Blomquist & Zukin, 1997), been linked to positive effects on citizens' civic knowledge, attitudes, and behaviors. In terms of civic knowledge and attitudes, public journalism–inspired news coverage has been found to enhance citizens' (1) interest in, knowledge of, and concern for election-year topics and local community problems (Chaffee, McDevitt, & Thorson, 1997; Chen, Thorson, Yoon, & Ognianova, 2002; Denton & Thorson, 1997, 1998; Huang, 2006; Meyer & Potter, 2000; Miller, 1994; Thorson, Friedland, & Anderson, 1997; Thorson, Shim, & Yoon, 2002); (2) trust in others (Denton & Thorson, 1997, 1998; Meyer & Potter, 2000); (3) willingness and perceived ability to take part in public problem-solving activities (Chaffee et al., 1997; Meyer & Potter, 2000; Thorson et al., 1997); and (4) positive attitudes toward participating news organizations (Denton & Thorson, 1997; Friedland & Nichols, 2002; Huang, 2006; Meyer & Potter, 2000; Miller, 1994; Rhodenbaugh, 1998; Thorson et al., 1997, Zang, 1995).

In turn, these positive changes in citizens' civic knowledge and attitudes have been found to enhance citizens' inclination to (1) engage in interpersonal discussion of election-year topics and local community problems (Chaffee et al., 1997; Chen et al., 2002; Friedland & Nichols, 2002; Friedland et al., 1998; Simmons, 1999; Thorson et al., 1997, 2002; Thorson, Ognianova, Coyle, & Lambeth, 1998; Vercelotti, 2001); (2) volunteer for and/or donate money to local civic organizations (Chaffee et al., 1997; Chen et al., 2002; Friedland, 2000; Friedland & Nichols, 2002; Thorson et al., 2002); (3) establish new civic organizations (Friedland, 2000; Friedland & Nichols, 2002); (4) contact public officials about local community problems (Friedland et al., 1998); (5) register to vote (Miller, 1994; Ruggiero & Craft, 2001); and (6) vote in elections (Bowers & Walker, 2003; Chaffee et al., 1997; Chen et al., 2002; Denton & Thorson, 1998; Friedland et al., 1998; Miller, 1994; Ruggiero & Craft, 2001). Aside from these positive effects on citizens' civic behaviors, a couple of studies by Friedland and colleagues (see Friedland, 2000; Friedland & Nichols, 2002; Nichols, Friedland, Rojas, Cho, & Shah, 2006) have found public journalism's news coverage to have an actual political impact, notably by prompting local government officials to make more public funds available for existing efforts to address given problems or even to change their public policies toward those problems.

While only a couple of studies have tried to determine which of public journalism's newswork behaviors have a particularly strong impact on citizens' civic knowledge, attitudes, and behaviors, a number of important findings have been made. First, research shows that initiatives that focus on a single problem over a sustained period of time are more effective overall than are initiatives that focus on multiple problems for shorter periods of time. In a comparative study of four public journalism initiatives, Thorson et al. (1997) found that the *Charlotte Observer*'s "Taking Back Our Neighborhoods," an initiative that focused solely on the problem of crime and ran for a considerable length of time, was more successful at enhancing citizens' interest in, knowledge of, and concern for this problem than were the three other initiatives that focused on several problems at once and did so for shorter periods of time. Moreover, Thorson et al. (1997) found that initiatives that aim to involve citizens in public problem-solving are more effective overall than are initiatives that only aim to involve citizens in public deliberation. Specifically, they found that, while the two problem-solving initiatives (the *Charlotte Observer*'s "Taking Back Our Neighborhoods" and the Binghamton, New York, *Press & Sun Bulletin*'s "Facing Our Future") also enhanced public deliberation, the two deliberative initiatives (the *Wisconsin State Journal*'s "We the People" and the *San Francisco Chronicle*'s "Voice of the Voter") did not inspire any public problem-solving activity. Moreover, in a study of an unnamed multiple-media initiative on the problem of unemployment, Thorson et al. (1998) found that knowledge of the problem was significantly higher among citizens who had been exposed to the initiative through newspaper and television (but not radio) coverage than among citizens who had only been exposed to the initiative through one of the three media. Relatedly, in a secondary analysis of data from Friedland and Nichols's (2002) study, Nichols et al. (2006) found that multi-media partnerships were significantly more likely than initiatives conducted by single news organizations to inspire citizens to join existing civic organizations or to create new ones.

Taken together, these findings suggest that the most effective public journalism initiatives are (1) conducted in collaboration between one or more newspapers and television stations, (2) focused on a single problem over a sustained period of time, and (3) aimed at involving citizens in both public deliberation and public problem-solving.

METHODOLOGICAL SHORTCOMINGS

While most of the empirical research on public journalism is well conceptualized, well executed, and well reported, some studies suffer from methodological problems relating to conceptualization, measurement, and interpretation. These shortcomings do not raise doubts about the validity of the body of research as a whole. But they do direct attention to deficiencies that future studies ought to address.

First, and most importantly, few of the studies were guided by clearly and fully explicated conceptual definitions of public journalism. Instead, many of the studies defined public journalism in very general (and vague) terms as a journalistic movement whose primary goals are to enhance civic commitment to and citizen participation in democratic processes. While public journalism advocates' failure to define public journalism as a journalistic philosophy in its own right might explain, if not legitimately justify, this absence of conceptual definitions, researchers could, as a second-best option, have developed operational definitions by distinguishing public journalism's practices from those of conventional, mainstream journalism. Here, studies of journalists' attitudes toward public journalism did a generally much better job than did studies of public journalism's news coverage and its impact on citizens. While most of the former studies operationalized public journalism in terms of its most prevalent practices, such as by distinguishing between "modest" and "bolder" approaches to public journalism (e.g., Voakes, 1999), many of the latter studies merely assumed that given news organizations were practicing public journalism either because they had participated in initiatives supported financially by such institutions as the Pew Center for Civic Journalism or because they themselves labeled their efforts as public journalism. One notable exception to this pattern is Meyer and Potter (2000), who operationalized public journalism in terms of seven commonly applied practices.

Although most of the studies of journalists' attitudes toward public journalism were guided by operational definitions of public journalism, some of the definitions applied were arguably too narrow and, in a few instances, even misleading. For example, in operationalizing what he termed "personal" and "institutional" public journalism, Bare (1998) defined public journalism in terms of individual journalists' or news organizations' commitments to help solve community problems. While problem-solving is certainly an important aspect of public journalism, it is not the only aspect and, as studies of journalists' attitudes toward public journalism show, most surely not the least controversial one. More problematically, a couple of studies equated public journalism with practices that arguably have little, if anything, to do with it. For example, Weaver and Wilhoit (1996) defined public journalism in part by journalists' efforts to develop the public's intellectual and cultural interests and to provide entertainment. Similarly, Heider et al. (2006) and Poindexter et al. (2006) defined public journalism in part as the reporting on interesting people and groups.

While Meyer and Potter's (2000) study, as previously mentioned, was based on one of the most clearly and fully explicated operational definitions of public journalism, this study suffered from other problems; problems that are shared by the five studies that draw on secondary analyses of their data (see Loomis, 1998; Maier & Potter, 2001; Rhodenbaugh, 1998; Ruggiero & Craft, 2001; Verykoukis, 1998). Meyer and Potter (2000) used their measure of twenty newspapers' before-hand intentions of doing public journalism to test for effects on citizens from the newspapers' subsequent election reporting. This seems counterintuitive considering that Meyer and Potter (2000) offered no evidence that the newspapers had publicized their before-hand intentions of doing public journalism. In the absence of such publicity, one would more logically expect citizens to be impacted by the newspapers' actual election reporting; that is, the publicly observable, physical manifestations of their privately held intentions.

Moreover, some of the studies suffered from various measurement problems. Most of the studies of public journalism's news coverage were quantitative content analyses. In such analyses, it is a commonly held norm that the researcher should not only offer explicitly defined (and accepted) variable operationalizations but also provide statistics summarizing the level of coder agreement. However, many of these studies did not fully explain how the variables under investigation were operationalized but instead merely listed variable labels, did not report the level of coder agreement, or underreported the extent to which coders agreed, such as by providing an overall, simple agreement coefficient that masked the reliability of individual variables. Relatedly, some of these studies were conducted solely by their authors. In such cases, coder reliability is of the weakest kind: "Intracoder agreement," or "stability," the coder's agreement with himself or herself over time. "Intercoder reliability," or "reproducibility," is a much stronger measure as it gauges the degree to which coding protocols yield similar results when applied by two or more coders, none of which, ideally, are the author (see Krippendorff, 2003). The idea is to demonstrate that the phenomenon being investigated exists independently—or outside the mind—of the person who designed the study. Finally, some of these studies did not make clear who performed the coding—whether the coding was done by the author, independent coders only, or some combination of the author and independent coders.

Like the content-analytic studies, some of the survey-based studies also suffered from measurement problems. Aside from failing to report response rates, some of these studies achieved response rates that fell well below the commonly accepted minimum of 50%, making it difficult to accurately generalize from the samples under investigation to the larger populations that those samples were supposed to represent. For example, the Campaign Study Group (2001) study reported a response rate of 70%, which, when calculated correctly, only amounted to 23.4%. The authors noted that out of a sample of 512 newspapers, 360 newspapers, or 70%, returned the questionnaire. However, it was also noted that the questionnaire was originally mailed to the three top editors at each of the 512 newspapers. So, the actual sample consisted of 1,536 editors, of which a reported 471 editors (30.7%) actually returned the questionnaires. Since only the senior-most editor's response was retained in those instances where more than one questionnaire was returned from the same newspaper, the actual response rate was 360 out of 1,536 editors, or 23.4%.

In addition to lack of information about, or poor, response rates, some of the survey-based studies did not detail the actual questions asked. This is clearly problematic considering that question wording is likely to influence responses. Moreover, some of these studies included questions that were "double-barreled," in the sense of simultaneously asking two or more questions. For example, Arant and Meyer (1998) posed the following double-barreled, agree–disagree statement: "My newspaper has an obligation not just to point out community problems and explain alternative solutions but also to set up meetings and organize programs to solve the problems." The problem with this statement is that a respondent could potentially agree (or disagree) with one or more of its four dimensions and still disagree (or agree) with the rest, making it difficult to interpret what an agree or disagree response actually meant to the respondent. Relatedly, Dickson and Topping (2001) asked their respondents whether their newspapers had participated in at least one public journalism "project" or "activity" within the previous 5 years. While this question is not double-barreled, its wording might inadvertently have inflated the number of respondents who answered yes to it by combining a measure of relatively strong commitment to public journalism (e.g., participation in a public journalism project), with the much broader (and more loosely defined) notion of public journalism activity. Indeed, Dickson and Topping's (2001) finding that almost three quarters (73%) of respondents work for news organizations that have been involved with public journalism in one form or another is much higher than those reported by Arant and Meyer (1998) and Friedland and Nichols (2002). A similar problem may have beset the Campaign Study Group (2001) study, which asked respondents whether they had used the "tools" and "techniques" of public journalism.

Finally, a couple of studies might have overestimated the differences in the news coverage of news organizations practicing public journalism and mainstream news organizations more generally as well as the impact of public journalism's news coverage on citizens. While the Campaign Study Group's (2001) assessment of differences in news coverage was based on journalists' self-reported behaviors rather than on any actual, comparative analyses of content, Friedland and Nichols's (2002) and Nichols et al.'s (2006) assessments of public journalism's impact on citizens were based on journalists', rather than on their own, evaluations of such impact. More generally, studies of public journalism's impact on voting might have exaggerated the actual level of such impact. While it is certainly likely that news organizations' inclusion of election–related mobilizing information and, more generally, emphasis on active citizen participation in democratic process have led to higher voter turnout, these studies did not take into account other possible causal factors. Indeed, the complexity of voting behavior makes it unlikely that increases in voter turnout was due only to public journalism–related content factors.

SUGGESTIONS FOR FUTURE RESEARCH

Aside from addressing the methodological shortcomings discussed above, future research ought to broaden the substantive scope of inquiry in a number of important directions. Here, I focus on general gaps in the empirical research literature as well as on more specific questions relating to how closely the practice of public journalism approximates the democratic ideals underlying my proposed public philosophy.

First, future research should expand on the range of news organizations under investigation. Although many studies have investigated public journalism's news coverage and its impact on citizens, much of what is currently known about these topics stems from studies of a small number of public journalism's earliest and most well-known practitioners, notably the *Charlotte Observer*, the *Wichita Eagle*, and the *Wisconsin State Journal*. While these news organizations, as mentioned in chapter 1, have served as sources of inspiration for numerous other news organizations, the generalizability of findings would clearly be enhanced by incorporating a much wider array of news organizations. After all, more than 300 newspapers, or about one fifth of all daily newspapers in the United States, have been involved with public journalism over the past decade (Friedland & Nichols, 2002).

Second, while researchers' virtually exclusive focus on locally–oriented public journalism initiatives is justified by the relative absence of larger-scale initiatives, future studies should examine the larger-scale initiatives that do exist. As mentioned in chapter 1, both National Public Radio and the Public Broadcasting Service have been involved with public journalism initiatives of a national scope. More generally, Friedland and Nichols (2002) found that 6% of U.S. public journalism initiatives have been conducted by newspapers with a daily circulation of 500,000 or more.

Third, future research should expand its scope of inquiry beyond public journalism–inspired election initiatives. Although a number of studies have looked at special reporting projects as well as at efforts to make public journalism an integral part of daily information-gathering and news-reporting practices, the predominant focus continues to be election reporting. This is both surprising and unfortunate considering that only about 10% of the U.S. public journalism initiatives conducted to date have focused on elections (Friedland & Nichols, 2002).

Finally, there is a general lack of independent, social–scientific research on the practice of public journalism outside the United States. While news organizations in about a dozen other countries have experimented with public journalism during the past decade, a topic I discuss in more detail in chapter 7, much of what is currently known about these initiatives stems from descriptive accounts by journalism scholars and practicing journalists who have been involved with designing and/or executing them.

In addition to filling these general gaps in the empirical research literature, future research ought to address a number of questions relating to my proposed public philosophy. First, while research shows that news organizations practicing public journalism quote more ordinary citizens, including women and minorities, than do mainstream news organizations more generally, little is known about how citizens are quoted. Do news organizations help nurture a genuinely deliberating public by highlighting citizens' underlying reasons for espousing certain opinions? Or, alternatively, do they merely offer citizens opportunities to state their opinions on given topics but without substantiating their claims? Similarly, to what extent do news organizations articulate the particular social locations from which citizens speak as a means to elucidate how those social locations affect their sense of problems and solutions? Are citizens presented as embodied beings who speak from particular social locations? Or, alternatively, are they presented as disembodied beings who do not speak from any particular vantage points? Finally, to what extent do news organizations offer citizens opportunities to challenge entrenched distinctions between topics of public interest and matters of private concern? Do news organizations offer citizens opportunities to introduce and comment on topics that traditionally have been rendered off-limits of public deliberation? Or, alternatively, do they only solicit citizen commentary on a limited range of predefined topics?

Second, future research should investigate news organizations' efforts to promote public deliberation off the news pages. While many studies have looked at public journalism's news coverage, little is known about the various citizen encounters, in the form of focus groups, roundtable discussions, and community forums, that news organizations sponsor and that help form the basis for their subsequent reporting. The absence of empirical research on this topic is both surprising and unfortunate considering that more than half (58%) of all U.S. public journalism initiatives conducted to date have featured some form of news media–sponsored public deliberation (Friedland & Nichols, 2002). Among many possible research concerns, future studies should investigate the structure and foci of such forums as well as the moderating roles news organizations play. Do news organizations tend to sponsor multiple forums in which members of specific social groups can deliberate about their particular concerns among themselves? Or, alternatively, do they tend to sponsor more encompassing forums in which members of various social groups are encouraged to jointly deliberate about problems of presumed common concern? And to the extent that the latter is the case, do news organizations make special efforts to promote participatory parity among members of different social groups?

Third, future research should investigate the extent to which news organizations work to create a critical public sphere about journalism in which citizens can publicly criticize news reporting on given topics and news organizations subsequently respond publicly to citizen criticism. While Friedland and Nichols (2002) found that almost half (47%) of all U.S. public journalism initiatives conducted to date have featured requests for citizen feedback, they did not elaborate on whether such feedback was publicized and publicly responded to or whether it merely served to inform journalists' work behind closed doors. Similarly, while many examples exist of news organizations offering citizens opportunities to participate in the setting of the news media agenda, little is known about how widespread that practice is and what role, precisely, citizens play in the agenda-setting process. Do citizens and journalists serve as genuine partners with equal opportunities to influence the news media agenda? Or, alternatively, do citizens merely serve in an advisory capacity for journalists who listen to citizens' suggestions but ultimately decide upon the news media agenda on their own?

Finally, while much is known about how public journalism's news coverage impacts citizens, little is known about the social distribution of that impact and, more broadly, about the nature of the problem-solving efforts that given public journalism initiatives help inspire. How are the effects of public journalism's impact distributed within given localities? Do public journalism initiatives tend to reduce differences in political knowledge and participation among dominant and subordinate social groups? Or, alternatively, do they tend to stabilize, or perhaps even widen, any preexisting differences among different social groups? Relatedly, do solutions that are eventually enacted by citizens and/or government officials tend to benefit all social groups within a given locality? Or, alternatively, do those solutions tend to favor the interests of certain dominant social groups?

FOUR

SCHOLARLY AND JOURNALISTIC CRITICISMS OF PUBLIC JOURNALISM

While mainstream journalists, as discussed in the previous chapter, have been found to be favorably disposed toward many of public journalism's practices, it is no exaggeration to say that public journalism has been and continues to be one of the most controversial, if not divisive, topics in journalism circles. Indeed, since the very first public journalism initiatives were carried out in the late 1980s and early 1990s, journalism scholars and practicing journalists alike have directed various more or less damning criticisms at public journalism. In this chapter, I summarize, analyze, and respond to the most significant of those criticisms by drawing on my proposed public philosophy and the empirical research literature on public journalism, as well as other relevant material. In so doing, I also further clarify and elaborate on my vision for public journalism and its implications for how I believe public journalism ought to be practiced.

I begin by responding to a number of criticisms regarding the very nature of public journalism, namely the claims that advocates have failed to clearly define public journalism as a journalistic notion and, more radically, that advocates have tried to build a religious movement rather than a journalistic notion proper. While I agree with scholarly critics that public journalism remains inadequately theorized, I contend that journalistic critics' use of religious metaphors to ridicule public journalism is best understood as a classic, if extreme, example of journalistic boundary-maintenance work aimed at ostracizing public journalism's newsroom practitioners from the realm of legitimate journalists.

Next, I respond to various criticisms regarding the commercial context of public journalism. While I agree with scholarly critics that advocates have failed to consider the potential constraints imposed by commercial media systems, I show that news organizations practicing public journalism have been able to promote broad-based citizen participation in democratic processes, despite managements' interest in catering to the demographically most attractive segments of the citizenry. Journalistic critics' more damning accusations that public journalism is merely a profit–oriented strategy embraced by managements to serve the commercial interests of media owners and advertisers, and that this profit orientation is likely to force journalists to self-censor their reporting for fear of offending audiences, are best understood as manifestations of increasing anxiety about a corporate colonization of journalism and its damaging impact on journalists' professional autonomy and the quality of news coverage. In this important respect, I argue, public journalism can be seen to have served as a critical incident; that is, as an opportunity for journalists to air, challenge, and negotiate their own boundaries of practice vis-à-vis the commercial institutions within which journalism operates.

Following this discussion of potential obstacles standing in the way of furthering public journalism's goals, I respond to criticisms regarding the very appropriateness of those goals, notably that journalists should engage in problem-solving, and the means used to achieve them (public opinion polls and news media–sponsored forums for public deliberation). While I disagree with the claim, advanced by both scholarly and journalistic critics, that journalists can and should try to remain politically neutral with respect to possible solutions to problems, I agree with scholarly critics that journalists should not exaggerate their power as agents of progressive political change by acknowledging that journalism is only one of many important political institutions. I also agree with scholarly critics that the use of public opinion polls to identify problems of concern to citizens is deeply problematic and should be abandoned, but argue that, in the absence of any viable alternatives to the news media–sponsored forums for public deliberation currently in use, journalists should instead try to make such forums as open and inclusive as possible. I conclude by briefly considering how advocates could more fully convince managements, editors, and rank-and-file reporters of the utility of public journalism.

THE NATURE OF PUBLIC JOURNALISM

The first and arguably most fundamental criticism concerns the very nature of public journalism. Briefly put, while some scholarly critics fault advocates for having failed to clearly define public journalism as a journalistic notion—to explicate whether public journalism is a journalistic philosophy, theory, or merely a set of practices (see, for example, Coleman, 1997; Meyer, 1998; Richards, 2000)—others fault advocates for having failed to clearly specify how public journalism differs from conventional, mainstream journalism (see, for example, Lichtenberg, 1999; Roselle, 2003; Zelizer, 1999). Still others, as mentioned in chapter 2, call on advocates to develop an explicit "public philosophy" for public journalism.

There can be little doubt that public journalism's founding scholarly and journalistic advocates have failed to clearly define public journalism as a journalistic notion. While advocates, as described in chapter 1, have advanced certain broad-based arguments about the relationship between journalism and democracy, how journalists should conceive of the public, and what role journalists should play in public life, those arguments do not add up to a coherent journalistic philosophy (or theory) in its own right. Indeed, my primary objective in chapter 2 was to heed scholars' call for an explicit public philosophy that could guide the adoption of specific goals and inspire the development of particular practices to help achieve those goals.

Nevertheless, advocates have, at least implicitly, tried to define public journalism through their challenges to conventional, mainstream journalism. As described in chapter 1, advocates have taken issue with various problematic aspects of contemporary election reporting and, more broadly, with the elite-centered focus of daily news coverage. Moreover, the actual practice of public journalism helps define it as a journalistic notion. As outlined in chapter 1, and described more formally in chapter 3, the empirical research literature shows that, as a journalistic notion, public journalism is centrally aimed at (1) reporting on problems of particular concern to citizens (e.g., by focusing more attention on substantive policy issues than on isolated political events), (2) covering those problems from the perspectives of citizens (e.g., by including more citizens, including women and minorities, as sources of information), and (3) involving citizens in efforts to address problems in practice (e.g., by including more mobilizing information about how to become involved in local community affairs). Thus, public journalism remains in the unfortunate situation of being defined more by its challenges to perceived flaws in conventional, mainstream journalism and by its own alternative practices than by any sustained, scholarly effort to define it as a journalistic philosophy (or theory) in its own right.

PUBLIC JOURNALISM AS A RELIGIOUS MOVEMENT

Contrary to most scholarly critics, who tend to see public journalism as a well-meaning, if underdeveloped, journalistic notion, many journalistic critics contend that public journalism is not a journalistic notion at all. Indeed, for metaphors to describe public journalism, journalists most often borrow from religion. While some journalists claim that public journalism is an "old-fashioned religion" (Ward, 1996, p. 23), others describe it as "the hottest secular religion in the news business" (Shepard, 1994, p. 29), a "New Age civic religion" (Hoyt, 1995, p. 30), or an effort to "convert the media from dispensers of salacious gossip into something more Good Samaritan–like" (Snow, 1996, p. A13). As such, public journalism's "gospel" (Cohn, 1995, p. 14; Corrigan, 1999, p. 19; Jurkowitz, 1996, p. 17; Shepard, 1994, p. 28), "evangel" (Corrigan, 1999, p. 19), "sermon" (Hoyt, 1996, p. 30), "doctrine" (Corrigan, 1999, p. 55), or "crusade of goodwill" (Villano, 1996, p. 32) rests on "several articles of faith" (Corrigan, 1999, p. 74; Stepp, 1996, p. 39) and "draws on a number of sacred texts" (Hoyt, 1995, p. 32).

Analogously, public journalism's founding scholarly and journalistic advocates, notably Jay Rosen and Davis Merritt, are described as "apostles" (Corrigan, 1999, p. 24), "high priests" (Cohn, 1995, p. 14), "preachers" (Shepard, 1994, p. 29), "proselytizers" (Shaw, 1999, p. 73), "evangelists" (Corrigan, 1999, p. 27; German, 2000, p. A25; Glaberson, 1994, p. D6), "civic crusaders" (Nofziger, 2000, p. B8; Shepard, 2000, p. 44; Stein, 1994, p. 15), and, most commonly, "gurus" (Cohn, 1995, p. 14; Corrigan, 1996, p. 15B; Corrigan, 1999, p. 28; Dubuisson, 1995, p. F2; O'Brien, 1996, p. 8; Revah, 1996, p. 8; Shepard, 1994, p. 29), who partake in "evangelic road shows" (Dennis, 1995, p. 48), a "crusade" (Corrigan, 1999, p. 76), or even a "holy war" (Stepp, 1996, p. 38), to call on journalists to enter "the promised land of community connectedness" (Hoyt, 1992, p. 47) or the "road to salvation" (Corrigan, 1999, p. 12). James Fallows, former editor of *US World & News Report* and another prominent advocate of public journalism, is described as "the media minister" who "blessed" public journalism (Hoyt, 1996, pp. 28–29).

Public journalism's newsroom practitioners, in turn, are described as "co-religionists" (Skube, 1999, p. 12L), "believers" (Shepard, 1994, p. 29), "members of a cult" (Jurkowitz, 1996, p. 17), or "converts" (Corrigan, 1996, p. 15B; Corrigan, 1999, p. 19; Jurkowitz, 2000, p. F1), who have experienced a "conversion" (Corrigan, 1999, p. 74) and who "bear witness" to public journalism (German, 2000, p. A25) while defending their newsroom experiments with a "religious fervor" (Effron, 1997, p. 14).

While these accusations are arguably too outlandish to merit a serious rebuttal, it is worth considering why journalists would condemn public journalism, its advocates, and newsroom practitioners in such strong terms. Most importantly, these attacks could be seen as a classic, if extreme, example of what many scholars, following Bennett, Gressett, and Haltom's (1985) seminal work on the topic, call "journalistic boundary-maintenance work" (see, for example, Bratich, 2004; Hindman, 2005; Ruggiero, 2004). That is, they could be understood as an effort to ostracize public journalism's advocates and, more specifically, its newsroom practitioners from the realm of legitimate journalists. But in contrast to most other instances of journalistic boundary-maintenance work, where the journalism community has reacted to individual journalists or news organizations that have strayed from commonly accepted journalistic norms and practices, the challenges posed by public journalism required a more extreme response. Specifically, by arguing that journalists should report on problems of concern to citizens and do so from citizens' perspectives rather than those of government officials, experts, and other elite actors, public journalism challenges the very foundation upon which mainstream journalists' cultural capital and authority are based: their privileged access to elite sources of information. This also explains why journalists from news organizations with some of the most privileged access to national and international elites, notably the *New York Times* and the *Washington Post*, have been among the strongest critics of public journalism (see, for example, Frankel, 1995; Raines, 1996; Yardley, 1996).

The use of religious metaphors in particular to facilitate this condemnation of public journalism could also be put in the context of Weaver et al.'s (2006) finding that the percentage of journalists who describe religion or religious beliefs as being very important to them (36%) is significantly lower than in the U.S. population at large (61%). That is, for journalists who pride themselves not merely on their rationality but specifically on their secular (if not anti-religious) habits of mind and who commit themselves only to professional principles, to accuse public journalism's newsroom practitioners of having been duped by religious fanatics is to strip them of any form of professionalism and ability to render professional judgments. Ironically, journalists' use of religious metaphors to condemn public journalism ignores how one of the cornerstones of mainstream, professional ideology—the ideal of objectivity—is itself, if not religious, then at least faith-based. As Schudson (1978, p. 6) puts it, the ideal of objectivity is based on "a faith in facts, a distrust of values, and a commitment to their segregation."

THE COMMERCIAL CONTEXT OF PUBLIC JOURNALISM

Aside from faulting advocates for having failed to clearly define public journalism as a journalistic notion, and casting doubts about whether public journalism should be regarded as a journalistic notion at all, scholarly and journalistic critics alike have expressed a number of concerns regarding the commercial context of public journalism. Many scholars criticize advocates for ignoring the potential constraints imposed by commercial media systems and, more specifically, for failing to acknowledge that public journalism's ability to promote broad-based citizen participation in democratic processes might be inherently limited by media owners' and advertisers' commercial interests in catering to demographically attractive segments of the citizenry, whose concerns are not necessarily the most politically compelling (see, for example, Calabrese, 2000; Hackett & Zhao, 1998; Iggers, 1998). Public journalism's financial dependence, some scholars claim, is masked by heavy reliance on support from such institutions as the Pew Center for Civic Journalism (see Cook, 1998; Glasser & Craft, 1998; Merrill, Blevens, & Gade, 2002). Other scholars argue that by appealing to the civic conscience of individual editors and reporters, and by casting journalism's problems as rhetorical rather than structural, advocates neither demand nor will inspire any fundamental changes to the commercial logic of news organizations (see Compton, 2000; Hardt, 1999; Martin, 2001). Still other, perhaps more cynical, scholars assert that public journalism's emphasis on addressing audience concerns is likely to serve the circulation and profit interests of media owners and advertisers (see Frank, 1998; McChesney, 1999; Richards, 2000).

To many journalists, public journalism is not merely likely to serve the circulation and profit interests of media owners and advertisers; it is, in fact, a deliberate, corporate strategy embraced by managements to advance such commercial concerns (see, for example, Greenberg, 1996; Peirce, 1994; Tracey, 2003). This commercial orientation, many journalists claim, is likely to force journalists who work for news organizations practicing public journalism to self-censor their reporting for fear of offending audiences and, by implication, media owners and advertisers (see, for example, Calamai, 1995; Hoyt, 1995; Shaw, 1999).

It is certainly true that public journalism's founding scholarly and journalistic advocates have ignored the potential constraints imposed by commercial media systems and, more precisely, public journalism's ability to further its goals, given media owners' and advertisers' interest in maximizing profits. Instead, advocates simply take the commercial foundations of news organizations as given. Indeed, in one of only a few explicit statements on this topic, Rosen (2000, p. 682) notes that, as a journalistic reform movement operating within mainstream, commercial news media, "public journalism is not an insurrection, or even a minor revolt against the structural forces at work. It did not propose and cannot sustain a challenge to the commercial regime in which the American press operates." It is thus also correct that advocates have neither demanded nor sought to inspire any fundamental changes to the commercial logic of news organizations. Instead, advocates presume that entrenched journalistic norms and practices can be challenged without altogether subverting the commercial foundations of news organizations. As Rosen (1991, p. 268) puts it, public journalism assumes "that journalism could indeed be different…despite the regime of private ownership, the ideology inherent in a professional outlook, and the general weaknesses of the public sphere." And there is evidence to suggest that democratic concerns and commercial interests occupy a perhaps uneasy coexistence within news organizations practicing public journalism. Most significantly, the Gannett newspaper company, one of public journalism's long-standing supporters, launched its still ongoing "Real Life, Real News" initiative in 2004. Explicitly aimed at increasing circulation and profits, notably through reader surveys conducted by the marketing departments of individual news outlets, this initiative encourages the company's news outlets to place more emphasis on the impact of news stories on readers' everyday lives. Contrary to public journalism's focus on engaging citizens in deliberation and problem-solving, as members of larger, politically involved publics, this initiative addresses citizens as individual consumers of news concerned with its impact on their private lives (see Gannett's web site, http://www.gannett.com).

Nevertheless, commercial imperatives do not necessarily prevent news organizations practicing public journalism from promoting broad-based citizen participation in democratic processes, as scholars fear. Aside from having sponsored community-wide deliberative forums in hundreds of cities (Friedland & Nichols, 2002) and, as the research on sourcing patterns shows, relying more on women and minorities as sources of information than mainstream news organizations more generally (see chapter 3), there is evidence that these news organizations have addressed politically unpopular problems of concern to commercially unpopular segments of the citizenry. According to Friedland and Nichols (2002), more than one fifth of the approximately 600 U.S. public journalism initiatives conducted to date—nearly all by commercial news organizations, with the exception of some by public broadcasters (see chapter 1)—have focused on such problems as racism, poverty, and inner-city crime. Other problems of particular concern to marginalized segments of the citizenry (especially minorities) include alcohol and drug abuse, child care, domestic violence, health care, homelessness, immigration, public housing, racial profiling, unemployment, and welfare. Thus, news organizations have spent considerable resources, both material and symbolic, addressing the plight of the most marginalized segments of the citizenry. Again, these are hardly the segments of the citizenry coveted by advertisers and, by extension, media owners. Thus, contrary to the fear that news organizations would only cater to demographically attractive segments of the citizenry, public journalism initiatives have not been geared toward the wealthy and powerful—the ones most attractive to management.

While it is certainly true that institutions such as the Pew Center for Civic Journalism have supported public journalism financially, including by funding initiatives on problems like racism, poverty, and inner-city crime (see Ford, 1998, 2001; Kramer, 1997, for various examples), there is no evidence that such support, which typically has amounted to $12–15,000, has even come close to covering the actual costs. Indeed, research shows that public journalism initiatives are costly (see Loomis, 1998; Meyer, 1998; Potter & Kurpius, 2000). This is not surprising considering that such initiatives, as discussed in previous chapters, tend to rely more heavily than does conventional, mainstream journalism on staff-written stories; expensive surveys, interviews, and focus groups with citizens; and elaborate visual displays, among other expenses.

More broadly, the vast majority of public journalism initiatives (90%) have focused on long-standing, deeply embedded community issues rather than on elections and other more newsworthy events (10%) (see chapter 1). This suggests, in turn, that news organizations have managed to avoid the commercially–oriented tendency for "episodic" (event-based), as opposed to "thematic" (issue-based), news reporting (see, for example, Bennett, 2006; Iyengar, 1991; Patterson, 1993).

Further evidence of the willingness of commercial news organizations to transcend narrow competitive agendas comes from the more than 160 multiple-media partnerships that have been formed to date (see chapter 1). Contrary to the fear that such inter-media alliances would homogenize news reporting (see Corrigan, 1999; Gartner, 1998; Grimes, 1999), research shows that news organizations have coordinated their reporting to maximize reach and impact while producing complementary, as opposed to overlapping, coverage (see Denton & Thorson, 1998; Thorson et al., 1997, 1998).

As to scholars' fear that public journalism's emphasis on addressing audience concerns is likely to serve the circulation and profit interests of media owners and advertisers, I would certainly hope that practicing public journalism is economically viable, as this would likely prompt even more news organizations to embrace it, a topic I return to later in the chapter. The question, rather, is whether the notion of public journalism has been embraced by managements to further purely commercial interests at the expense of citizens' democratic needs.

The most damning accusations, made by many journalists, that public journalism is indeed a profit-centered strategy embraced by managements to serve the commercial interests of media owners and advertisers, and that this profit orientation is likely to force journalists who work for news organizations practicing public journalism to self-censor their reporting for fear of offending audiences, find little empirical support. While the charge of self-censorship is refuted, at least in part, by research showing that many public journalism initiatives have addressed controversial problems such as racism, poverty, and inner-city crime, research also shows that the factors predisposing given news organizations to practice public journalism include the civic attitudes of their top managers. In a study of the 19 largest publicly held newspaper companies in the United States, Loomis and Meyer (2000) found that companies whose top managers expressed more concern for social responsibility than for generating profits were significantly more likely to practice public journalism than were companies whose top managers embraced profits over social responsibility. Thus, while it might be correct, as scholars fear, that appealing to the civic conscience of individual editors and reporters will not inspire any fundamental changes to the commercial logic of news organizations, Loomis and Meyer's (2000) findings suggest that top managers with civic consciences can and do ensure that news organizations are guided by more than a concern for profit. Importantly, journalists' claim that newspaper companies such as Gannett and Knight-Ridder have embraced public journalism primarily out of a concern with generating profits (see Hoyt, 1995; Paterno, 1996; Villano, 1996) was also refuted. Both companies scored higher on social responsibility than on profit orientation. Nevertheless, as previously noted, Gannett's launch of its "Real Life, Real News" initiative and continuous support of public journalism suggests that concerns for profit and social responsibility occupy a perhaps uneasy coexistence within individual news organizations. However, the controversial nature of many public journalism initiatives (and especially ones that address politically unpopular problems of concern to commercially unpopular segments of the citizenry), coupled with the very costliness of practicing public journalism, suggests that these particular problems are better positioned as general critiques of contemporary, mainstream journalism than as problems particular to public journalism.

While these accusations find little empirical support, it is worth considering why journalists, as in the case of the claim that public journalism is a religious movement, would advance such comparatively much more extreme attacks than scholars. Most importantly, these accusations could be understood as a manifestation of journalists' own inability to halt, or even to criticize, the increasing corporate colonization of all journalism, including at their own news organizations. In this important respect, public journalism could be seen to have served as what Zelizer (1992, p. 67) calls a "critical incident"; that is, as an opportunity for journalists "to air, challenge, and negotiate their own boundaries of practice" vis-à-vis the commercial institutions within which journalism operates.

Research shows that journalists' anxiety, if not distress, about the profit orientation of news media and the damaging impact that orientation has on their professional autonomy and the quality of news coverage has increased dramatically over the past decade and a half, a time frame that coincides with the emergence of public journalism as a journalistic reform movement. In a survey of more than 550 top managers, mid-level editors, and rank-and-file reporters across the United States, the Pew Research Center (1999) found that 68% of editors and 75% of reporters were worried about the increasing corporatization of news media, as evidenced by buyouts of individual news organizations by diversified corporations and newspaper companies. They believed that business and financial pressures stemming from the profit orientation of corporate news media were undermining their professional autonomy and compromising the quality of news coverage. Such pressures, 65% of editors and 74% of reporters stated, had forced them to cater to news audiences by blurring the boundaries between news and entertainment. In a subsequent survey of more than 200 rank-and-file reporters across the United States, the Pew Research Center (2000) found that 41% and 30% of respondents, respectively, agreed that corporate owners and advertisers exerted a strong influence on which topics were covered or emphasized. Perhaps most importantly, this survey found reporters largely willing to acknowledge self-censorship. Thirty-six percent and 29% of respondents, respectively, stated that newsworthy stories were ignored to avoid damaging the financial interests of corporate owners or advertisers. Interestingly, of those reporters who admitted to having avoided newsworthy stories, only 19% said that superiors had sent them signals to do so. The majority (52%) had decided to self-censor reporting either on their own or based on the anticipated reactions of superiors. Most recently, the Pew Research Center (2004) found, in a survey of almost 550 top managers, mid-level editors, and rank-and-file reporters, that, when asked to mention the leading problems facing journalism today, the vast majority of respondents mentioned business/financial pressures and the declining quality of news coverage.

These findings stand in stark contrast to those of only a decade and a half ago. In their 1992 survey of more than 1,500 U.S. journalists, Weaver and Wilhoit (1996) documented a continuing decline in journalists' perceptions of their professional autonomy since 1982. Yet, among the 52% of respondents who mentioned internal-organizational constraints as contributing to diminished autonomy, only 9% cited profit-driven priorities as the most significant source. Similarly, among the 34% of respondents who mentioned external-organizational constraints as contributing to diminished autonomy, only 8% cited advertiser pressure as the most significant source.

Such data, then, suggest that journalists' accusations stem from their own fears about the damaging impact of news media's profit orientation rather than from any reasoned and reasonable assessment of public journalism. Journalists' self-understanding as autonomous professionals who decide upon the form and content of news reporting without interference from extra-journalistic actors and considerations is perceived, not illegitimately, as being threatened by media owners' and advertisers' commercial concerns with satisfying the interests of news audiences. Unable to launch a successful attack on their own employers (or future employers), and certainly unable to provide any plausible alternatives or solutions, they scapegoat public journalism instead.

PUBLIC JOURNALISM'S FOCUS ON PROBLEM-SOLVING

Scholarly and journalistic critics alike have not only raised concerns about public journalism's ability to further its goals within commercial media systems but have also taken issue with the very appropriateness of some of those goals, notably that journalists should engage in problem-solving. Many journalists contend that their sole professional responsibility is to report on problems and that any effort on their part to also engage in problem-solving would represent an abdication of that responsibility (see, for example, Eisner, 1994; Frankel, 1995; Greenberg, 1996). Other journalists fear that, if they were to engage in problem-solving, they would risk compromising their political neutrality by being forced to take sides among conflicting political interests, become advocates for particular political interests, or even succumb to dominant political interests (see, for example, Byrd, 1995; Cohn, 1995; Rosenfeld, 1995).

While some scholars agree that public journalism's focus on problem-solving could render journalists vulnerable in the face of dominant political interests (see Craig, 1996; Hodges, 1997; Ryan, 2001), most scholars do not take issue with the notion of problem-solving per se but fault advocates for exaggerating journalists' power as agents of progressive, political change (see, for example, Dzur, 2002; Goidel, 2000; Mancini, 1997).

It is certainly true that public journalism's explicit focus on problem-solving distinguishes it from conventional, mainstream journalism. Nevertheless, critics' distinctions between merely reporting on problems and also engaging in efforts to solve problems and, more broadly, between political neutrality and political advocacy, are arguably untenable. Indeed, one of the most important lessons of the vast scholarly literature on "news framing" (see, for example, Entman, 1993; Johnson-Cartee, 2004; Reese, Gandy, & Grant, 2001) is that there is no politically neutral standpoint from which to select and report on problems. Every time journalists choose to report on certain problems, from certain perspectives, using certain sources of information, they either implicitly or explicitly suggest that certain problems are more in need of public attention than others and that certain ways of understanding and addressing those problems are more appropriate than other possible ones. Put differently, the claim that journalists can remain politically neutral is both illusionary and counterproductive. It is illusionary because news reporting will by necessity always be based on the perspectives of certain sources of information, and counterproductive because pretending otherwise merely serves to deflect attention away from the particular political interests embedded within those perspectives. Public journalism, as discussed in previous chapters, aims to address both of these issues. First, it admonishes journalists to openly acknowledge the particular interests that guide their reporting. Second, it argues that journalists should challenge the interests embedded within conventional, mainstream journalism by reporting on problems of concern to citizens and do so from the perspectives of citizens rather than elite actors.

While the distinctions between problem-reporting and problem-solving, and between political neutrality and political advocacy, are untenable in a very fundamental sense, there is little reason to fear that the way in which public journalism is practiced has forced journalists into overt political advocacy in a more immediate, practical sense. Indeed, rather than advocating their own solutions to given problems, or endorsing those of other political actors, journalists have merely sponsored forums for citizen deliberation, encouraged citizens to become more involved in local community affairs through participation in local civic organizations, and, as part of election initiatives, offered citizens opportunities to ask candidates for office questions about what they plan to do to address given problems. In this important respect, the charge of political advocacy is better directed at my proposed public philosophy than at the actual practice of public journalism. As discussed in chapter 2, I would argue that journalists, in the interest of promoting social equality, should advocate specific political proposals on their own, endorse those of relevant politicians and candidates for office, and actively partner with special interest groups that seek to further given political ends. This more politically activist approach to problem-solving, however, would not force journalists to succumb to dominant political interests. Quite the contrary, it would require journalists to scrutinize all political interests as well as expose and condemn those whose agendas are at odds with the overarching goal of promoting social equality. But it would, on many occasions, require journalists to take sides among conflicting political interests. Indeed, journalists should not only help ensure that the concerns of the most marginalized segments of the citizenry are articulated and heard, but also seek to advance their particular concerns.

While I thus disagree with the argument that journalists can and should try to remain politically neutral, I agree with scholars that journalists should not exaggerate their power as agents of progressive, political change by acknowledging that journalism is only one of many important political institutions. While journalists can promote political change by sponsoring and reporting back on citizen deliberations, encouraging citizens to continue their deliberations and act upon their outcomes within civic and political organizations, advocating particular political proposals on their own, endorsing those of special interest groups, and applying pressure on relevant government officials, they cannot on their own ensure that citizens' deliberations are sustained over time, that given citizen solutions are enacted, or that government officials implement given policy recommendations in practice.

PUBLIC JOURNALISM'S USE OF PUBLIC OPINION POLLS AND DELIBERATIVE FORUMS

Finally, but not least importantly, a number of scholarly critics have raised concerns about the means public journalism's newsroom practitioners use to further their goals, notably public opinion polls (to identify problems of concern to citizens) and deliberative forums such as roundtable discussions, community forums, and town hall meetings (to offer citizens opportunities to debate those problems among themselves). Several scholars argue that the use of public opinion polls runs counter to the very idea of public journalism. Specifically, by equating public opinion with the aggregate of individual opinions, public opinion polls measure the opinions of individuals as opposed to the opinions of publics as well as accentuate the privateness, as opposed to the publicness, of public opinion by not offering citizens opportunities to publicly articulate and justify their opinions (see Glasser & Craft, 1998; Heikkila & Kunelius, 1996; Iggers, 1998).

I certainly agree that the use of public opinion polls to identify problems of concern to citizens, a method used in approximately one third of the 600 U.S. public journalism initiatives conducted to date (see Friedland & Nichols, 2002), is deeply problematic. Indeed, by asking individual citizens predetermined questions in a format that does not allow them to discuss their opinions, and their underlying reasons for espousing those opinions, with others, public opinion polls run counter to the very notion of a deliberating public engaged in a process of common deliberation (see chapter 2). Moreover, instead of offering journalists a genuine opportunity to learn what is on citizens' minds, when given the chance to elaborate on their concerns at length, in their own words, and through interaction with others, public opinion polls merely offer journalists a superficial understanding of where individual citizens stand in relation to problems predefined by journalists themselves as being of potential concern. In this important respect, the use of public opinion polls also runs counter to the notion, discussed in chapter 2, that citizens should serve as genuine partners in the process of setting the news media agenda. In effect, public opinion polls ask citizens to respond to an agenda already set by journalists rather than to independently (and publicly) help formulate an agenda of their own.

It would seem, then, that the most viable solution would be to use deliberative forums such as roundtable discussions, community forums, and town hall meetings not only to facilitate public deliberation on given problems, but also to determine which problems the public is to deliberate about in the first place. But, as mentioned, scholars have also greeted such forums with concern, arguing that they tend to privilege those citizens who have the time and skills to participate (see Pauly, 1999; Peters, 1999; Schroll, 1999).

One possibility, of course, could be to abandon the use of deliberative forums altogether and, instead, merely encourage citizens to conduct their deliberations within existing civic and political organizations. But this would relieve journalists of their responsibility for facilitating, as opposed to merely promoting, active citizen participation in democratic processes and, more importantly, leave the question unresolved as to how journalists should identify which problems are of concern to citizens. In the absence of any viable alternatives, the best option, I believe, would be to try to make the deliberative forums currently in use as open and inclusive as possible to avoid privileging certain participants. Aside from offering citizens (and members of marginalized social groups in particular) various material and/or symbolic incentives to participate, ranging from financial remuneration to a promise to subsequently report back on the outcomes of their deliberations, journalists could, as discussed in chapter 2, make special efforts to ensure that the concerns of marginalized social groups are articulated and heard, including by sponsoring separate discursive spaces for members of different social groups before bringing all the participants together within a joint discursive space and avoid privileging certain topics and modes of deliberation.

ENHANCING NEWSROOM COMMITMENT TO PUBLIC JOURNALISM

Having summarized, analyzed, and responded to the most important criticisms of public journalism, it might be useful to briefly consider how advocates could more fully convince managements, editors, and rank-and-file reporters of the utility of public journalism. After all, while about one fifth of all daily newspapers in the United States as well as numerous television and radio stations have experimented with public journalism, many more news organizations remain unconvinced about or, as the criticisms examined here suggest, even hostile to the very idea of public journalism.

Aside from the obvious need to define public journalism more clearly—both in and of itself and vis-à-vis conventional, mainstream journalism—advocates ought to be much more explicit about how public journalism's political goals relate to managements' commercial concerns. The perhaps strongest argument to be made in favor of public journalism is that those goals and concerns might in fact be complementary rather than mutually exclusive. As discussed in chapter 3, research shows that citizens, and members of marginalized social groups in particular, would like journalists to report on possible solutions to problems as well as sponsor deliberative forums where they can discuss those problems among themselves. Simply put, by embracing public journalism, managements would not only be able to help further citizens' democratic needs but, in all likelihood, also be able to increase circulation figures (especially among members of marginalized social groups) and thereby profits on behalf of media owners and advertisers. While it is certainly heartening that the factors predisposing given news organizations to practice public journalism include the civic attitudes of its top managers, it would be unrealistic to expect all, or even the majority, of top managers to commit to public journalism solely out of a concern for social responsibility. Thus, pointing out that the twin concerns of social responsibility and profit might in fact be complementary could substantially increase the number of news organizations practicing public journalism.

If convincing managements of public journalism's political *and* economic viability is important, it is arguably no less important to address the various objections of editors and rank-and-file reporters. After all, they are the ones who are ultimately charged with designing and implementing given public journalism initiatives in practice. And here, advocates are likely to face even tougher challenges. As discussed, many journalists continue to associate, if not equate, public journalism with the worst tendencies in contemporary journalism, notably an obsessive profit orientation, a diminished sense of professional autonomy, and a declining quality of news coverage. The challenge, then, would be to convince journalists that their distrust of public journalism might be more a reflection of their anxieties about the increasing corporate colonization of journalism than an expression of any reasonable assessment of public journalism. Indeed, a good argument could be made that, by engaging in public journalism, journalists would better be able to use whatever professional autonomy they do possess in the service of progressive political change and, in the process, produce news reporting that is more meaningful to citizens.

FIVE

CITIZENS AND ELITE ACTORS
IN PUBLIC JOURNALISM

If, as discussed in previous chapters, one of public journalism's central tenets is that journalists should focus their reporting on problems of concern to citizens, and that journalists should do so from the perspectives of citizens rather than government officials, experts, and other elite actors, how do journalists incorporate the perspectives of citizens and elite actors in practice? In chapter 3, I showed that the research on sourcing patterns has had mixed results. On one hand, many studies have found news organizations practicing public journalism to feature more ordinary citizens, including women and minorities, as sources of information than mainstream news organizations more generally. Yet, when it comes to the overall sourcing pattern, the results are more inconclusive. While some studies have found that news organizations practicing public journalism quote more citizens than elite actors, other studies have found that news organizations quote an equal number of citizens and elite actors or even quote more elite actors than citizens.

In this chapter, I contribute to the literature on sourcing patterns by discussing how one of the most widely acclaimed and longest-running public journalism initiatives, the *Akron* (Ohio) *Beacon Journal's* Pulitzer Prize-winning race relations campaign "A Question of Color," positioned citizens and elite actors as sources of information about various race-related problems confronting the city of Akron. While the campaign itself lasted less than a year, the *Beacon Journal's* efforts to address the problems examined continue to this day through the "Coming Together Project," a local civic organization that the newspaper helped establish after the campaign ended to improve race relations in Akron. Although the "Question of Color" campaign is the central focus of the analysis, I will, where relevant, draw parallels to other prominent public journalism campaigns on race relations.

After a brief overview of the "Question of Color" campaign, I summarize the results of a quantitative content analysis of sourcing patterns. The analysis shows not only that more citizens were quoted more often than were all elite actors combined but also that citizens were allowed to speak more directly to readers than were elite actors. Next, I conduct a critical textual analysis of the campaign informed by my proposed public philosophy for public journalism. Contrary to the quantitative content analysis, this analysis reveals that the campaign accorded elite actors a much more prominent role than citizens, notably by limiting citizens' contributions to the recounting of personal experiences with racism while quoting at length elite actors' more general reflections on the causes and consequences of various race-related social inequalities. Thus, from a methodological perspective, the chapter suggests that to obtain an accurate impression of news organizations' sourcing behavior, quantitative content analyses of sourcing patterns ought to be complemented by critical textual analyses of how the testimony of sources is used to illuminate given topics. Following this discussion, I describe what the *Akron Beacon Journal* did to inspire citizens to address the problems examined during the campaign, using my proposed public philosophy to offer suggestions to what the *Beacon Journal* could have done differently and better. I conclude by considering the *Beacon Journal*'s efforts to help create a critical public sphere about its race reporting.

THE "QUESTION OF COLOR" CAMPAIGN

In late February 1993, the *Akron Beacon Journal* launched a 10-month-long public journalism campaign called "A Question of Color." This campaign, which subsequently was awarded the 1994 Pulitzer Prize for public service journalism, comprised 30 articles that appeared in five installments. Inspired by the racially motivated assault on Rodney King and the subsequent riots in Los Angeles in 1992, the original goal was to examine various race-related problems confronting Akron, Ohio, a city with a long and torturous history of tension between its White and Black citizens. While the original goal was only to examine various race-related problems, the *Beacon Journal* decided to broaden the scope with the publication of the second installment. As I describe in more detail later, the *Beacon Journal* tried to involve citizens in efforts to improve race relations by offering practical solutions to many of the problems examined and by helping to establish a local civic organization, the "Coming Together Project," which still exists today. Like the *Beacon Journal*, other news organizations have expanded on the original scope of their campaigns. For example, midway through its 1996 "Through the Prism" race relations campaign, the Riverside, California, *Press-Enterprise* decided to also focus its reporting on possible solutions to problems. But in contrast to the *Beacon Journal*, the *Press-Enterprise* limited its own involvement to reporting on what citizens in other cities had done to address problems similar to those examined (see Ford, 2001).

In the article inaugurating the campaign, the *Akron Beacon Journal* noted that it would explore the "impact [of race] on life in the Akron-Canton area .... [How] Blacks and Whites think and feel about themselves and one another, how they're different, how they're alike" ("Race: The Great Divide," 1993, p. A1). To that end, the *Beacon Journal* used several of the information-gathering tools commonly applied by news organizations practicing public journalism, notably a telephone survey, in-depth interviews, and focus groups.

First, the *Akron Beacon Journal* conducted a telephone survey in collaboration with faculty from the University of Akron's Survey Research Center to identify problems of concern to citizens. As a result of this survey, five problems appeared as particularly salient: crime, criminal justice, education, employment, and housing. Each of these problems subsequently became the focal point of one of the installments. Next, the *Beacon Journal* arranged for two outside moderators to conduct focus groups with White and Black citizens about the problems identified. For each problem, three sets of focus groups were held: one all White, one all Black, and, upon completion of these focus groups, one comprising all the participants. Finally, the *Beacon Journal* conducted in-depth interviews about each of the problems with various elite actors, including government officials (notably members of the city council and the board of education, city planners, judges, prosecutors, and police officials) and experts (notably within the disciplines of Black studies, economics, law, political science, social work, and sociology). Like the *Beacon Journal*, many other news organizations have used telephone surveys, in-depth interviews, and focus groups to guide their reporting projects on race relations, including the *Charlotte Observer* ("Side by Side," 1997), the *Cincinnati Enquirer* ("Neighbor to Neighbor," 2001), the *Columbus Dispatch* ("The Color Chasm," 1999), the *San Francisco Chronicle* ("About Race,"

1998), and the *St. Paul Pioneer Press* ("The New Face of Minnesota," 2000) (see Ford, 2001).

The *Akron Beacon Journal*'s information-gathering approach, as should be apparent, was consistent with central tenets of public journalism and, more specifically, with my proposed public philosophy. Indeed, the *Beacon Journal* not only focused its information-gathering on problems of concern to citizens but also let the outcomes of the focus groups set the agenda for the subsequent interviews with elite actors, thereby allowing citizens to set the agenda for their testimony rather than ask citizens to respond to an already-established elite actor agenda. Perhaps most importantly, by organizing separate focus groups with White and Black citizens before hosting one comprising all the participants, the *Beacon Journal* helped create multiple discursive spaces in which members of dominant (e.g., Whites) and subordinate (e.g., Blacks) social groups could deliberate about their particular concerns among themselves before doing so jointly.

A QUANTITATIVE CONTENT ANALYSIS
OF SOURCING PATTERNS

If the *Akron Beacon Journal* went to great lengths to solicit the views of citizens, it arguably did as much to incorporate their views in the various articles. To analyze the "Question of Color" campaign's use of citizens and elite actors as sources of information, I conducted a quantitative content analysis of "source dominance" and "source prominence," two of the most widely applied measures of sourcing behavior. Following Stempel and Culbertson (1984), I operationalized source dominance as the number of sources quoted and their frequency of mention, and source prominence as the number of lines of full quotations and partial quotations/paraphrases. Since the campaign only comprised 30 articles, I analyzed all the articles rather than a sample. Table 5.1 summarizes the results.

The results show that, while the "Question of Color" campaign quoted many citizens and elite actors, it quoted considerably more citizens. Indeed, the results reveal not only that more citizens were quoted more often than were government officials and experts combined (e.g., source dominance), but also that citizens' views appeared more in the form of full quotations than in the form of partial quotations/paraphrases (e.g., source prominence). The ratio of this latter measure was 3.28, 0.65, and 0.90 for citizens, government officials, and experts, respectively. Put differently, while the views of

Table 5.1
Sourcing Patterns in "Question of Color" Campaign

	Number of Sources	Frequency of Mention	Full Quotations	Partial Quotations/ Paraphrases
Citizens	103	477	1211	369
Government officials	40	206	288	443
Experts	23	117	155	174
Total	166	800	1654	986

citizens tended to be presented in the form in which they were originally expressed, the views of government officials and experts were more often paraphrased by reporters.

BIFURCATION OF CITIZEN AND ELITE ACTOR TESTIMONY

Despite the *Akron Beacon Journal*'s efforts to elevate the role of citizens relative to elite actors in both the information-gathering and reporting stages, the "Question of Color" campaign did not succeed at creating a genuine public sphere for citizen–elite actor deliberation. This becomes evident when considering how the testimony of citizens and elite actors was used to illuminate the various problems under investigation. At the most general level, the campaign did not help bring a genuinely deliberating public into being (see chapter 2). Instead of providing citizens and elite actors with opportunities to deliberate about the various problems examined, the campaign effectively bifurcated their testimony. Although the articles interspersed the testimony of citizens and elite actors, their respective contributions spoke to different topics. Overall, while the articles quoted citizens' concrete experiences with racism through the recounting of personal anecdotes, the articles quoted elite actors' more general reflections on the causes and consequences of various race-related social inequalities.

Thus, instead of creating a genuine public sphere for citizen–elite actor deliberation, the "Question of Color" campaign helped nurture two separate spheres of argument, what Goodnight (1981) calls a "personal sphere" and a "technical sphere," respectively, each associated with different epistemologies and modes of discourse. Briefly put, while citizens spoke concretely about incidents of racism rooted in personal experience, elite actors spoke more abstractly about problems of racial inequality rooted in impersonal reflection and empirical research.

While no studies have investigated whether public journalism initiatives, for lack of a better term, tend to personalize the testimony of citizens and generalize the testimony of elite actors, there is evidence that personalization of citizen testimony has been a prominent feature of even some of the most widely celebrated initiatives. Most notably, in his study of the *Wichita Eagle*'s "People Project," Riede (1995, p. 14) found that "virtually every story [began] either with a quote from a citizen about an issue concerning him or her or an anecdote intended to put a human face on the issue."

PERSONALIZATION OF CITIZEN TESTIMONY

While personalization of social problems, or the narrative technique "of representing social life through individual portraits" (Parisi, 1998, p. 236), makes for compelling story-telling by humanizing what could otherwise appear as impersonal stories, this narrative technique is also problematic. First, by recounting citizens' personal experiences with racism rather than their views on broader problems of race-related social inequality, the "Question of Color" campaign could be seen to have positioned citizens as objects (or victims) of social problems rather than as subjects (or centers of consciousness) capable of inserting those experiences within a broader context. In this important respect, the campaign's personalization of citizen testimony runs counter to public journalism's central tenet that journalists should position citizens as active participants in, as opposed to passive spectators to, debates about given problems (see chapter 1). This argument does not imply that the *Akron Beacon Journal* should not have offered citizens opportunities to recount their personal experiences with racism, at length and in their own words. Rather, it implies that to position citizens as active participants in the debates, the *Beacon Journal* should also have offered them opportunities to comment on broader problems of race-related social inequality.

Moreover, the personalization of citizen testimony is at odds with the *Akron Beacon Journal*'s own goal of offering readers a nuanced understanding of how racism impacts different social groups within the city of Akron. Consider the following example. In an article reporting on some of the Black focus group participants' experiences with racism, one of the participants recounted the following incident:

"If anyone doubts that racism exists, just listen to what happened at my husband's job the other day," said a middle-aged mother of two, raising her hand as if to swear to the truthfulness of her story. She asked to remain anonymous because she feared reprisals against her husband. A White man who works with her husband was upset at being passed over for a promotion in favor of a Black coworker, the woman said. He apparently thought the Black man was less qualified than him and attributed his own lack of advancement to reverse discrimination. So, she said, "This guy came to work in a Ku Klux Klan outfit, hood, medals, everything," but only got a slap on his wrist from his White supervisors. "All they did was give him two days off to cool down. If that had been a Black man (and he did something similar) he would have been fired on the spot," she fumed (Chancellor, 1993, p. A7).

The problem with this and the numerous other personal anecdotes is that they do not make clear to readers the relations between race and other interacting social signifiers, notably class and gender (see chapter 2). No contextual information was provided about the particular workplace in which this incident took place. Did it occur on the shop floor of a large factory or in the executive suites of a prestigious law firm? Would the supervisors have reacted as they did if the perpetrator and/or victim had been a woman instead?

Thus, while the *Akron Beacon Journal* explored in depth how White and Black citizens differed in their experiences with racism, including by challenging entrenched distinctions between topics of public interest and matters of private concern by examining instances of racism in the workplace (e.g., "economic privacy") and in the home (e.g., "domestic privacy") (see chapter 2), the *Beacon Journal* failed to examine how those experiences could have been influenced by other interacting social signifiers, notably class and gender. These interacting subject positions, which possibly were articulated by citizens themselves during the focus groups, were dismissed as uninteresting or irrelevant by the reporters.

This failure to articulate the interrelations between race, class, and gender is all the more surprising, if not odd, considering that statistics quoted by the *Akron Beacon Journal* showed that, while Blacks are discriminated against as a group, lower income Black women are most particularly vulnerable to discrimination (see Kirksey, Holley, & Paynter, 1993). Relatedly, it is worth noting that, while the *Beacon Journal* stated that it deliberately selected the focus group participants to represent a "diverse" cross section of citizens (see "The Focus Groups," 1993), the majority of those quoted, judging from their job descriptions and first names, were middle-class men.

While the "Question of Color" campaign never broached the question of class, the interrelation between race and gender was only touched upon once. In an article describing a Black focus group discussion about why Blacks end up in the criminal justice system more often than do Whites, the reporter wrote:

> As the group debated whether the disproportionate number of Black arrests resulted from targeting Blacks, [Patty Conners, one of the focus group participants] caught herself apologizing for her opinions. "What the hell am I doing?" she asked herself. Conners believes that addressing this problem and others involving race and crime requires people to remove their masks. "Do Blacks and Whites get treated equally in the justice system?" she asked. "No, I don't think so." But then, she suggested, neither do women. "This country is ruled by...the White middle-class man," she said. "If you don't fit that, you're used, abused and thrown out. Women get it too." (Love, 1993, p. A5)

Ironically, the "Question of Color" campaign's personalization of citizen testimony does not represent a challenge to conventional, journalistic practices, but rather mirrors such practices closely. Where mainstream journalism typically personalizes public affairs coverage, and election reporting in particular, by focusing more attention on the personal attributes and private lives of politicians and candidates for office than on their views on given policy issues (see, e.g., Bennett, 2006), the "Question of Color" campaign personalized its coverage by recounting citizens' personal experiences with racism rather than their views on broader problems of race-related social inequality. Thus, contrary to what appears to be the practice of public journalism more generally (see chapter 3), the campaign's use of the narrative technique of personalization lead to "episodic," as opposed to "thematic," reporting. Episodic reporting is problematic, Iyengar (1991) argues, because it makes it difficult for audiences to understand how seemingly disparate events are related and to appreciate the broader social, political, and economic forces that impact those events.

Following my proposed public philosophy, the *Akron Beacon Journal* could have done several things differently and better. First, instead of merely recounting citizens' personal experiences with racism, the *Beacon Journal* could have offered citizens opportunities to elaborate on how other interacting social signifiers aside from race might have influenced their particular experiences with racism. While it is certainly possible that the *Beacon Journal* did so during the focus group discussions, the resulting articles did not reflect this. Second, and relatedly, the *Beacon Journal* could have offered citizens opportunities to insert those experiences within a broader context by reflecting on how their personal experiences with racism relate to deeper problems of race-related social inequality. Again, while it is certainly possible that the *Beacon Journal* did so during the focus group discussions, the resulting articles did not bear this out. Finally, but not least importantly, the *Beacon Journal* could have experimented with alternative modes of framing, including by producing, as did the *Colorado Springs Gazette* (see chapter 1), multiple versions of the same article, each written from a specific perspective (defined by race, class, and gender as well as along other possible dimensions).

While the *Akron Beacon Journal* did not produce multiple versions of the same article, it did experiment with other modes of framing, notably by casting many of the problems examined as "open-ended questions" rather than as "closed-ended answers." Consider the following two examples.

In an article examining potentially discriminatory practices within Akron's educational system, the reporters posed the following rhetorical questions after having discussed why White students on average receive higher grades than Black students:

> When does a "C" reflect racism by the professor and when does it simply reflect "C" work? Who should decide? Who decides what role African cultures played in the evolution of Western civilization? If historians have determined the role was minimal, is it racist to portray it that way? Or is it simply good history? How much does it matter if all or most of the historians are White? (Kirksey, Jenkins, & Paynter, 1993, p. A14)

Similarly, in an article examining potentially discriminatory employment practices, the reporters posed the following rhetorical questions after having discussed why the unemployment rate is much higher for Blacks than for Whites:

> To what degree…does racial bias in hiring or promotion remain a factor in Black economic woes? Are most African-Americans doomed to second-class citizenship as long as Whites control most of the

wealth-generating businesses in this region and nation? To what extent are economic opportunity and prosperity...a question of color; to what extent a question of hard capitalism? (Cannon, Know, & Paynter, 1993, p. A6)

The *Akron Beacon Journal's* use of open-ended questions is noteworthy in at least two important respects. First, by implying that potentially discriminatory practices relating to education and employment are too complex to be approached from a single authoritative perspective, such questions might stimulate readers to reflect on those practices from multiple perspectives rather than from one racially motivated perspective, such as the "White perspective" or the "Black perspective." In this sense, the use of open-ended questions might stimulate readers to engage in what Habermas (1990, 1993), as discussed in chapter 2, calls "ideal role-taking" or "reciprocal perspective-taking"—taking into consideration the perspectives of others rather than elevating their own perspective to an indisputable standard. Second, the significance of this approach could be seen to lie in the fact that it encourages readers to engage in actual conversation with others—preferably of a different race—if they are to develop a more nuanced understanding of such practices.

More generally, the *Akron Beacon Journal* could be seen to have combined dialogical and deliberative modes of public discourse (see chapter 2). Specifically, the *Beacon Journal* applied a dialogical mode of public discourse to deliberative ends when, in reporting back on the focus groups with White and Black citizens, it preserved the to-and-fro of argument rather than merely summarized their outcomes in their own words. Similarly, the *Beacon Journal* applied a deliberative mode of public discourse to dialogical ends when, in casting many of the problems examined as open-ended questions, it encouraged citizens to further discuss those problems during actual conversation with others.

GENERALIZATION OF ELITE ACTOR TESTIMONY

If the *Akron Beacon Journal's* use of citizen testimony left much to be desired, its use of elite actor testimony, notably that of various experts on race-related problems, was no less problematic, albeit for different reasons. First, it is worth noting that most of the expert testimony consisted of unsubstantiated speculations about the causes and consequences of various race-related social inequalities rather than the results of empirical studies. Throughout the "Question of Color" campaign, the *Beacon Journal* quoted the views of many experts as to why racial inequality relating to crime, criminal justice, education, employment, and housing persists despite rigorous antidiscrimination laws. Second, in the few instances where the *Beacon Journal* did quote experts who had done actual empirical research on racial inequality, the studies mentioned did not relate directly to Akron. Instead, the experts were quoted as trying to generalize the findings from studies of other cities, even nationwide studies, to the problems confronting Akron. Yet, it is questionable whether the results of those studies helped illuminate the specific problems of concern to Akron. While the findings were in some instances contradicted by statistics supplied by the *Beacon Journal* itself, in other instances *Beacon Journal* statistics revealed that the problems confronting Akron were of a different, possibly much more serious nature. Consider the following two examples.

In an article examining the reasons for the increasing income gap between Whites and Blacks in Akron, Cannon et al. (1993) quoted studies conducted by Professor John Kasarda, an economist at the University of North Carolina at Chapel Hill. Kasarda's studies of San Francisco had shown that, compared to other ethnic groups, notably Chinese, Black consumers were significantly less likely to frequent Black-owned businesses. Yet, contrary to Kasarda's studies, statistics supplied by the *Akron Beacon Journal* showed that Akron Blacks were frequenting Black-owned businesses at a level comparable to that of other ethnic groups. In fact, *Beacon Journal* statistics revealed that the increasing income gap between Whites and Blacks in Akron had little, if anything, to do with a lack of "Black solidarity" toward Black-owned businesses, and more to do with a pervasive racism that made it difficult for Black entrepreneurs to obtain business loans. Not only did Black entrepreneurs experience difficulties obtaining business loans, when successful, they received much less funding than did their White counterparts (see Cannon, 1993).

Similarly, in an article examining the reasons why White students generally outperform Black students in Akron's public schools, Kirksey, et al. (1993) quoted nationwide studies conducted by Professor Jawanza Kunjufu, a sociologist at the University of Chicago. Kunjufu's studies had shown that educational disparities between White and Black students could be attributed in part to the fact that White students spend more time studying than do Black students. As Kunjufu put it, "Among many Black students, the very act of not working hard has been elevated to a virtue—to a kind of badge of true Blackness" (p. A13). While the *Akron Beacon Journal* did not quote statistics showing differences in the study habits of White and Black students in Akron, it did supply statistics suggesting other, possibly much more serious, economic reasons for those educational disparities. Specifically, *Beacon Journal* statistics revealed that the increasing racial segregation of neighborhoods in Akron was eroding the tax base needed to finance public education in predominantly poor, Black neighborhoods. As the reporters themselves commented, "Whether intended or not, there are clear racial implications to a system of 'public' education whose property-tax–based funding apparatus so obviously seems to favor the sons and daughters of the affluent and White" (p. A12).

While it is difficult to determine why the *Akron Beacon Journal* did not quote experts who had done actual empirical research on the particular problems facing Akron, it is worth noting that few of the experts quoted were themselves from Akron. Indeed, of the 23 experts mentioned, only 5 were associated with institutions of higher education in Akron (the College of Wooster and the University of Akron). This is surprising, if not odd, considering that faculty from the University of Akron's Survey Research Center conducted the initial telephone survey on which the entire campaign was based.

IN SEARCH OF SOLUTIONS

While the "Question of Color" campaign's original goal, as mentioned earlier, was only to examine various race-related problems confronting the city of Akron, the scope of the campaign took an unexpected turn with the publication of the second installment. Disappointed with the initial lack of public attention, it was decided, as Dale Allen, one of the editors responsible for the campaign, recounted, to go "beyond consciousness raising [to make it possible for] readers who wanted to be part of the solution to come together to set a community agenda" (quoted in Merritt, 1998, p. 99). In announcing the campaign's expansion (see Dotson & Allen, 1993), the *Akron Beacon Journal* promised to help local civic organizations "in the process of improving race relations" (p. A1). Representatives of local civic organizations were encouraged to contact the newspaper if they were interested in signing up for "multiracial partnerships that can work toward common goals" (p. A11). The *Beacon Journal* hired two facilitators, a White retired minister and a Black retired school principal, to match up local civic organizations "with shared interests" (p. A1). Representatives of more than 200 local civic organizations soon contacted the newspaper. At the same time, the *Beacon Journal* carried many articles that offered readers practical solutions to the problems examined during the campaign (see, for example, Knox, Cannon, & Paynter, 1993; McEaney, Allen, & Paynter, 1993; Outlaw, Harris, & Paynter, 1993).

Subsequently, in 1995, the *Akron Beacon Journal* helped establish a new civic organization to serve as an umbrella organization for the various partnerships that were formed. This "Coming Together Project," which continues to this day, sponsors various activities for participating member organizations, middle and high-school students, and the city of Akron at large, including lectures on race relations, interracial student gatherings, and an annual "Unity Walk." The "Coming Together Project" gained national attention in 1997 when President Clinton chose Akron as the site for his first town hall meeting on race, citing the initiative as the primary reason behind his decision.

While the *Akron Beacon Journal* should be commended for its efforts to promote problem-solving both on and off the news pages, there are reasons to question both its underlying approach to problem-solving and the particular forms of citizen intervention it sought to inspire. Most generally, the *Beacon Journal*'s problem-solving efforts were based on the problematic assumption that the root of the "race problem" was a lack of communication and that increased opportunity for interracial interaction would lead to consensual solutions to common problems. This "consensual" approach to problem-solving ignored how White and Black citizens were likely to have (and in Akron indeed did have) vastly different experiences with and views on racism, although citizens' views, as mentioned earlier, were never fully articulated.

Following my proposed public philosophy, the *Akron Beacon Journal* would better have served both its public journalism goals and its social goals by adopting a more "conflictual" approach to problem-solving aimed at recovering underlying conflicts of interest and perspective. The *Beacon Journal* could have sponsored separate discursive spaces for White and Black citizens to deliberate among themselves before doing so jointly. This would have offered Blacks opportunities to articulate their particular concerns prior to interacting with Whites. More specifically, the *Beacon Journal* could have helped organize roundtable discussions modeled after, but larger than, its small-scale focus group discussions. The *Beacon Journal* could even have provided White and Black citizens with designated sections—distinctive discursive domains—in which to present their particular positions in their own words. Moreover, the *Beacon Journal* could have encouraged White and Black citizens to reflect on how racial self-understandings affect their sense of problems and solutions and to reflect on how some social inequalities might damage certain participants' very ability, literally and affectively, to participate (at all, much less on an equal footing) in a search for solutions. The *Beacon Journal* reported, for example, that while more than 30% of Akron's Blacks were living below the poverty level, only 8% of Whites were (see Kirksey, Holley, and Paynter, 1993). Is it fair to ask poor Blacks, who struggle on a daily basis to make ends meet, to participate in a discourse of consensus, counterfactually presented as color-free and abstract, with Whites, who presumably understand and know much less about Blacks than Blacks know about them? That is, why should poor Blacks be expected to yield equally to Whites for the sake of consensus?

Moreover, the *Akron Beacon Journal* could have promoted a more expansive form of citizen intervention. Consider the following example. Toward the very end of the "Question of Color" campaign, the *Beacon Journal* carried a major article titled "Prisoners of Violence" (Harris, Outlaw, & Paynter, 1993), which examined why more crimes in Akron are committed by Blacks than Whites. The article quoted statistics showing that the prevalence of crime in a given neighborhood is related to the socioeconomic status of its inhabitants. Thus, higher crime rates are to be found in poor Black neighborhoods than in affluent White neighborhoods. The *Beacon Journal* also carried two smaller companion articles offering readers advice on how to avoid being victimized. First, in an article titled "Securing Your Home" (1993), the *Beacon Journal* included suggestions from the Akron Police Department on how to protect one's home against potential intruders. Second, in an article titled "Keeping a Vigil" (1993), the *Beacon Journal* included suggestions on how to organize neighborhood watch groups.

These companion articles are noteworthy for several reasons. First, the suggestions offered can hardly be said to confront the underlying causes of crime. Indeed, if implemented, they would merely serve to keep some of the symptoms of crime at a distance. Second, the suggestions offered either depended on individual intervention (e.g., how to protect one's home against potential intruders) or local, citizen-based intervention (e.g., how to organize neighborhood watch groups). Neither of these suggestions, however, acknowledged the need for more deep-seated, systemic intervention. If it is correct, as *Akron Beacon Journal* statistics showed, that the prevalence of crime is related to socioeconomic status, then one would clearly have to implement political measures aimed at raising the income levels of Blacks such as by offering various incentives to pursue education.

This incongruity between the *Akron Beacon Journal's* own investigations into the scope of given problems and its efforts to inspire citizens to address those problems is mirrored in the "Coming Together Project." Consider the *Beacon Journal's* coverage of why White students generally outperform Black students in Akron's public schools. The *Beacon Journal's* own investigations revealed, as mentioned earlier, that the increasing racial segregation of neighborhoods was eroding the tax base needed to finance public education in predominantly poor, Black neighborhoods. Yet, instead of advocating political measures aimed at ameliorating this problem, the "Coming Together Project" merely brings White and Black students together to discuss racism. However, the problem is not a lack of mutual understanding and respect between White and Black students, but rather a lack of equal educational opportunities. While the "Coming Together Project" thus departs from the mainstream journalistic stance of neutrality by advocating local, citizen-based intervention, it does not fundamentally challenge the status quo. Indeed, the "Coming Together Project" and, by implication, the *Akron Beacon Journal*, continues to avoid highlighting how the political system is fundamentally unjust to certain social groups (e.g., Blacks), leaving untouched the implication that citizens' failure to get sufficiently involved explains the political system's malfunctions. Surprisingly, while scholarly observers have ignored this problematic aspect of the "Coming Together Project," no less than President Clinton expressed similar concerns during his town hall meeting on race in Akron:

> How does [the "Coming Together Project"] result in less discrimination
> in the workplace or in the school, or people helping each other to succeed
> in school or at work? Can you give me any examples about what it's done
> other than make people feel good for an hour or so on Sunday or some
> other church event? (Clinton, 1997, p. 1959)

The *Akron Beacon Journal's* problematic approach to problem-solving is reflected in many other public journalism–inspired race relations campaigns. Like the *Beacon Journal*, other news organizations have engaged citizens in efforts to improve interpersonal race relations, rather than in efforts to address more deep-seated, systemic problems, such as by encouraging readers to form interracial friendships (the *Sacramento Bee's* 1999 "Getting

Along"), socialize with people of a different racial background more gener-
ally (the *Yakima* [Washington] *Herald-Republic*'s 2000 "Race in the Yakima
Valley"), or attend multi-racial church services (the Wilmington, Delaware,
News Journal's 1998 "The Turning Point"). Similarly, like the *Beacon Jour-
nal*, other news organizations have helped establish new civic organizations
to formalize those efforts, including the New Orleans *Times-Picayune*'s
"Eracism" ("Together Apart: The Myth of Race," 1994); the Riverside,
California, *Press-Enterprise*'s "Coalition for Finding Common Ground"
("Through the Prism," 1996); and the Utica, New York, *Observer-Dispatch*'s
"Bridge-Builders" ("Building Bridges," 1995) (see Ford, 2001).

The important question, then, is what could the *Akron Beacon Journal*
have done to promote a more viable approach to problem-solving. Following
the problem-solving model outlined in chapter 2, the *Beacon Journal* should
have advocated interventions that corresponded to the nature of given problems under investigation. This would have required the *Beacon Journal* to
consider whether given problems could adequately be addressed by citizens
themselves, or whether those problems required more deep-seated, systemic
intervention by government officials. Second, the *Beacon Journal* should have
considered whether given problems could adequately be addressed through
local intervention, whether citizen-based or governmental, or whether those
problems required intervention of a broader regional, state, national, or even
international scope.

Thus, instead of engaging citizens in mere feel-good efforts that, at best,
would only partially address the symptoms of problems, the *Akron Beacon
Journal* should have inspired citizen deliberation about the real problems
at stake and the measures needed to resolve those problems, including by
sponsoring debates between citizens, experts, and government officials.
Instead of positioning citizens as sources of complaint, as able only to articulate problems (e.g., by recounting their personal experiences with racism),
citizens should have been offered opportunities to question experts and
government officials directly and to propose and negotiate solutions. For
example, if the system for financing local public schools was responsible for
educational inequalities between White and Black students, then the *Beacon
Journal* should have encouraged debate about what could be done to correct
the property tax problem. Would offering Blacks incentives to move to traditionally White neighborhoods work? Could proportionally more tax money
be distributed to predominantly Black neighborhoods?

Moreover, *Akron Beacon Journal* reporters could have joined those debates themselves, including by examining the advantages and disadvantages of various alternatives and by applying pressure on relevant government officials. *Beacon Journal* reporters could also have endorsed politicians or candidates for office that in their view advocated the most viable courses of action. Finally, *Beacon Journal* reporters could have challenged the measures of educational success themselves. For example, are SAT scores or grade point averages the best ways to assess and compare student performance?

These suggestions do not imply that the *Akron Beacon Journal* should have reported on educational inequalities and other race-related social problems at the expense of other important problems or that the *Beacon Journal* should have endorsed/rejected politicians or candidates for office solely on the basis of their stands on such problems. Rather, they imply that the *Beacon Journal* should have stimulated serious, sustained deliberation about various race-related social problems instead of merely engaging citizens in efforts to address surface-level manifestations of problems.

A CRITICAL PUBLIC SPHERE ABOUT RACE REPORTING

If the *Akron Beacon Journal*'s approach to problem-solving left (and continues to leave) much to be desired, the *Beacon Journal* satisfied another important requirement of my proposed public philosophy, namely to help create a critical public sphere about its race reporting. During the focus group discussions, the Black citizens had voiced a number of complaints about the *Beacon Journal*'s crime coverage, notably that (1) Black men are depicted primarily as criminals, (2) while stories about Black criminals often receive front-page exposure, stories about White criminals are often buried inside the newspaper, and (3) while stories about Black criminals are often accompanied by pictures, most stories about White criminals carry no pictures (see Chancellor, 1993; Harris, Outlaw, & Paynter, 1993; Holley, Kirksey, & Paynter, 1993; Love, 1993; Outlaw et al., 1993). Toward the very end of the "Question of Color" campaign, the editors in charge decided to publicly respond to these and other criticisms by inviting 17 of the *Beacon Journal*'s editors and reporters, nine White and eight Black, to participate in focus group discussions about the newspaper's coverage of White and Black crime. Each participant was asked to review two months' worth of newspapers (July and August of 1993), paying particular attention to the crime coverage. As did the *Beacon Journal* during its focus group discussions with White and Black citizens, during one evening in late December, the newspaper held three focus group discussions: one all White, one all Black, and, later than evening, one comprising all the participants.

In the article reporting on those in-house discussions (see Dyer, 1993), the *Akron Beacon Journal* publicly responded to the Black citizens' complaints by quoting in considerable detail the participants' views on this topic and by offering concrete examples of differential coverage. While no explicit reasons were given as to why White and Black crime were covered differently, Dale Allen did note the disproportionate number of Black editors (4 out of 31) and reporters (22 out of 145) at the newspaper, which could insinuate a reason for the differential coverage. Indeed, the *Beacon Journal* not only responded to the Black citizens' complaints but also took actual steps to address them. Shortly after the campaign ended, the *Beacon Journal* appointed several additional Black columnists to create a more equitable distribution of White and Black columnists at the newspaper (see Canedy, 2000). While few news organizations have gone to the same lengths to publicize, respond to, and address citizens' complaints, several other news organizations turned the gaze inward during their own race relations campaigns. For example, while the *Indianapolis Star* formed an internal committee to look at the way minorities were covered as part of its 1993 "Blacks and Whites: Can We Get Along?" campaign, the New London, Connecticut, *Day* ("Two Races, Two Worlds," 1999); the Wichita Falls, Texas, *Times Record News* ("About Face," 1997); and the *Winston-Salem* (North Carolina) *Journal* ("Dividing Lines," 1998) all carried articles that examined how their lack of newsroom diversity had historically impacted their race coverage (see Ford, 2001).

Importantly, the *Akron Beacon Journal*'s in-house discussions also revealed highly racialized tensions in the newsroom itself. As had Black citizens more generally, the Black journalists complained both that the *Beacon Journal* depicted Black men primarily as criminals and that Black criminals received more sensationalized front-page exposure than did White criminals. Conversely, the White journalists complained that Blacks "not only are underplayed in negative stories but overplayed in positive stories" (Dyer, 1993, p. A6). Specifically, the White journalists complained that the *Beacon Journal*, which then had and still has a Black publisher and several high-ranking Black editors, "is trying so hard to be perceived as nonracist that fairness and honesty have suffered, that the truth is sometimes sugarcoated in the name of sociological engineering" (Dyer, 1993, p. A6). Even Bob Dyer, the White journalist who wrote the article about the in-house discussions, subsequently conceded that he and his colleagues were surprised by the racial tensions in the newsroom: "You know, we were like any other part of society. We didn't have a clue" (quoted in Canedy, 2000, p. 177). In 1999, Bob Dyer, now a columnist, argued in print with a fellow Black columnist over the word "niggardly," creating a furor that, once again, polarized the newsroom (see Canedy, 2000).

Despite the *Akron Beacon Journal*'s continuous efforts to improve race relations through the "Coming Together Project," and the appearance of much racial tension in the newsroom itself, the *Beacon Journal* reverted to its prior approach to race coverage when the "Question of Color" campaign ended after 10 months. Race-related topics appeared (and continue to appear) only in the context of newsworthy, breaking events. That the *Beacon Journal* resumed its conventional approach to race coverage is perhaps not surprising, at least if the journalistic philosophy of Dale Allen is representative of the rest of the newsroom staff. The article reporting on the in-house discussions quoted Mr. Allen as asserting that "all stories get judged on the basis of...what's happened in the last 24 hours" (Dyer, 1993, p. A6). Indeed, when a White (and somewhat controversial) columnist who had participated in the "Question of Color" campaign asked whether a newspaper should ever be concerned about the social implications of its reporting, Dale Allen responded:

> I think we have a responsibility to understand that what we do, and how we do it, has an impact on the community. But I also think that you have to leaven that with the prime reason we're here: That's to report the news. That's our essential raison d'etre. It overshadows all else. (Dyer, 1993, p. A6)

Given the importance White and Black citizens had attributed to race-related topics, one might suspect that the *Akron Beacon Journal* would not as easily have been able to revert to its prior approach to race coverage had it institutionalized (as discussed in chapter 2) more formal mechanisms for involving citizens in setting the news agenda. Indeed, had deliberating citizens been working in partnership with editors and reporters, the *Beacon Journal* might have been compelled to make race-related topics a consistent—even prominent—feature of its regular public affairs coverage.

SIX

THE CONSENSUS CONFERENCE MODEL AS A PUBLIC JOURNALISM TOOL

The previous discussion of the *Akron Beacon Journal*'s "Question of Color" campaign showed, among other issues, that the campaign did not engage citizens, experts, and government officials in actual deliberation and, more broadly, accorded these actors different, if not unequal, roles in the problem-solving process. In this chapter, I introduce a deliberative method known as the "consensus conference model" whereby the *Beacon Journal* and other news organizations practicing public journalism could engage citizens and experts more interactively and equitably in the search for solutions to given problems while at the same time involve government officials in the process of implementing those solutions in practice.

Following a broad overview of the consensus conference model—its main features, historical roots, possible uses, and relations to other prominent deliberative methods—I examine in more detail each stage of the actual consensus conference process. Specifically, I discuss how these stages could be modified to best approximate central tenets of public journalism and, more specifically, my proposed public philosophy. Next, I summarize the empirical research literature on the impact of consensus conferences on citizens, experts, and government officials. I conclude by briefly considering what news organizations interested in sponsoring consensus conferences could do to enhance their political impact.

THE CONSENSUS CONFERENCE MODEL

The consensus conference model has become a widely applied means of engaging citizens and experts in efforts to identify possible solutions to contentious societal problems and of prompting government officials to carry out the proposed solutions in practice. Since 1987, when the first consensus conference was convened in Denmark, more than 50 such conferences have been held in various countries worldwide, notably Australia, Canada, Denmark, Holland, the United Kingdom, and the United States (see Loka Institute, 2005).

Briefly put, the consensus conference model revolves around a so-called citizen panel. The citizen panel is a collection of typically 10–16 individuals who have been charged by the conference organizers to examine and formulate solutions to a problem of broad public concern. Over the course of two preparatory meetings and a main conference, as I describe in more detail later, the citizen panel formulates a series of questions relating to the overall problem, participates in the selection of experts to address those questions, engages in extensive questioning of and interaction with experts, deliberates about the experts' responses, and then arrives at recommendations as to how the problem in question should be resolved. The final outcome of the citizen panel's deliberations is a so-called consensus statement that is presented to invited government officials as well as to the public at large at the end of the conference (see Andersen & Jaeger, 1999; Fixdal, 1997; Grundahl, 1995, for detailed overviews of the consensus conference model).

The main objectives of the consensus conference model, all of which are congruent with the goals of public journalism more generally, are thus to facilitate citizen–expert interaction, to contribute to political deliberation and action, and to inspire public debate. And, like public journalism (see chapter 1), the model promotes a form of deliberative democracy that combines features of direct-participatory and representative democracy. While consensus conferences offer citizens opportunities, in consultation with experts, to formulate solutions to given problems, citizens do not enact those solutions themselves but present them to government officials in the form of consensus statements to be used as input for further political deliberation and action.

The consensus conference model was developed by the Danish Board of Technology, a publicly financed institution established by the Danish Parliament in 1985 to promote active citizen participation in science and technology assessment. The Danish model was inspired, in turn, by the so-called consensus development conference model, developed by the U.S. National Institutes of Health in the late 1970s to bring experts together to assess the safety and efficacy of various medical technologies as a way of transferring new medical knowledge and devices into clinical practice (see Ash & Lowe, 1984; Jacoby, 1995; Joergensen, 1995, for historical overviews and current applications of the consensus development conference model). While consensus development conferences only feature interaction among experts on a relatively narrow range of medical topics, Danish-style consensus conferences feature interaction among citizens, experts, and government officials on a wide range of topics within science and technology.

The consensus conference model is thus based on the underlying assumption that citizens can and should be actively involved in science and technology assessment rather than merely act as passive receivers of scientific and technological information provided by experts. This understanding of the role of citizens, which is consistent with public journalism's central argument that citizens should be addressed as active participants in, as opposed to passive spectators to, debates about given problems, has deep roots in Danish civic and political culture. Specifically, it is rooted in a historically high level of awareness of and critical engagement with societal problems among citizens, a self-consciousness about their rights and responsibilities as citizens, and a general openness toward achieving consensus through debate and negotiation nurtured by the fact that no single political party has had an absolute majority in the Danish Parliament for more than a century. More recently, the model's emphasis on active citizen engagement with science and technology assessment can be traced back to a tradition of critical public debate that began with popular resistance toward nuclear energy in the 1970s. In 1974, a broad-based Danish grassroots organization, the Organization for Information on Nuclear Energy, was formed. It was so successful at mounting opposition to the Danish Parliament's plans to introduce nuclear energy that Parliament decided not to build nuclear power plants in Denmark—a decision that is still in effect today. The nuclear energy debate subsequently fueled various other public debates about science and technology, including biotechnology, the environment, and the uses of information technology (see Cronberg, 1995; Joss, 1998; Toft, 1996, for discussions of the consensus conference model's historical roots).

While the consensus conference model has deep roots in Danish civic and political culture, the model is, as the many experiments with it worldwide show, applicable to other countries. Equally important, while the model, likely as a result of having been developed by the Danish Board of Technology, has primarily been used to examine contentious problems of science and technology, there is nothing about the model, as Durant (1995, p. 79) notes, that "makes it uniquely suited to dealing with scientific and technological issues." Rather, Joss and Durant (1995, p. 203) argue, consensus conferences "are potentially useful whenever communities are faced with complex issues about which it is unreasonable to expect everyone to be equally well-informed. In this sense, consensus conferences offer themselves as a potentially constructive contribution to democratic life in general." Indeed, the model is particularly well-suited to many of the problems examined by public journalism initiatives. While some of these problems, as discussed in chapter 2, can be adequately addressed by citizens themselves, whether within a given locality or on a broader scale, many problems are sufficiently complex to benefit from extensive citizen–expert interaction and, equally important, require political intervention to be resolved, whether at the local, state, regional, national, or international level. And indeed, the organizers of consensus conferences have not only been successful at securing the involvement of government officials at various political levels, but also, as I describe in more detail later, at prompting government officials to implement citizens' recommendations in the form of actual legislation.

The significance of the consensus conference model as a public journalism tool comes into even sharper focus when compared to other prominent deliberative methods. Since numerous such methods exist (see Rowe & Frewer, 2005, for an overview of more than 100 deliberative methods currently in use), I focus here on the three most commonly applied methods that, to a greater or lesser extent, feature interaction among citizens, experts, and government officials, namely "deliberative opinion polls," "citizens juries," and "scenario workshops."

Despite some minor variations, a deliberative opinion poll generally follows a relatively fixed set of procedures. Briefly put, the organizers recruit, via a telephone survey, a statistically representative, random sample of citizens that ranges in size from approximately 130 to 450. During the 2- to 4-day event, the participating citizens are polled individually on a series of questions relating to the overall topic, receive background information about it in the form of detailed briefing documents written by the organizers, participate in small group deliberations moderated by trained facilitators, ask questions of a panel of invited experts as a plenum, and are then polled individually again at the end of the event. Government officials are sometimes, but not always, invited to hear and comment on the final polling results (see, for example, Ackerman & Fishkin, 2004; Fishkin, 1995; Fishkin & Farrar, 2005).

Although deliberative opinion polls, like consensus conferences, feature interaction between citizens and experts, consensus conferences accord citizens a much more prominent role in the process. First, while consensus conferences offer citizens opportunities to set the agenda for their interactions with experts by formulating a series of questions relating to the problems examined, participating in the selection of experts to address those questions, and engaging in extensive questioning of experts, deliberative opinion polls offer citizens no opportunity to participate in the selection of experts and only little opportunity to question them, especially considering the large number of participants. Moreover, while consensus conferences offer citizens opportunities to formulate their own solutions to given problems, and to do so in their own words, deliberative opinion polls merely poll individual citizens on a series of predetermined questions at the beginning and at the end of the event, thereby limiting citizens' opportunity to engage in actual deliberation and problem-solving. Finally, while consensus conferences always conclude with citizens presenting their recommendations to invited government officials, government officials only occasionally attend deliberative opinion polls. Thus, while deliberative opinion polls, as discussed in previous chapters, represent an important advance over conventional public opinion polls, consensus conferences better approximate public journalism's goal of strengthening citizens' agenda-setting, deliberative, and problem-solving power.

If the design of the deliberative opinion poll limits is usefulness as a public journalism tool, this is even more so the case for citizens juries. A citizens jury resembles a conventional jury in that a randomly selected, but demographically representative, sample of typically 18–24 citizens is brought together to deliberate about a predetermined problem on five or more occasions. In contrast to deliberative opinion polls, where the participating citizens are asked a series of predetermined questions relating to the overall topic, the citizens jury is only asked one or a few questions (the "charge"), which it is supposed to address during its deliberations. The citizens jury hears testimony from various preselected experts who present alternative solutions to the problem in question, deliberates among itself, and then chooses among the presented solutions the one it believes to be most appropriate (see, for example, Coote & Lenagham, 1997; Crosby & Nethercut, 2005; Smith &

Wales, 2000). Unlike deliberative opinion polls, where government officials sometimes, but not always, are invited to hear and comment on the final polling results, government officials have expressed little interest in and only rarely attend citizens juries. In both cases, however, and in sharp contrast to the consensus conference model, participating citizens are effectively asked to respond to an already-established expert agenda rather than to set the agenda for expert testimony themselves.

Scenario workshops follow similar, albeit not identical, procedures as citizens juries. Briefly put, in a scenario workshop, which typically lasts two days, a number of citizens, business representatives, experts, and government officials are invited to debate the relative desirability of several predefined visions (or scenarios) for how given public problems could be resolved. During the course of the workshop, the participants examine the presented scenarios, identify strengths and weaknesses of each of them, and then select the scenario they believe to be most appropriate for addressing the problem in question (see, for example, Andersen & Jaeger, 1999; Bilderbeek & Andersen, 1994; Joss, 2002). While scenario workshops, like deliberative opinion polls and citizens juries, limit citizens' agenda-setting, deliberative, and problem-solving power by offering them little opportunity to define the problems examined or to formulate their own solutions to them, they differ from those other deliberative methods by formally making citizens only one of several equally important actors in the problem-solving process. While such a design could be seen as one possible way of equalizing the role of citizens relative to other actors, it is more likely that the three other types of actors, given their economic (business representatives), technical (experts), and political (government officials) knowledge and/or power, would be able to dominate the process.

STAGES OF THE CONSENSUS CONFERENCE PROCESS

While the consensus conference model strengthens citizens' opportunities to engage in agenda-setting, deliberation, and problem-solving relative to other prominent deliberative methods, news organizations practicing public journalism might find it appropriate to implement certain changes to the actual consensus conference process before adopting this model in practice. These changes would bring the conference process more in line with central tenets of public journalism and, more specifically, with my proposed public philosophy. To appreciate how and why this is the case, it is useful to consider the different stages of the process in some detail.

The conference process typically begins with the organizers selecting a problem and thereafter publicly announcing that a conference will be held on that problem. Interested individuals are invited to apply for membership on the citizen panel and are asked to submit approximately one page about themselves, their knowledge of the problem, and their reasons for wanting to participate. Unlike deliberative opinion polls and citizens juries, where participating citizens are randomly selected, organizers generally aim to compose the citizen panel of individuals from varied sociodemographic backgrounds who, moreover, have neither any particular knowledge of the problem nor represent special interest groups.

Certain changes to this initial stage of the conference process are in order. First, instead of selecting the problem to be examined on their own, it would be appropriate for the sponsoring news organizations to choose the topic in consultation with citizens. Indeed, one of the central tenets of public journalism, as discussed in previous chapters, is that citizens should be offered opportunities to participate in the setting of the news media agenda. Moreover, while it is clearly appropriate to select a sociodemographically diverse citizen panel, the requirements that panelists should not be knowledgeable about the problem in question or represent special interest groups are problematic. While such requirements, as some scholars note, might help broaden the range of participants and perspectives beyond those of scientific experts and powerful special interest groups commonly involved in public policy debates (see Einsiedel & Eastlick, 2000; Guston, 1999; Joss & Durant, 1995), the exclusion of especially marginalized special interest groups is problematic. Their participation on the citizen panel would, as other scholars note, bring diverse perspectives to bear on the problem examined, expose the inherently value-laden nature of all public policy debates, and exert political pressure on government officials (see Barns, 1995; Marris & Joly, 1999; Purdue, 1999). Thus, inviting representatives of various special interest groups to serve on the citizen panel might help create a more informed debate in which given problems are examined in broader social, political, and economic terms rather than in narrow technical, or even technocratic, terms.

More broadly, the implied distinction between politically "ignorant"/ "inactive" (e.g., ordinary citizens) and "knowledgeable"/"active" (e.g., representatives of special interest groups) individuals runs counter to the very idea of public journalism. It essentially suggests that "authentic" citizenship depends on one not being knowledgeable about important societal problems and doing little to try to address those problems in practice. Moreover, such a distinction could undermine one of the central goals of consensus conferences, namely to strengthen citizens' role in public policy debates. In a study of the 1994 U.K. consensus conference on genetically modified foods, Barns (1995) found that the panelists' lack of knowledge about the problem made it difficult for them to question the invited experts' narrow but technically complex agendas. With no substantive knowledge of the problem, the panelists had little choice but to ask factual questions, as opposed to questions that inquired into its social, political, and economic ramifications and, as a result, ended up accepting, rather than challenging, the technocratic discourse within which experts' responses were framed. In another study of this conference, Levidow (1998) summed up this problem by concluding that, instead of "democratizing technology," the conference ended up "technologizing democracy."

Once the citizen panel has been formed, the panelists typically undergo a period of preparation for the main conference. The citizen panel meets during two preparatory weekends, 8–10 and 4–5 weeks before the main conference. During those meetings, the panelists receive detailed briefing packets on the problem in question developed by the organizers, hear testimony from a number of invited experts, and, on the basis of this introduction to the problem, set the agenda for the main conference by formulating a series of questions to be addressed by a more comprehensive panel of experts during that event. The citizen panel also participates in the selection of experts for the main conference. While some organizers merely ask the panelists which types of experts they would like to see appear at the conference, others offer panelists opportunities to compose the expert panel from a predrawn list of possible candidates, or even to select the expert panel on their own (see Fixdal, 1997; Hendriks, 2005; Joss, 1995).

It is useful to convene such preparatory meetings for several reasons. Aside from enhancing the panelists' knowledge of the problem in question, the opportunity to formulate questions relating to the problem and participate in the selection of experts to address those questions might strengthen the citizen panel's agenda-setting power vis-à-vis experts. Yet, the fact that the organizers and invited experts brief the panelists on the problem prior to the main conference could reduce their ability to set the agenda on their own. Indeed, the briefing packets and oral presentations by invited experts have been found to exert a strong influence on the formulation of the citizen panel's questions and its choice of experts for the main conference (see McKay & Dawson, 1999). One possible solution could be to invite a diverse range of experts, including representatives of various special interest groups, to help prepare the briefing packets, brief the citizen panel in person during the preparatory meetings, and assist the citizen panel with identifying suitable experts for the main conference. Such a procedure was followed during the 1996 Norwegian consensus conference on genetically modified foods where representatives of 25 different special interest groups were invited by the organizers to help prepare the briefing packets and to propose suitable experts for the main conference (see Fixdal, 1997).

There are other reasons why the panelists should participate in the selection of experts for the main conference, either on their own or in collaboration with the organizers and representatives of various special interest groups, rather than simply accept the organizers' choices. Scholars note not only that having the organizers select the expert panel might foster cynicism among the panelists (Grundahl, 1995) but also that panelists have proven themselves perfectly capable of critically evaluating the professional credentials, institutional affiliations, and particular agendas of experts. Indeed, the citizen panel often spends considerable time considering how best to ensure a balanced mix of experts, thus exhibiting a high level of political sophistication (Durant, 1995).

The main conference typically follows a 4-day schedule. On the first day of the conference, the invited experts present their responses to the questions formulated by the citizen panel in the form of extended presentations. While the experts are expected to respond to questions that fall within their particular areas of expertise, two or more experts are often encouraged to address each question. On the morning of the second day, the panelists discuss the answers provided by the experts as well as ask follow-up questions. During the afternoon of the second day, as well as the entire third day, the citizen panel retires behind closed doors to work through the answers and formulate a consensus statement that outlines how the problem examined should be addressed. Finally, on the morning of the fourth day, the panelists present the consensus statement at a news conference as well as submit it to invited government officials.

The design of the main conference could be adopted by news organizations practicing public journalism without any modifications. Consistent with central tenets of public journalism, the citizen panel not only sets the agenda for interaction with experts but also, and equally important, receives testimony from several experts on each question. This not only situates the panelists in a prominent position vis-à-vis experts, but also offers them opportunities to compare different, and possibly conflicting, answers to given questions and to draw out the values that are embedded within those answers by playing out disagreeing experts against one another. The importance of having several experts respond to each question is further underscored by the fact that experts, known to vehemently disagree among themselves, tend to react more favorably toward each other's views when faced with the citizen panel. Internal, professional disagreements, even paradigm struggles, are downplayed when broader questions of the role of expert knowledge in public policy debates are on the agenda (see Cronberg, 1995). This, in turn, also underscores the importance of having representatives of various special interest groups on the citizen panel, as these individuals are much more likely than ordinary citizens to have detailed knowledge of the problem in question and, thereby, to be able to compel experts to publicly acknowledge salient disagreements. Finally, the fact that the citizen panel formulates the consensus statement without interference from experts might, at least in part, make up for the often secretive processes through which experts participate in public policy-making.

While the design of the main conference could be adopted without any modifications, there are reasons to question the stipulation that the citizen panel should reach a final consensus. Some scholars argue that it is important to reach consensus, given that the presence of dissensus could be interpreted by government officials as though broadly agreed-upon public solutions to problems are not feasible (Kluver, 1995), and that government officials might thereby be inclined to dismiss the political significance of the entire process (Andersen & Jaeger, 1999). Yet such a pursuit of consensus is problematic from a public journalism perspective. As discussed in chapter 2, a search for consensus is likely to suppress awareness of conflicting views among citizens, create barriers for genuinely open citizen deliberations, and might even help bolster those views that manage to make themselves appear as if they represent the views of all citizens. Following my proposed public philosophy, I would argue that the panelists should be encouraged to articulate their different, and possible conflicting, views by making salient differences the very focal point of deliberation. Thus, instead of requiring the citizen panel to reach an all-encompassing consensus on all aspects of the problem examined, the panelists should be encouraged to elaborate on which aspects they could agree and not agree and why. And indeed, despite the stipulation that the citizen panel should reach a final consensus, conference organizers have in practice allowed for a variety of outcomes. While some organizers insist that the citizen panel reach a consensus on all aspects of the problem, others allow the citizen panel to disregard aspects it could not agree upon, articulate majority and minority views in the form of so-called split statements, or, in rare instances, to merely outline the range of views expressed and reasons put forward in support of those views (see Cronberg, 1995; Fixdal, 1997; Hudspith & Kim, 2002).

THE IMPACT OF CONSENSUS CONFERENCES

Since the mid-1990s, a number of empirical studies have investigated the impact of consensus conferences on citizens, experts, and government officials. These studies show that consensus conferences are associated with various positive outcomes that, as should become apparent, are congruent with the hoped-for effects of public journalism.

Studies of consensus conferences held in Australia, Canada, Denmark, Holland, the United Kingdom, and the United States have found them to have a number of positive effects on participating citizens, notably by strengthening their (1) substantive knowledge of given problems, (2) confidence about engaging in interaction with experts, (3) sense of citizenship, and (4) trust in political problem-solving processes (see Andersen & Jaeger, 1999; Einsiedel & Eastlick, 2000; Guston, 1999; Hamlett, 2002; Hudspith & Kim, 2002; Joss, 1995; Kluver, 1995; Mayer, de Vries, & Geurts, 1995; McDonald, 1999; McKay & Dawson, 1999).

Scholars attribute citizen panelists' enhanced knowledge and confidence about interacting with experts to the iterative (e.g., two preparatory meetings and a main conference) and interactive (e.g., extensive interactions between citizens and experts) features of the consensus conference model. These positive outcomes, in turn, are reflected in the sophistication and specificity of questions asked of experts and in the complexity of citizen deliberations and the resulting recommendations to government officials. Similarly, citizen panelists' enhanced sense of citizenship and trust in political problem-solving processes manifest in subsequent political involvement. Following participation in a consensus conference, citizens tend to become more involved in various political activities, including by accepting invitations to serve on governmental advisory boards, testifying at public hearings attended by government officials, giving presentations in their local neighborhoods and workplaces, and writing articles for local news media (see Andersen & Jaeger, 1999; Einsiedel & Eastlick, 2000; Guston, 1999). While less research has focused on the impact of consensus conferences on participating experts, available evidence points to an important outcome, namely that experts tend to become more appreciative of citizens' abilities to learn about and pass judgment on complex problems (see Einsiedel & Eastlick, 2000; Guston, 1999; Mayer & Geurts, 1998). Taken together, these findings suggest that there is no compelling reason for news organizations practicing public journalism to delimit citizens' problem-solving activities to participation in local, community-based interventions or, as the case of the *Akron Beacon Journal*'s "Question of Color" campaign showed, to surface-level manifestations of problems. Citizens, it appears, are both capable of formulating solutions to complex problems in consultation with experts and willing to help implement those solutions in collaboration with government officials.

Finally, but not least importantly, research has uncovered various positive effects on government officials. According to government officials who have attended a consensus conference, the resulting citizen recommendations offer them insight into the range of views citizens hold on given problems and, more specifically, how citizens perceive the wider social, political, and economic ramifications of given problems. This is information that experts, given their often narrow technical expertise and agendas, are unable to provide (see Andersen & Jaeger, 1999; Einsiedel & Eastlick, 2000; Joss, 1998). In turn, this might explain why citizen panelists from several consensus conferences have been invited to serve on governmental advisory boards relating to the particular problems examined. Moreover, in a study of all 179 members of the Danish Parliament, Joss (1998) found that those who had attended a consensus conference used the resulting citizen recommendations as a source of personal information, as input for internal party discussions, and during wider parliamentary deliberations. Indeed, Joss (1998) found that of the 13 consensus conferences held in Denmark between 1987 and 1995, 8 were subsequently mentioned in parliamentary proceedings. Similarly, Einsiedel and Eastlick (2000) found that government officials who had attended the 1999 Canadian consensus conference on food biotechnology subsequently made extensive, positive reports about the process and outcome of the conference to colleagues within the Departments of Health and Agriculture and the Food Inspection Agency. Likewise, following the 2000 Canadian consensus conference on solid waste management, government officials who had attended the conference subsequently engaged in extensive discussions about the resulting citizen recommendations and, more generally, applauded the process as a valuable means of gaining input from the general public (Hudspith & Kim, 2002).

Perhaps most importantly, consensus conferences have been found to have an impact on actual legislation, a particularly impressive finding considering that the citizen panel only serves in an advisory capacity, with no legal mandate to influence legislation. Among the many Danish consensus conferences that have had an impact on legislation, four in particular are worth mentioning: (1) the conference on food irradiation (1989) led to legislation prohibiting this kind of food preservation; (2) the conference on human genome mapping (1989) led to legislation prohibiting the use of genetic screening for hiring and insurance purposes; (3) the conference on infertility (1993) led to legislation requiring that physicians register information on different treatment options with the Danish Board of Health; and (4) the conference on integrated agricultural production (1994) led to legislation establishing the Danish Council of Agriculture to support such agricultural production (see, for example, Joss & Durant, 1995; Kluver, 1995; Mayer & Geurts, 1998). Similarly, following two consensus conferences on food biotechnology in Australia and New Zealand in 1999, an Office of Gene Technology was established in Australia to oversee regulatory topics not covered by existing agencies with biotechnology jurisdictions (Andersen & Jaeger, 1999), while the New Zealand Food Authority was required to enforce the labeling of all genetically modified foods (Einsiedel, Jelsoee, & Breck, 2001). Likewise, following the 2000 Canadian consensus conference on solid waste management, the City of Hamilton adopted a solid waste management plan, of which 9 of the 18 new provisions were similar to those recommended by the citizen panel (Hudspith & Kim, 2002). In sum, consensus conferences have managed to address some of the major complaints that citizens who have participated in deliberative forums often direct against them, namely that such forums have no political impact whatsoever, are used to legitimate political decisions that have already been made behind closed doors, or are convened merely to give the appearance of public consultation without there being any genuine intent to act on the resulting citizen recommendations (see, for example, Button & Matson, 1999; Levine, Fung, & Gastil, 2005; Ryfe, 2002).

MAXIMIZING THE POLITICAL IMPACT
OF CONSENSUS CONFERENCES

While consensus conferences have had much political impact, especially in Denmark, scholars speculate that this impact might be due in large part to their institutional setting and timing. Specifically, scholars attribute the extensive political impact of the Danish consensus conferences to their institutionalization through the Danish Board of Technology and to the fact that the problems examined at those conferences were deliberately selected to coincide with given parliamentary debates on those problems.

This does not imply, however, that news organizations, in the absence of formal, institutional ties to government, would be unable to exert an equally strong political impact. Indeed, most consensus conferences around the world, including many that have been shown to have had a political impact, have been sponsored by various non-governmental institutions, including non-profit foundations (e.g., in New Zealand and the United States), museums (e.g., in Australia and the United Kingdom), and universities (e.g., in Canada and Holland). Rather, to enhance their chances of having a political impact, news organizations would need to move beyond their antagonistic relationship to government and, equally important, time the hosting of such conferences to coincide with the making of political decisions on given problems. Instead of presuming, as many news organizations practicing public journalism appear to do, that governmental involvement is inadequate at best and detrimental at worst (see chapter 2), news organizations ought to see government officials as important partners in the problem-solving process by encouraging them to consider solutions formulated by citizens themselves. Similarly, to make the conferences as relevant to them as possible, news organizations ought to consider the political saliency of given problems and choose those that are of most concern to citizens and government officials alike. While it is certainly commendable, as discussed in previous chapters, that the vast majority of public journalism initiatives have focused on long-standing political problems of concern to citizens rather than on elections and other more immediately newsworthy events, the lack of explicit connections to extant policy debates might inadvertently have limited their actual political impact.

SEVEN

THE PRACTICE OF PUBLIC JOURNALISM WORLDWIDE

While most of the experimentation with public journalism has taken place in the United States, like-minded initiatives have been carried out in other parts of the world, including Africa (Malawi, Senegal, Swaziland), the Asia/Pacific Rim (Australia, Japan, New Zealand), Europe (Denmark, Finland, Sweden), and South America (Argentina, Columbia, Mexico). In this chapter, I provide a broad overview and discussion of the practice of public journalism worldwide, with a particular focus on how public journalism is practiced in Denmark. The Danish projects are particularly interesting not only because they have differed the most from those in the United States but also because they have furthered important aspects of my proposed public philosophy for public journalism.

I begin with a relatively brief description of the various non-U.S. projects that have been carried out to date since these projects have resembled their U.S. counterparts in almost all respects. Indeed, the only substantive difference is that news organizations in some countries have promoted more direct interaction between citizens and government officials than has typically been the case in the United States. Next, I describe in more detail how the Danish projects have differed from their U.S. counterparts. I show that, in contrast to U.S. news organizations, Danish news organizations have advocated their own solutions to given problems and debated those solutions with other relevant actors, made consistent efforts to both highlight and address the concerns of marginalized segments of the citizenry, and encouraged citizens to formulate substantive solutions to problems while using experts as citizen–advisors. I conclude by considering why the Danish projects have differed from their U.S. counterparts in these important respects. I argue that, while the more activist journalistic stance assumed by the Danish news organizations could be attributed to a more activist professional self-understanding among Danish journalists, this activism, and especially the prominent role accorded citizens vis-à-vis experts, could also be seen as a manifestation of the increasing populism of Danish news media more generally.

ASIA/PACIFIC RIM (AUSTRALIA, JAPAN, NEW ZEALAND)

The Australian experiments with public journalism date back to 1997 when the Australian Broadcasting Corporation (ABC), the national public broadcasting service, conducted a telephone survey and several community forums in Queensland to identify the problems local residents were most concerned about. Following these forums, the ABC sponsored two larger-scale town hall meetings, broadcast live on ABC Radio and Television, in which local residents could discuss their most pressing concerns and relay those concerns directly to a number of invited government officials. The broadcasts were followed by talk-back radio programs devoted to further discussions of those concerns among local residents themselves (Hippocrates, 1999).

In 1998, the *Courier Mail*, a regional newspaper based in Queensland, launched a more comprehensive, two-year-long race relations project called "Public Journalism, Public Participation and Australian Public Policy: Connecting to Community Attitudes." Inspired by the *Akron Beacon Journal*'s "Question of Color" campaign, the *Mail* sponsored two community forums on race relations in Queensland and New South Wales, respectively, which together were attended by more than 600 local residents. Subsequently, the *Mail* reported back on the outcomes of these forums, carried articles that described local, citizen-based initiatives to improve race relations, and solicited much reader feedback in the form of opinion columns, letters to the editor, and hotline comments (Romano, 2001).

The following year, in 1999, five local newspapers from the Rural Press Publishing Group in New South Wales conducted a series of focus groups with teenagers as part of their joint "Project Youth." The media partners went to schools and youth centers to identify problems of particular concern to teenagers and subsequently devoted much coverage to their concerns (Petralia, 2004).

Most recently, in 2000, the *Latrobe Valley Express*, a local newspaper in Victoria, did a project on the state of public transportation. The *Express* sponsored a community forum where local residents could discuss their concerns and subsequently devoted considerable coverage to discussions of what could be done to address those concerns (Romano & Hippocrates, 2001).

Unlike in Australia, where the public journalism projects carried out to date have focused on long-standing problems of concern to citizens, those in New Zealand have all been conducted in conjunction with specific elections. The first project was launched during the 1996 national elections. Three regional newspapers, the *Manawatu Evening Standard*, the *Press*, and the *Waikato Times*, used several information-gathering tools to identify topics of concern to voters, including a telephone survey and voters' panels in which the participants were asked to comment on the performance of the different political parties. The media partners subsequently carried in-depth stories about the topics identified and asked candidates from the various parties to respond to voter-generated questions. Inspired by the *Charlotte Observer*'s 1992 "Your Voice, Your Vote" election project, the participating news organizations threatened to insert a block of white space with the words "no response," if the parties refused to answer any of the voter-generated questions. And, as in Charlotte, this happened only once when the National Party, the governing party at the time, declined to respond to a question. After one of the media partners, the *Press*, inserted a block of white space under the National Party's name, which appeared next to the answer of the rival New Zealand First Party, the National Party did not refuse to answer any subsequent questions. The project culminated in a series of town hall meetings, sponsored by the media partners, in which the candidates responded to questions formulated by a voters' panel in front of a live audience (McGregor, Comrie, & Campbell, 1998).

In 1999, a similar project was carried out by the *City Voice*, a local newspaper in Wellington, in conjunction with the national elections that year. The *Voice* did in-depth interviews with almost 300 eligible voters, asking them to rank-order a list of election topics. The highest-ranked topics subsequently became the focus of a series of town hall meetings in which voters were invited to ask representatives of the different political parties what they were planning to do to address those topics. Two additional meetings were added to cover two referenda presented to voters—a proposal to reduce the number of MPs and a proposal to implement more stringent crime measures. Each meeting was preceded by news stories in the *Voice* and followed by extensive coverage of its outcomes (Venables, 2001).

Two of the media partners from the 1996 project, the *Press* and the *Waikato Times*, teamed up with two other regional newspapers, the *Evening Post* and the *Otago Daily Times*, to take a public journalism approach to their coverage of the 2001 local elections. The media partners conducted a telephone survey to identify the topics of concern to voters and subsequently reported on those topics in a series of background articles, ran profiles of each of the local candidates for office, and carried voter-generated questions to the candidates. As in 1996, the media partners threatened to insert a block of white space with the words "no response," if the candidates refused to answer any of the voter-generated questions. Once again, this happened only once, when the *Post* carried through on its threat when one of the candidates declined to respond to a question. Like in 1996, the project culminated in a series of town hall meetings, sponsored by the media partners, in which the candidates responded to questions formulated by a voters' panel in front of a live audience (Ewart, 2003).

In addition to these project-based initiatives, steps have been taken in both Australia and New Zealand to make public journalism an integral part of daily news practices. Since 2004, APN News & Media, an international newspaper company that owns 23 regional newspapers in Australia and New Zealand, has been involved with a public journalism–inspired initiative called "Readers First." As part of the still-ongoing initiative, newspapers operated by APN News & Media try to focus their reporting on problems of concern to citizens from their perspectives. This is accomplished by identifying citizen concerns through ongoing telephone surveys and focus groups, and by using more ordinary citizens and fewer elite actors as sources of information in news stories (Ewart & Massey, 2006).

Like in Australia and New Zealand, several public journalism projects have been carried out in Japan. The Japanese experiments with public journalism date back to 1995 when the *Asahi Shimbun*, one of the largest national newspapers, did a project on public dissatisfaction with the established political parties. Following a telephone survey of more than 2,000 registered voters, the *Shimbun* did in-depth interviews with almost 70 non-party–supporting citizens, the results of which appeared in the paper. The *Shimbun* subsequently relayed the interviewed citizens' questions and concerns to representatives of the five major parties and carried their answers in the paper (Ito, 2005). Similarly, as part of its coverage of the 2001 national elections, the *Tokyo Shimbun*, a Tokyo-based regional newspaper, solicited voter-generated questions and relayed the candidates' answers in a series of articles (Ito, 2005).

In 1999 and 2002, the *Shinano Mainichi Shimbun*, a regional newspaper based in the Nagano Prefecture, did two projects, on nursing care and child rearing. The *Shimbun* sponsored and subsequently reported back on a series of community forums in which local residents discussed the problems among themselves. The *Shimbun* also launched web sites, eventually used by more than 800 individuals, where residents could discuss those problems further (Perry, 2004).

In 2003, the *Kahoku Shimpo*, a regional newspaper based in the Miyigo Prefecture, did a project on the problem of unregistered chemicals in the food industry. The *Shimpo* offered suggestions to what citizens could do to address the problem and created a web site where citizens could discuss the problem among themselves as well as with representatives of the food industry (Perry, 2004). Also in 2003, the *Chugoku Shimbun*, a regional newspaper based in the Hiroshima Prefecture, did a project on the increase in youth gang activity in Hiroshima. The *Shimbun* did in-depth interviews with victims of gang violence, asked local residents what they believed could be done to address the problem, and encouraged residents to help solve the problem themselves, including by reaching out to young gang members (Perry, 2004).

Aside from being the first Japanese newspaper to experiment with public journalism, the *Asahi Shimbun* is also the one that has done the most to make public journalism an integral part of its daily news practices. Since 2000, the *Shimbun* has had a "Section for Civic Welfare" in which participating journalists try to cover problems of concern to citizens from their perspectives. Journalists affiliated with this section regularly meet up with group of citizens to discuss their concerns, report back on those concerns in the news pages, and even help set up meetings between citizens and government officials. For example, in 2002, the "Section for Civic Welfare" carried a series of articles on the lack of pediatric care in the Tohoku Prefecture. As part of the series, journalists sponsored three community forums in which parents and physicians discussed their concerns, reported back on the outcomes of these forums, and subsequently set up meetings where parents and physicians could relay their concerns directly to relevant government officials (Ito, 2005). Other Japanese news organizations have made efforts to enhance interaction between citizens and journalists. The *Tokyo Shimbun* has since

1990 held a yearly day of discussions between readers and senior editors, the results of which are subsequently summarized in the paper (Ito, 2005).

EUROPE (FINLAND AND SWEDEN)

As in the Asia/Pacific Rim, news organizations in several European countries, including Finland and Sweden, have experimented with public journalism. The Finnish projects date back to 1997 when *Aamulehti*, a regional newspaper based in Tampere, did a project related to the local city budget. Inspired by the *Wisconsin State Journal's* "We the People" project in Madison, Wisconsin, *Aamulehti* convened a 12-member budget jury, which was charged with formulating a budget proposal. *Aamulehti* subsequently reported back on the outcomes of the budget jury's deliberations and, more broadly, explained to readers the actual political processes through which the city's budget comes into being (Kunelius, 2001).

In 1998–1999, the *Savon Sanomat*, a regional newspaper based in Kuopio, did three small-scale projects that related to intergenerational conflicts in Kuopio, citizens' lack of opportunities to influence local political processes, and the national elections of 1999. As part of the projects, which all followed similar procedures, the *Sanomat* sponsored a series of community forums where local residents could discuss those problems among themselves and, in the case of the second and third projects, could relay their concerns directly to invited government officials and candidates for office, respectively (Heikkila, 2000).

More recently, in 2003, the *Helsingin Sanomat*, the largest national newspaper, did a project in conjunction with the national elections that year. The *Sanomat* conducted a telephone survey to identify topics of concern to voters, focused its reporting on those topics, solicited voter-generated questions, and relayed the candidates' answers in the news pages (Ruusunoksa, 2005a). Similarly, in 2004, *Aamulehti* did a project in conjunction with the local elections that year. *Aamulehti* sponsored a series of community forums where voters could ask questions of local candidates for office and subsequently reported back on the outcomes of these forums (Ruusunoksa, 2005b).

Aside from these project-based initiatives, several news organizations have taken steps to make public journalism an integral part of their daily news practices. Since 1999, the *Savon Sanomat* has had a weekly section devoted to coverage of local public problems reported from citizens' perspectives. This section includes several features, including articles that carry citizen-generated questions to local government officials, articles that report back on the answers obtained, and articles that include citizen feedback on coverage, obtained through regular meetings with groups of citizens. Likewise, since 2003, the *Uutispaiva Demari*, a local newspaper affiliated with the Social Democratic Party, has had a weekly section called "Citizen Channel," which offers readers opportunities to ask questions of party representatives and comment on their responses. The *Demari* has also instituted novel story forms, including a so-called Democracy Barometer in which journalists assess given political decisions in terms of their potential impact on citizens' opportunities to influence democratic processes. Finally, since 2004, the *Ita-Hame*, a local newspaper in Heinola, has had a civic reporter whose responsibility it is to meet up with groups of local residents on a regular basis to identify and report back on their concerns, including by setting up meetings where residents can relay those concerns directly to relevant government officials (Ruusunoksa, 2006).

Unlike in Finland, only a few Swedish news organizations have experimented with public journalism. In 1998, two local newspapers, *Goteborgsposten* and *Vestmandlands Lans Tidning*, based, respectively, in Gothenburg and Vestmandland, carried out separate projects in conjunction with the national elections that year. Both papers conducted telephone surveys to identify topics of concern to voters and subsequently covered those topics in depth, including by carrying answers from various party representatives to voter-generated questions (Becksmo & Stjernfeldt, 2001).

More significantly, *Dagens Nyheter*, the largest national newspaper, has since 1999 had a mobile newsroom. The mobile newsroom travels to different parts of Sweden for 4–6 weeks at a time to report on problems of concern to local residents from their perspectives. Journalists affiliated with the mobile newsroom sponsor community forums in which local residents can discuss their concerns, report back on the outcomes of these forums, and offer residents opportunities to subsequently evaluate their coverage of those concerns (Beckman, 2003).

SOUTH AMERICA (ARGENTINA, COLUMBIA, MEXICO)

Like in Europe, news organizations in several South American countries, including Argentina, Columbia, and Mexico, have experimented with public journalism. In 1999, *Clarin* and *La Nacion*, the two largest national newspapers in Argentina, did a joint project called "Citizens Agenda" in conjunction with the election for mayor of Buenos Aires and a convention held to draft a new city charter. With the financial support of the United States Information Agency, *Clarin* and *La Nacion* convened a series of community forums in which voters were invited to discuss the topics they believed should drive the newspapers' election coverage, sponsored meetings where voters could relay their concerns directly to the mayoral candidates, and subsequently reported back on the outcomes of these forums and voter-candidate encounters (Mwangi, 2001).

As in Argentina, Columbia's largest national newspaper, *El Tiempo*, did a project in 1997 in conjunction with the local elections that year. *El Tiempo* conducted a telephone survey to identify the topics voters were most concerned about, sponsored a series of community forums where voters could discuss those concerns, and subsequently reported back on the results of the survey and the forums, including by summarizing the candidates' positions on those topics. In 1998, a large network of newspapers (*El Columbiano, El Mundo, El Tiempo*), television (Teleantioquia, Telemedellin, Telepacifico), and radio (Caracol, RCN, Todelar) stations launched a still-ongoing project, called "Citizen Voices," which is aimed at offering citizens opportunities to discuss a wide variety of problems of concern to them. The media partners have sponsored numerous community forums on such problems as crime (1998), violence (2003), and poverty (2004) (London, 2004).

While news organizations in Columbia have made efforts to regularize the practice of public journalism, none have gone as far as the newspaper company Groupo Reforma in Mexico. Since 1991, Groupo Reforma, a family-owned newspaper company consisting of four major newspapers in Mexico's largest cities (Guadalajara, Mexico City, Monterrey, and Saltillo), has operated a network of so-called editorial councils that offers citizens opportunities to formally participate in news media agenda-setting, decision-making, and performance evaluation. The primary goals of these editorial councils, which meet weekly, are to help the newspapers determine which problems citizens would like to see covered, how citizens would like to see those problems reported, and to obtain citizen feedback on coverage. Every year, editors of each major section at all Groupo Reforma newspapers—hard news sections, feature sections, and zoned suburban editions—recruit an editorial council consisting of 12 or more citizens. From a single editorial council in 1991, this formalized mechanism for citizen participation in journalistic processes has evolved into a comprehensive network of 63 editorial councils with more than 900 participants in 2005 (Chavez, 2005).

AFRICA (MALAWI, SENEGAL, SWAZILAND)

As in South America, news organizations in several African countries, including Malawi, Senegal, and Swaziland, have experimented with public journalism. In 1998, four Swazi news organizations, the Swaziland Broadcasting Corporation (television), the Swaziland Broadcasting and Information System (radio), the *Swazi Observer*, and the *Times of Swaziland*, collaborated on two projects that dealt with criminal activities preventing the routine operations of rural health care clinics ("Rural Health Care: The Human Side of Crime on Health Care") and rape, incest, and other forms of sexual violence ("Rape/Incest Issues: Far from the Headlines, Closer to the Heart"). During the projects, which were supported financially by the United States Information Agency, the media partners focused on the problems under investigation from the perspectives of citizens, including by reporting on what citizens themselves could do to address them and describing grassroots efforts already underway. Since the projects ended, two of the media partners, the *Observer* and the Swaziland Broadcasting Corporation, have made efforts to routinize the practice of public journalism by, respectively, instituting a weekly section that reports back on the outcomes of newspaper-sponsored community forums in which local residents discuss particular problems of concern to them and by producing a weekly program that focuses on the specific problems facing rural communities (Gillis & Moore, 2004).

Like the Swaziland Broadcasting Corporation, the Malawi Broadcasting Corporation (MBC), the national public broadcasting service, has also taken steps to make public journalism an integral part of its daily news practices. With the financial support of the George Soros Foundation, the MBC has since 2000 developed a comprehensive network of so-called listening clubs at the village level in which local residents listen together to its radio programming, discuss which problems they would like to see covered in the future, and give feedback on past programming (Moore & Gillis, 2005).

Finally, since 2000, Radio Oxy-Jeunes, a local radio station based in Senegal's capital of Dakar, has taken several steps to focus its programming on problems of concern to local residents. First, the station has instituted a number of novel programming formats, including *Dialogue Council*, a weekly program in which a local mayor is invited to discuss, with a live audience of his or her constituents, particular problems of concern to residents identified through in-depth interviews prior to the broadcasts. As part of the live broadcasts, the interviews are played for response by the mayors, and listeners are invited to call in with follow-up questions. When, after three editions of the program, the mayors refused to participate because of the tough questioning and criticism, the station continued the programs in their absence. Following public outcry, no mayor has subsequently refused an invitation to appear. Moreover, Radio Oxy-Jeunes has instituted a weekly program called *The Bus*. Similar to *Dagens Nyheter*'s mobile newsroom, journalists from the station travel to different parts of the country, do in-depth interviews with local residents to identify problems of concern to them, and offer residents opportunities to discuss those concerns among themselves during the live broadcasting of the program (Mwangi, 2002).

This brief overview shows that there are few differences in the way public journalism is practiced around the world. Like their U.S. counterparts, news organizations in other countries use various information-gathering tools to identify problems of concern to citizens, including telephone surveys, in-depth interviews, and focus groups; sponsor community forums where citizens can discuss those problems among themselves; report on problems from the perspectives of citizens rather than government officials, experts, and other elite actors; offer citizens opportunities to evaluate their coverage; and engage in various efforts to make public journalism an integral part of daily news practices. Indeed, the only substantive difference is that news organizations in some of these countries promote more direct interaction between citizens and government officials than is typically the case in the United States. Instead of relaying citizens' questions and concerns to government officials, news organizations in several countries regularly set up meetings where citizens can do so themselves.

There are several plausible explanations for the many similarities identified. First, it is worth noting that most of the non-U.S. projects were conceived in close collaboration with university faculty who had spend time in the United States on various research fellowships and/or had learned about the U.S. experiments with public journalism through the scholarly and popular press. To take just a few examples, faculty from the Queensland University of Technology, the Universidad Pontificia Bolivariana, and the University of Tampere have played leading roles in the design of the various projects in Australia, Columbia, and Finland, respectively (see Heikkila, 2000; Hippocrates, 1999; London, 2004). Indeed, many of the non-U.S. projects, as mentioned earlier, were deliberately designed to emulate practices applied by some of public journalism's earliest and most well-known U.S. practitioners, notably the *Akron Beacon Journal*, the *Charlotte Observer*, and the *Wisconsin*

State Journal. Second, several of the non-U.S. projects, as previously mentioned, were been supported financially by U.S.-based governmental and non-governmental organizations like the United States Information Agency (Argentina and Swaziland) and the George Soros Foundation (Malawi). Without invoking an overly simplistic cultural imperialism hypothesis, it is certainly possible that these funding agencies played a role in how the various projects in these countries were designed.

While these factors might, at least in part, explain the many similarities identified, it still remains somewhat puzzling that the non-U.S. projects, especially those in Africa, Asia, and South America, have not differed more substantially from their U.S. counterparts. Indeed, considering the long tradition for development journalism on these three continents, one would expect the participating news organizations to have assumed a much more activist, journalistic stance, including by focusing attention on problems of particular concern to the most marginalized segments of the citizenry, advocating their own solutions to given problems under investigation, and working directly with non-governmental organizations to help address those problems in practice. Surprising as it might appear, one has to turn to Denmark, a wealthy, Western European country, to find evidence of such journalistic activism.

THE FIRST DANISH PUBLIC JOURNALISM PROJECTS

Like the various non-U.S. projects carried out to date, the first Danish experiments with public journalism resembled their U.S. counterparts. In 1997, *Aarhus Stiftstidende* and *Fyens Stiftstidende*, two regional newspapers based, respectively, on the peninsula of Jutland and the island of Funen, took a public journalism approach to their coverage of the local elections that year. As part of its "Voters' Election" project, *Aarhus Stiftstidende* conducted a telephone survey to identify the topics voters were most concerned about and on which they wanted the paper to report. The survey showed that voters were most concerned about the state of local public schools, the influx of immigrants and refugees, the living conditions of the elderly, and the lack of affordable housing. Subsequently, *Aarhus Stiftstidende* covered those topics in depth and had the candidates respond to voter-generated questions relating to each of them. Similarly, as part of its "Your Election" project, *Fyens Stiftstidende* covered each of Funen's 32 municipal districts in depth. Each day leading up to the election, the paper focused on one district by examining the particular problems facing it. *Fyens Stiftstidende* also contacted 75 eligible voters from each district who were asked to formulate questions to the candidates. From the approximately 700 questions received, 350 were forwarded to the candidates and their responses appeared in the paper (Hansen, 1999).

JOURNALISTIC ACTIVISM

While the first Danish election projects replicated practices commonly applied in the United States, notably telephone surveys aimed at identifying topics of concern to voters, in-depth coverage of those topics, and various forms of voter-candidate interaction, subsequent projects have differed substantially from their U.S. counterparts. *Jyllands-Posten Koebenhavn*, the Copenhagen edition of *Morgenavisen Jyllands-Posten*, a regional newspaper based in Jutland, launched in 1998 a project called "The Uneven School." The primary goal of this project was to examine the reasons behind the increasing ethnic segregation of public schools in Copenhagen and, as one of the editors in charge put it, to explore what could be done "to further the integration of children of a non-Danish ethnic background" (Rosendal, 2001, p. 1).

Although the project's overall premise—to examine the causes of and identify possible solutions to a pressing social problem—was similar to many U.S. projects, *Jyllands-Posten Koebenhavn* took a much more activist, journalistic approach. Indeed, journalists involved with the project not only advocated their own solutions to the problem, but also solicited critical commentary from other relevant actors, notably school officials, parents, and students, thereby positioning themselves, as discussed in chapter 2, as active participants in the problem-solving process. For example, in an article examining the increasing ethnic segregation of public schools on Vesterbro, the neighborhood with the highest concentration of people of a non-Danish ethnic background, journalists presented two different solutions. A more ethnically integrated school system could be obtained, they suggested, by either busing children of a non-Danish ethnic background to other schools in Copenhagen or by establishing a central registration to ensure than all schools on Vesterbro would receive an equal number of those children. The two principals quoted in the article, from local public schools with predominantly Danish and non-Danish children, rejected both proposals and, instead, advocated increased social interaction among parents. The most viable solution to the problem of ethnic segregation, they argued, would be to fight mutual prejudice among parents, an effort, they acknowledged, that local public schools, including their own, had failed to honor (see Rosendal

& Bro, 1998). In other articles, journalists advocated and debated alternative solutions to the problem of ethnic segregation, such as to market schools with predominantly non-Danish children to Danish parents, to combine schools serving respectively Danish and non-Danish children, and even to circumscribe parents' abilities to choose their children's schools on their own.

Moreover, in contrast to U.S. projects, where one of the central goals, as discussed in chapter 2, has been to focus attention on problems of presumed shared concern to all citizens, *Jyllands-Posten Koebenhavn* made efforts to highlight the particular concerns of marginalized segments of the citizenry. Aside from carrying conventional, balanced accounts contrasting two or more conflicting views on given problems, the paper carried many articles that were written from the perspectives of specific publics, with a minimum of editorial interference. These included articles recounting the views and experiences of inter-ethnic couples who had decided to send their children to ethnically segregated schools, children of inter-ethnic couples attending ethnically integrated schools, and children of non-Danish ethnic background attending ethnically integrated and segregated schools.

Jyllands-Posten Koebenhavn's comparatively more activist stance is reflected in many other, more recent, projects. In 2000, Koebenhavns Radio, a local Copenhagen-based radio station affiliated with Danmarks Radio, the national public broadcasting service, launched a project that was aimed at addressing various traffic-related problems in Copenhagen. As part of the "Traffic Project," journalists at the station not only produced a web site where listeners could post their own solutions and discuss them with other listeners but also presented four detailed proposals for how problems such as accidents, air pollution, and congestion could be resolved. In a follow-up project called "Traffic Life" in 2001, Danmarks Radio, Koebenhavns Radio, and *Politiken*, a major national newspaper, took these efforts to solve traffic-related problems beyond the news pages by contacting local police precincts with the highest concentration of accidents to encourage them to conduct regular traffic checks. As during the "Traffic Project," one of the media partners, *Politiken*, carried a regular column called "Reader Debate" where interested readers could offer their own solutions to traffic-related problems (Henriksen, 2001). Also in 2001, *Jyllands-Posten Koebenhavn*, Koebenhavns Radio, and TV Danmark/Local Rapporten, a local Copenhagen-based commercial television station, collaborated on a project that was aimed at finding ways to ease the integration of immigrants into Danish society. As part of their joint "Project Bridge-Builder," the two broadcasters offered immigrants opportunities to articulate their particular concerns by inviting recent immigrants from seven different countries to produce their news and other programming on several occasions. *Jyllands-Posten Koebenhavn* contacted local businesses to encourage them to offer internships to recent immigrants attending business high schools in Copenhagen. Moreover, the media partners encouraged residents to call in with possible solutions and produced a web site where they could discuss those solutions among themselves (Rasmussen, 2001). In 2002, five Funen-based news organizations, *Fyens Amts Avis*, *Fyens Stiftstidende*, Radio Fyn, TV Danmark2, and TV2/Fyn, collaborated on a project, called "A Time to Live," which was aimed at finding ways to reduce stress in the workplace. As part of the project, journalists from the participating news organizations offered various suggestions to how employers could help their employees better balance the conflicting demands of work and home life (Joergensen, 2002). Similarly, in 2003 and 2004, DR Midt & Vest, a local Jutland-based radio station affiliated with Danmarks Radio, launched two projects, "A Living Future" and "Senior Citizens at Work," which focused, respectively, on the increasing depopulation of the rural parts of Denmark and the employment problems of the elderly. As part of the projects, journalists from the station offered various suggestions to how these problems could be addressed (Kambsgaard, 2005; Kambsgaard & Stephansen, 2003). Most recently, in 2005, Danmarks Radio and *Politiken* collaborated on a project, called "How Difficult Can It Be," which was aimed at addressing the employment problems experienced by citizens of a non-Danish ethnic background. As did the media partners during "Project Bridge-Builder," Danmarks Radio and *Politiken* offered citizens of a non-Danish ethnic background opportunities to articulate and discuss their particular concerns by inviting recent immigrants to report on the obstacles they had encountered and by creating a web site where immigrants could discuss those obstacles among themselves. The media partners also contacted local businesses to encourage them to offer internships or paid employment to recent immigrants (see the project's web site, http://www.dr.dk/p1/hvorsvaert).

Several Danish news organizations have also taken steps to make public journalism an integral part of their daily news practices. In 2003, *Berlingske Tidende*, a major national newspaper, launched a still-ongoing initiative called "Closer to the Readers," which is aimed at identifying which problems citizens are most concerned about and how citizens would like to see those problems covered. As part of the initiative, *Berlingske Tidende* has established an internal research group that, so far, has done in-depth interviews with more than 3,000 citizens as well as focus groups with more than 400 regular readers (Soendergaard, 2005). Similarly, in 2005, *Fyens Amts Avis*, a Funen-based regional newspaper, launched a still-ongoing initiative called "Closer," which, like *Dagens Nyheter* in Sweden, features a mobile newsroom. Journalists affiliated with the mobile newsroom travel to different parts of Funen to identify problems of concern to local residents, sponsor community forums where residents can discuss those concerns among themselves, and actively solicit criticism and suggestions for future stories (Joergensen, 2005).

CITIZEN-EXPERT INTERACTION

Aside from assuming a more activist, journalistic stance than their U.S. counterparts, the Danish news organizations have differed from those in the United States by their use of citizens and experts. Although one of the central goals of U.S. projects, as discussed in previous chapters, has been to involve citizens in the development of solutions to given problems, citizens and experts have, with few exceptions (most notably, the "We the People" project in Madison, Wisconsin), been assigned unequal roles in the problem-solving process. Specifically, while citizens have been encouraged to design and enact local, community-based solutions, the development of more far-reaching, systemic solutions has been relegated to experts. The Danish projects, in contrast, have involved citizens in the development of substantive solutions to problems, while using experts as citizen-advisors, thereby effectively reversing the roles played by citizens and experts in most U.S. projects. Indeed, all of the Danish projects have engaged citizens and experts in a form of interaction that resembles that of the consensus conference model. While there is no evidence that the participating news organizations deliberately sought to emulate, or were even aware of, the Danish consensus conferences, it is not surprising that these news organizations, given their roots in a highly egalitarian civic and political culture, would promote a similar form of citizen–expert interaction.

During its "Traffic Project," Koebenhavns Radio convened a 10-member citizen panel, selected from among more than 500 volunteers, which was charged with formulating a strategic plan for how various traffic-related problems could be resolved within the next 10–15 years. As during consensus conferences more generally, Koebenhavns Radio also arranged for a number of experts on traffic-related problems to meet with the panel.

Each expert was assigned 20 minutes for a brief presentation, after which the panelists would ask questions and discuss the topics raised internally. Subsequently, Koebenhavns Radio arranged for some of the experts to remain on standby, should the panelists decide to call them in for further advice; 25 of the experts who volunteered to serve as citizen-advisors were called in on several occasions. Like Koebenhavns Radio, the media partners responsible for the "Traffic Life," "Project Bridge-Builder," "Time to Live," "Living Future," "Senior Citizens at Work," and "How Difficult Can It Be" projects also convened citizen panels, which were charged with formulating substantive solutions to the problems examined and arranged for various experts to meet with the panels on several occasions. The final recommendations of the respective citizen panels were, as during consensus conferences more generally, presented at public hearings attended by prominent government officials, including the Mayor of Copenhagen ("The Traffic Project"), the Secretary of Transportation ("Traffic Life"), the Secretary of the Interior ("Project Bridge-Builder"), the chairpersons of the two largest unions representing employers and employees ("Time to Live"), the Secretary of Agriculture ("A Living Future"), the Secretary of Employment ("Senior Citizens at Work"), and the Secretary of Integration ("How Difficult Can It Be").

POLITICAL ACTIVISM OR POPULISM?

While it is difficult to determine with any degree of conclusiveness why the Danish public journalism projects have differed from their U.S. counterparts in these important respects, several plausible explanations should be considered. First, the more activist, journalistic stance assumed by the Danish news organizations could be attributed to a more activist professional self-understanding among Danish journalists. Lund, Jensen, and Marosi (2001) found, in a national survey of more than 800 print and broadcast journalists, that while 97% of respondents believe that journalists should hold government officials responsible for solving societal problems, 94% of respondents believe that journalists should help increase citizen participation in democratic processes. Indeed, while about two thirds (67%) stated that journalists should help set the agenda for political debate, almost three quarters (73%) stated that journalists should help citizens formulate solutions to pressing social problems. While these figures might, at least in part, explain why Danish news organizations have not only encouraged citizens to formulate substantive solutions to given problems but have also advocated specific solutions on their own, the results of another survey might account for the efforts made to both highlight and address the concerns of marginalized segments of the citizenry. Esmark and Kjaer (2000) found, in a national survey of 150 print and broadcast journalists, that while almost three quarters (72%) of respondents believe that journalists should ensure that all political interests are equally represented in public debate, almost one third (31%) believe that journalists should serve as mouthpieces for individuals and groups with little or no political influence.

U.S. journalists, in contrast, define their primary professional responsibilities as information investigation, analysis, and dissemination. While journalists, as discussed in chapter 3, have been found to be favorably disposed toward many of public journalism's practices, three of the most important role functions continue to be investigating government claims (71%), providing analysis of complex problems (51%), and getting information to the public quickly (59%) (see Weaver et al., 2006).

Differences in the professional self-understanding of Danish and U.S. journalists could, in turn, be explained by differences in the historical development of the Danish and U.S. press systems, notably their degree of party political attachments. In contrast to the United States, where the evolution from a party–political to a commercial press has all but dissolved the tradition of partisan advocacy (Schudson, 1978), the Danish press, like many of its European counterparts (Patterson, 1998), has retained its historically strong party–political affiliations. Indeed, despite a gradual de-party-politicization of the Danish press since the 1960s, 22 of the 37 daily newspapers remain associated with particular political parties or ideologies (Soellinge, 1999).

While the journalistic activism displayed by the Danish news organizations could be attributed to an activist professional self-understanding among Danish journalists, this activism, and especially the prominent role accorded citizens vis-à-vis experts, could also be seen as a manifestation of the increasing populism of Danish news media more generally. Hjarvad (2000) argues that over the past decade, a minor "revolt" has taken place among local and regional news organizations situated in the provinces against the perceived elitism of the Copenhagen-based, national news media. News organizations such as *Aarhus Stiftstidende* and *Fyens Stiftstidende*, which, as mentioned earlier, launched the first Danish public journalism projects, have made a conscious effort to form a contrast to the Copenhagen-based, national news media's top-down approach to news reporting. Conceiving of themselves as "voices of the people," provincial news organizations have begun to center their daily news coverage around problems of concern to citizens rather than the central political institutions of Danish society and to use citizens rather than experts, government officials, and other elite actors as their primary sources of information. Hjarvad (2000) notes that, while this populist approach to news reporting began among news organizations situated in the provinces, it has in recent years made inroads among the Copenhagen-based, national news media, including Danmarks Radio, another prominent news organization that has been involved with public journalism. Examples of Danmarks Radio's increasing populism include *19Direkte*, a daily television news program launched in 1999 where citizens formulate and debate solutions to pressing social problems among themselves and on which no experts or government officials appear (Braun, 2004).

Thus, while the tradition of political advocacy among Danish news organizations might have made it possible for individual journalists to take stands on policy issues and promote political action on the part of citizens, it is likely that the increasing populism of Danish news media has served to turn those efforts against conventional channels for political problem-solving, especially political parties. It should be noted that populism and mistrust of established political parties are part of a broader trend in Western Europe that, among other factors, could be attributed to the perceived crisis of the welfare state, anxieties associated with the loss of national sovereignty within the European Union, and the threat of immigration from the Third World (see, for example, Betz, 1994; Hayward, 1996; Parkin & Taggart, 2000).

The increasing populism of Danish news media might not only help explain the prominent role accorded citizens vis-à-vis experts, but also mirrors the actual historical trajectory of public journalism experimentation. While the first projects were launched by regional newspapers situated in the provinces (e.g., *Aarhus Stiftstidende* and *Fyens Stiftstidende*), many subsequent projects have been carried out by Copenhagen-based, national (e.g., Danmarks Radio and *Politiken*), and local (e.g., *Jyllands-Posten Koebenhavn*, Koebenhavns Radio, and TV Danmark/Lokal Rapporten) news organizations. *Jyllands-Posten Koebenhavn* is a particularly interesting case in point. Its several forays into public journalism could be seen as a conscious effort on the part of its parent company, *Morgenavisen Jyllands-Posten*, to bring its populist approach to news reporting to the nation's capital. Indeed, its first project, "The Uneven School," was launched only a couple of months after the Copenhagen edition was introduced. The extensive involvement of Copenhagen-based, national, and local news organizations stands in stark contrast to the United States, where the vast majority of projects, as described in chapter 3, have been carried out by local news organizations situated outside the major metropolitan areas.

EIGHT

FROM PUBLIC JOURNALISM TO THE PUBLIC'S JOURNALISM?

The public journalism movement has undergone a remarkable evolution over the course of merely a decade and a half. From its relatively humble beginnings as occasional, special projects among a handful of small-scale and medium-sized newspapers in the United States, hundreds of newspapers of all sizes as well as many television and radio stations worldwide have experimented with public journalism, including by making various public journalism practices an integral part of their routine newsroom operations. In this final chapter, I summarize the most recent data on the practice of public journalism as well as discuss whether the newer, citizen-based venues for news reporting, deliberation, and problem-solving are furthering the democratic ideals that have animated the public journalism movement thus far and, according to my more activist vision for the movement, ought to animate the future practice of public journalism.

Drawing on various sources of evidence, I begin by offering a general profile of the state of public journalism today. I show that, while the public journalism movement continues to attract new and committed newsroom supporters, and news organizations more generally are taking important steps to nurture a critical public sphere about journalism, news organizations are doing more to facilitate interaction between their newsroom staff and audiences than to facilitate interaction among citizens themselves and between citizens and government officials. Simply put, while the public journalism movement continues to expand, of the two gaps that inspired the movement in the first place—between news organizations and their audiences and between citizens and government—news organizations are, at least at the present time, doing more to bridge the former than the latter.

Following this broad overview of the current state of public journalism, I examine in more detail whether Internet-based media of communication, notably citizen-produced weblogs, hyper-local community web sites, the South Korean online newspaper *OhmyNews*, and the global *Indymedia* network, are furthering the democratic ideals that have animated, and in my opinion ought to animate, the public journalism movement. I argue, first, that the appearance of citizen-produced weblogs does not, as many scholarly and journalistic observers speculate, herald the dawn of a new "public's journalism." I show, among other issues, that such weblogs contain little independent, original news reporting, tend to re-mediate the news reporting and commentary of mainstream news organizations and, by implication, the views of their elite sources of information, and primarily inspire citizen interaction among individuals of similar political persuasions. In these important respects, I conclude, the discourse of citizen-produced weblogs not only runs counter to public journalism's democratic ideals but in fact falls far behind the movement's actual accomplishments.

Next, I examine the modes of operation and content of so-called hyper-local community web sites. I show that, while such community web sites, unlike citizen-produced weblogs, feature independent, original news reporting, they suffer from a journalistic division of labor whereby the newsroom staff takes on responsibility for reporting on local public issues and events while residents report on their private interests and concerns. More generally, I argue, such sites promote a vision of community as a unified site bounded by shared values and goals while failing to acknowledge that most contemporary communities are fragmented into multiple social groups with different, if not conflicting, interests.

Finally, I consider several efforts to promote citizen-based news reporting, deliberation, and problem-solving on a much broader scale, namely the South Korean online newspaper *OhmyNews* and the global *Indymedia* network. I show, first, that despite its much larger scale, *OhmyNews* operates in terms of the same problematic journalistic division of labor as hyper-local community web sites and, more generally, that its news reporting mimics that of mainstream news media.

By contrast, I show that the *Indymedia* network promotes alternative, citizen-based news reporting and commentary that counteracts that found in mainstream news media, respectful interaction among participants of various political persuasions, and political activism on behalf of progressive social, political, and economic change. In these important respects, I argue, the discourse found on the *Indymedia* network represents one of the best approximations of what a genuinely public's journalism might look like. I conclude by noting that the recent proliferation of citizen-based media of communication does not diminish the responsibility of mainstream news organizations for trying to further public journalism's democratic ideals.

THE STATE OF PUBLIC JOURNALISM TODAY

In the most comprehensive study of the practice of public journalism to date, Friedland and Nichols (2002) found that 45% of the more than 600 U.S. initiatives had been carried out by news organizations that had been involved with public journalism for 5 or more years. While such statistics could legitimately be interpreted as evidence of a strong and enduring commitment to public journalism among many news organizations, they might also indicate that, whether on the basis of short-term experimentation or philosophical principle, many news organizations remain fundamentally unchanged by public journalism. Although no study of comparable scope has been undertaken during the past 5 years, there is reason to believe that the public journalism movement continues to be characterized by a similar "half-step approach."

There is much evidence that the public journalism movement continues to attract new newsroom supporters, committed to making public journalism an integral part of their routine information-gathering, news-reporting, and performance-evaluation practices. Since 2001, when the Associated Press Managing Editors (APME) launched its still-ongoing "National Credibility Roundtables Project," an initiative aimed at enhancing the relationship between newspapers and their readers, approximately 200 newspapers, many of which were not involved with public journalism during the time frame (1994–2002) of Friedland and Nichols' (2002) study, have adopted various public journalism practices. Specifically, many newspapers have begun to: (1) make efforts to identify topics of particular concern to citizens, such as by holding regular, if informal, meetings with groups of readers to learn about their concerns, instituting formal reader panels charged with suggesting story topics, and dispatching reporters to different parts of their circulation areas, especially minority neighborhoods, to meet with local residents to gather story ideas; (2) report on those topics from the perspectives of citizens;

and (3) solicit and respond to citizen feedback through regular question/answer columns and citizen–journalist e-mail groups (see Associated Press Managing Editors [APME], 2002, 2003; Brickman, 2005; Brown, Thorson, & Fleming, 2006; Quinland, Bucco, & Berens, 2004). Importantly, Brown et al.'s (2006) comparative study of newspapers that had and had not participated in the APME initiative showed that, while newsroom commitment to these and other public journalism–inspired practices were highest among newspapers that had been involved with the initiative, efforts to include citizens in information-gathering, news-reporting, and performance-evaluation was also high among the other newspapers. This finding attests, as Brown et al. (2006, p. 21) note, to "the ongoing impact of some of [public journalism's] core ideas."

Moreover, during the past couple of years, many news organizations have taken important steps to nurture what I referred to in chapter 2 as a critical public sphere about journalism. Specifically, a growing number of news organizations in the United States and abroad, including the BBC, CBS, the *Guardian*, the *Houston Chronicle*, and the *New York Times*, have incorporated so-called editorial weblogs on their online sites where senior editors explain specific editorial decisions; invite questions, comments, and feedback from readers; and subsequently respond to reader concerns (see Dube, 2007, for a listing of dozens of editorial weblogs). Even more impressive, many news organizations, including the *Dallas Morning News*, the *Sacramento Bee*, the *Seattle Post-Intelligencer*, the *Spokesman-Review*, and the *Wichita Eagle*, have incorporated so-called editorial board weblogs on their online sites where members of the editorial board, either individually or as a collective, outline their ideas for upcoming editorials, discuss those ideas with interested readers, and subsequently respond to reader comments on the published editorials. While some news organizations, like the *Seattle Post-Intelligencer*, announce each day, following their editorial board meetings, which topics they are contemplating for the next day's edition, other news organizations, like the *Dallas Morning News*, invite comments from readers as those topics are still being discussed at meetings of the editorial board (see Glaser, 2004; Outing, 2005; Willey, 2003). Simply put, many news organizations are not only making their editorial decisions more transparent but are also holding themselves more publicly accountable for those decisions through direct interaction with citizens.

As in newsrooms, there is evidence that the public journalism movement continues to make inroads in journalism classrooms. In the most comprehensive study to date, Dickson et al. (2001) found that, while 12% of U.S. journalism programs have specific courses devoted to public journalism, public journalism is a topic for discussion or is taught as a journalistic practice in 84% of programs. Again, while no study of comparable scope has been undertaken during the past 6 years, there are many current examples of public journalism–inspired courses, even entire programs, including at some of the most prestigious U.S. journalism schools. For example, in 2006, the Reynolds School of Journalism at the University of Nevada launched a master's degree program in interactive environmental journalism. As part of this program, students are taught how to use new technologies to promote deliberation among citizens, experts, and government officials about given environmental problems. Similarly, in 2006, the University of Alabama launched a unique partnership, known as the "Ayers Family Institute for Community Journalism," between its School of Communication and Information Science and the *Anniston Star*, a local newspaper. As part of this partnership, master's degree students in journalism receive instruction in public journalism–inspired news reporting methods at the university while gaining practical newsroom experience at the paper. The University of Missouri's School of Journalism, with a $31 million grant from the Donald W. Reynolds Foundation, is currently in the process of establishing a journalism research and training institute aimed at bringing citizens, practicing journalists, and journalism scholars together to discuss and experiment with ways to strengthen journalism's democratic role (see the web sites of the respective institutions for further details).

While the public journalism movement continues to attract new and committed newsroom (and classroom) supporters, there is reason to question the depth of commitment of at least some of the current initiatives. First, it is important to note that the various efforts to make editorial decisions more transparent and publicly accountable were initiated in the wake of the recent newsroom scandals at such high-profile, elite news organizations as CBS, CNN, *Newsweek*, the *New York Times*, and *USA Today*. To take just two prominent examples, CBS's editorial weblog, the *Public Eye*, was created following the scandal surrounding the disputed authenticity of documents, originally presented at CBS News' *60 Minutes*, showing that President George W. Bush had received preferential treatment during his service in the Texas Air National Guard. Similarly, the *New York Times*' editorial weblog, the *Public Editor's Journal*, was created following the scandal surrounding journalist Jayson Blair's dishonest reporting. The reactive, as opposed to proactive, nature of these and other editorial weblogs makes one wonder whether the underlying motivation is to truly make editorial decisions more transparent and publicly accountable or whether the underlying motivation is to enhance news organizations' diminished credibility with audiences. Indeed, one might fear that, once the recent newsroom scandals begin to fade from public memory, many of the current initiatives will quickly be abandoned. Moreover, while the editorial (board) weblogs currently in existence have not inspired any scholarly research, my own informal review of some of these weblogs shows that they leave much to be desired. For example, while many editorial weblogs are indeed used to explain specific editorial decisions and to respond to reader questions and comments, perhaps not surprisingly, few address, or even acknowledge, the more fundamental factors that influence the news production process, notably the commercial interests of media owners and advertisers, organizational pressures and work routines, and various information-gathering and news-reporting conventions. Similarly, while many editorial board weblogs do indeed inspire discussions of specific editorial topics and editorials, few include discussions of what editorial board members are trying to achieve in a broader political sense through their editorial activity.

More broadly, the most recent empirical research on how news organizations use the interactive capabilities of their online sites shows that, while news organizations do much to promote interaction between their newsroom staff and audiences, they do considerably less to promote interaction among citizens themselves and between citizens and government officials. For example, while virtually all online newspapers feature general newsroom e-mail addresses, directories of individual staff e-mail addresses, and opportunities for readers to submit letters to the editor online, less than half offer readers opportunities to interact directly with one another through such features as discussion forums (45%), links to external discussion sites (21%), and community chat forums (2%). Indeed, only 19% of online newspapers include e-mail links to government officials mentioned in given news stories and none provide opportunities for readers to interact directly with government officials such as in the form of online chat forums (see Greer & Mensing, 2006; Rosenberry, 2005; Ye & Li, 2006).

CITIZEN-PRODUCED WEBLOGS

While mainstream news organizations, as the prior discussion shows, continue to aspire to many of the democratic ideals that have animated the public journalism movement, a growing number of scholarly and journalistic observers speculate that the appearance of various citizen-based venues for news reporting, deliberation, and problem-solving will allow citizens themselves to carry those ideals forward. Indeed, many observers anticipate the emergence of what Schudson (1999, p. 122) refers to as a "fourth model of journalism"; that is, a model of journalism "in which authority is vested not in the market, not in a party, and not in the journalist but in the public." One of the clearest expressions of this supposed shift from public journalism to the public's journalism (see, for example, Friedland, 2003; Heinonen & Luostarinen, 2005; Witt, 2004a), which is also referred to as the "second phase of public journalism" (see Nip, 2006), is that of Leonard Witt (2004b, p. 3), current president of the *Public Journalism Network*:

> Public journalism's tenets have the best chance of being advanced by the public using weblogs and other electronic communication tools. Citizens, who are so much a part of the public journalism philosophy, no longer have to be invited into the mix. They are part of the mix.

In the following sections, I discuss whether some of the most prominent, Internet-based media of communication, notably citizen-produced weblogs, hyper-local community web sites, the South Korean online newspaper *OhmyNews*, and the global *Indymedia* network, are indeed furthering public journalism's democratic ideals as well as the ideals embedded within my own more activist vision for the movement. I begin by considering the case of citizen-produced weblogs. This particular medium of communication has, as the quote above suggests, not only inspired much speculation among scholarly and journalistic observers but has also attracted by far the most research attention.

While the technology behind weblogs has been around since the early 1990s, this particular web site format gained rapidly in popularity in the late 1990s with the appearance of easy-to-use, freely available software such as Blogger, LiveJournal, and Weblogger (Blood, 2002; Lasica, 2002; Mortensen & Walker, 2002). Indeed, from an estimated 30,000 weblogs in 1998 (Amis, 2002), the number of citizen-produced weblogs has grown exponentially to about 52 million (*Technorati*, 2006). Although it is difficult to determine with any degree of precision how many of these weblogs deal with news and current affairs, content analyses showing that approximately 17% of weblogs cover such topics, either exclusively or in part (Papacharissi, 2004), would put the number of politically–oriented weblogs, at around 8.8 million. Such weblogs have been found to be the second most read type of weblogs behind personal or family weblogs (Whelan, 2003).

If the availability of easy-to-use, freely available software helped increase the popularity of weblogs, their wider visibility and speculations about their democratizing potential owe much to several high-profile cases of their alleged ability to force topics onto the mainstream news media agenda and inspire changes within the realm of politics and journalism. Most prominently, many observers claim that the concerted publicity of thousands of weblog writers forced Senator Trent Lott (R–MS) to resign as Senate Majority Leader following his racially insensitive remarks at former senator Strom Thurmond's (R–SC) 100th birthday celebration. During that event, Trent Lott suggested that the world would have been better off if segregationist Strom Thurmond had won the 1948 U.S. presidential election. While the celebration was broadcast live on the cable television network C-SPAN, Trent Lott's remarks initially attracted only little attention in the mainstream news media. In the following day's edition, the *New York Times* merely published a photograph from the event and the *Washington Post* carried a brief article on an inside page. It was only after Trent Lott's remarks appeared on the popular weblog *Talking Points Memo* as well as on numerous other weblogs that the mainstream news media began to devote significant coverage to the event (see, for example, Bloom, 2003; Bowman & Willis, 2003; Wright, 2003). Similarly, many observers claim that the negative fallout from many of the aforementioned newsroom scandals owes much to the influence of citizen-produced weblogs. Among other recent incidents, the concerted publicity of thousands of weblog writers has been credited with leading to: (1) the resignation of the *New York Times*' executive editor Howell Raines and managing editor Gerald Boyd following revelations about journalist Jayson Blair's dishonest reporting; (2) the firing of four senior CBS News executives after information began to circulate that disputed the authenticity of documents, originally presented at CBS News' *60 Minutes*, showing that President George W. Bush had received preferential treatment during his service in the Texas Air National Guard; and (3) the firing of CNN executive Eason Jordan following his remarks at the World Economic Forum that U.S. troops had deliberately targeted American journalists during the war in Iraq (see, for example, Palser, 2005; Pein, 2005; Smolkin, 2004).

In addition to their alleged ability to steer mainstream news media coverage, scholarly and journalistic observers situate the democratic significance of citizen-produced weblogs in their capacity for independent, original news reporting. Many observers claim that, in contrast to mainstream news media's centralized, top-down approach to news reporting, with their reliance on elite sources of information, weblogs facilitate a decentralized, bottom-up approach to news reporting by turning traditionally passive news consumers into active news producers (see, for example, Gillmor, 2004; Rothenburg, 2003; Rutigliano, 2004). One of the most widely cited, if not celebrated, examples of ordinary citizens engaging in independent, original news reporting is Salam Pax, an anonymous Iraqi architect. During the war in Iraq, Salam Pax used his weblog, *Where is Raed?* to file regular eyewitness reports on life in Baghdad before, during, and after the allied bombing. Salam Pax juxtaposed what he and relatives witnessed with what was reported in mainstream Western and Arab news media (see, for example, Bowman & Willis, 2003; Matheson & Allan, 2003; Reynolds, 2004).

Finally, scholarly and journalistic observers claim that the interactivity of weblogs, and especially the practice of linking to and commenting on other Internet-based materials, gives rise to a radically different kind of news discourse than the one found in mainstream news media. Specifically, the practice of juxtaposing news reporting and commentary from a wide range of sources, which one observer refers to as an act of "consumptive production" (Rothenburg, 2003), is seen to facilitate a "multiperspectival" (Bruns, 2005), "multivocal" (Gorgura, 2004), or "intertextual" (Gallo, 2003) form of news discourse. By juxtaposing news reporting and commentary from a diverse range of sources, observers claim, weblog writers not only challenge the narrow range of topics and sources featured in mainstream news media (Gorgura, 2004), but also allow potential readers to compare and contrast a multiplicity of competing truth claims (Gallo, 2003). As one observer argues:

> The heavy reliance on hyperlinks points to a model of knowledge in which the truth of what is happening in the world cannot be channeled exclusively through one news text. Instead, the weblog can be thought of as claiming a more contingent authority in its use of multiple hyperlinks. (Matheson, 2004, p. 457)

Taken together, these features of the citizen-produced weblog, notably its ability to steer mainstream news media coverage; its capacity for independent, original news reporting; and its juxtaposition of news reporting and commentary from a diverse range of sources, has led scholarly and journalistic observers to characterize the discourse of citizen-produced weblogs as "amateur journalism" (Lasica, 2003), "folk journalism" (Mortensen & Walker, 2002), "grassroots journalism" (Gillmor, 2004), and "personal journalism" (Allan, 2002).

While scholarly and journalistic observers speculate that the appearance of citizen-produced weblogs signifies the dawn of a new public's journalism, capable of furthering the democratic ideals that have animated the public journalism movement, the empirical research literature tells a very different story. First, although it is possible that at least some of the recent political and newsroom scandals were brought to wider public attention through the concerted publicity of thousands of weblog writers, there is little evidence that citizen-produced weblogs forced those scandals unto the agenda of mainstream news media. The Trent Lott scandal, which remains one of the most widely cited examples of the ability of weblog writers to steer mainstream news media coverage, owes much to the influence of mainstream news organizations. While Trent Lott's remarks, as mentioned earlier, were initially publicized on the popular weblog *Talking Points Memo*, his remarks were reported by two mainstream news organizations, the online magazine *Slate* and the *Washington Post*, before they gained widespread attention in the mainstream news media. Indeed, many of the early links to the story were to the *Slate* article rather than to the article on *Talking Points Memo* (see Baoill, 2004). In turn, Ashbee (2003) shows, in a detailed study of the scandal, that the mainstream news media's decision to pursue the story and Trent Lott's subsequent resignation as Senate Majority Leader may have had more to do with preexisting dissensus within the Republican Party about his leadership skills than with any influence on the part of weblog writers. Similarly, while CNN executive Eason Jordan's remarks were initially publicized on *Forumblog.org*, an independent weblog devoted to coverage of the World Economic Forum, his remarks were reported by a number of mainstream news organizations, including the *New York Post*, the *Wall Street Journal*, and the *Washington Post*, before they gained widespread attention in the mainstream news media (see Nip, 2006).

More generally, aside from the widely cited example of Salam Pax, and the case of a number of weblog writers who were invited to cover the 2004 Democratic and Republican Party conventions (see Meraz, 2005), there is little evidence of any independent, original news reporting. Ironically, even Salam Pax is no longer an independent reporter; having been located by the

Guardian in May 2003, he now writes for its online counterpart, the *Guardian Unlimited*, as well as the BBC (Tew, 2006).

While the absence of independent, original news reporting is obviously a severe limitation in itself, the democratic significance of citizen-produced weblogs might reside, as observers claim, in their challenges to the narrow range of topics and sources featured in mainstream news media. Specifically, the vast array of alternative news providers available on the Internet (see Atton, 2005) could afford weblog writers the opportunity to cover a wide range of topics using an ideologically diverse range of sources, thereby facilitating what observers call a "multiperspectival," "multivocal," or "intertextual" form of news discourse. Yet research shows that weblog writers do not challenge mainstream news media's narrow range of topics and sources. In much the same way that the topics discussed in other popular, citizen-based media of communication like electronic bulletin boards follow the agendas of mainstream news media (see Roberts, Wanta, & Dzwo, 2002), many studies have found that the topics discussed on citizen-produced weblogs follow the narrow range of topics featured in mainstream news media. Even more problematically, these studies show that, rather than juxtaposing the news reporting and commentary of an ideologically diverse range of sources, weblog writers juxtapose the accounts of a narrow range of elite mainstream news organizations, including the *New York Times*, the *Wall Street Journal*, and the *Washington Post* (see Adamic & Glance, 2005; Davis, 2005; Delwiche, 2003; Halavais, 2002a; Harper, 2005; Himelboim & Southwell, 2005; Hopkins & Matheson, 2005; Messner & Terilli, 2005; Reese, Rutigliano, Hyun, & Jaekwan, 2005; Reynolds, 2005; Wallsten, 2005; Welsh, 2005).

The same pattern of mainstream news media influence on weblog coverage has been found with respect to so-called warblogs, or weblogs devoted to the U.S. government's "War on Terrorism." In two content analyses of selected warblogs, Wall (2004, 2005) found that their primary sources of information, both in terms of news reporting and commentary, were elite U.S. and U.K. mainstream news organizations such as the BBC, CNN, the *New York Times*, and the *Times*. Only about 5% of links were to alternative news providers, of which only a handful were to alternative media in the Middle East. "This reliance on mainstream media is notable," Wall (2004, p. 13) correctly notes, "because it raises the question of whether the [war]blogs are supplying significantly different perspectives than mainstream media outlets." Like Wall, several other researchers (see Halavais, 2002b; Redden, 2003; Redden, Caldwell, & Nguyen, 2003) have found, as Redden (2003, p.

162) puts it, that warblogging "depends upon the re-mediation of mainstream media content." While warblogging, as Redden et al. (2003, p. 77) correctly note, "would lose relevance if it departed too far from mainstream agendas of broad social concern," the heavy reliance on mainstream news media is problematic. Like weblog coverage more generally, warblogs' re-mediation of mainstream news media perspectives serves to strengthen, as opposed to challenge, the views of their elite sources of information, notably U.S. government officials. Indeed, considering the strong influence of mainstream news media on warblog coverage, and their support of the U.S. government's war in Iraq more generally (see, e.g., Coe, Domke, Graham, John, & Pickard, 2004), it should come as little surprise that most warblog writers have been found to be supportive of the war (see Johnson & Kaye, 2004).

Thus, rather than influencing mainstream news media, as observers claim, research shows that weblog writers not only follow their agendas but also rely on them for information on given topics. Considering that mainstream news media coverage tends to be "indexical" (see Bennett, 1990) of the degree of elite consensus or dissensus on given topics, weblog writers are more likely to point potential readers toward a narrow range of views that reflect the state of elite opinion than toward a multiplicity of competing truth claims that can be compared and contrasted. Ironically, weblog writers' reliance on mainstream news media and, by implication, their elite sources of information, thus not only runs counter to public journalism's democratic ideals but in fact falls far behind the movement's actual accomplishments. As discussed in previous chapters, public journalism is not only based on the idea that the news should be reported from the perspectives of ordinary citizens rather than societal elites, the empirical research literature shows that news organizations practicing public journalism rely more on citizens as sources of information than do mainstream news organizations more generally.

Given the influence of mainstream news media on weblog coverage, it is indeed ironic, as Wall (2005) notes, that so many weblog writers cultivate a sense that they are outsiders from corporate-run, mainstream news organizations. Rather than challenging the dominance of mainstream news media, either through their own reporting or by linking to and commenting on that of an ideologically diverse range of alternative news providers, weblog writers help strengthen their dominance by further circulating, if not amplifying, their discourse. Indeed, weblogs' "derivative" (Andrews, 2003; Baoill, 2004; Carroll, 2004), if not "parasitic" (Halavais, 2002b), relationship to mainstream news media makes it more accurate to characterize the blogosphere as an "online echo chamber of mass-mediated political views" (Singer, 2005, p. 192) than as an "alternative sphere of news and views" (Redden, 2003, p. 162).

While only a few studies have looked at the commentary that weblog writers often attach to their hyperlinks, available evidence suggests that such commentary also serves to further circulate, if not amplify, the views of mainstream news media's elite sources of information. While one study found that weblog writers simply link to given news stories without attaching much evaluative commentary (see Reese et al., 2005), another study found that the commentary falls within the narrow discursive parameters of political elites. In a textual analysis of selected warblogs' coverage of the war in Iraq, Wall (2006) found that, while the discourse of pro-war weblog writers closely followed that of the Bush administration, the discourse of anti-war weblog writers closely followed that of the Democratic Party leadership. Overall, Wall (2006, p. 122) thus concluded, both of these main frames—pro and anti—reflect "a lack of originality or alternativeness....This leads to the question of whether [war]blogs are indeed offering alternative perspectives overall or are they simply offering more personal, potentially more visceral versions of existing public discourses?"

This lack of originality or alternativeness on the part of weblog writers also manifests itself in their resistance to engage in genuine deliberation across ideological divides. In contrast to mainstream news organizations practicing public journalism, which have at least tried to promote broad-based citizen deliberation, research on inter-weblog linking patterns shows that weblog writers primarily interact with those of similar political persuasions. Simply put, while conservatives link to other conservatives, liberals link to other liberals (see Ackland, 2005; Adamic & Glance, 2005; Davis, 2005; Hargittai, Gallo, & Kane, 2005; Reese et al., 2005; Welsh, 2005). And in the rare instances where conservative and liberal weblog writers do link to one another's postings, their commentary most often consists of "straw-man arguments" whereby the political positions of others are cited simply to be repudiated as being fundamentally flawed (see Davis, 2005; Hargittai et al., 2005).

If mainstream news media dominate the discourse of the blogosphere as a whole, a small number of weblog writers have become highly influential within the blogosphere. Indeed, in much the same way that elite mainstream news organizations like the *New York Times*, the *Washington Post*, and the major television networks set the agenda for numerous smaller news organizations and, apparently, also for citizen-produced weblogs, a phenomenon commonly referred to as "inter-media agenda-setting" (see, e.g., McCombs, 2005), these highly influential weblog writers function as what could be called "inter-weblog agenda-setters." In a study of 433 weblogs, Shirky (2003) found that, while the top 12 weblogs received 20% of all incoming weblog links, the top 50 received 50% of all such links. In a more recent, but smaller scale study of 36 weblogs, Halavais (2004) found an even more skewed distribution; the top seven weblogs received 50% of all incoming weblog links. Similarly, in a study of 104 weblogs, Meraz (2005) found that the top 10 weblogs received 52% of all incoming weblog links.

The highly skewed distribution of inter-weblog links, a phenomenon that has been found to characterize the distribution of links on Internet web sites more generally (see Barabasi & Albert, 1999), and politically–oriented web sites in particular (see Hindman, Tsiotsiouliklis, & Johnson, 2003), suggests, as Jacobs (2003, p. 10) correctly notes, that an "internal hierarchy" has emerged in the blogosphere. Indeed, it shows that the topics discussed in the blogosphere do not arise more or less spontaneously through interaction among thousands of weblog writers or, as Bowman and Willis (2003, p. 9) claim, that weblog discourse "is the result of many simultaneous, distributed conversations," but rather that those conversations are initiated by a select group of weblog writers. And to the extent that these weblog writers, as the prior discussion shows, take their cues from mainstream news media coverage, rather than vice versa, they serve as intermediaries or, in the language of Katz and Lazarsfeld's (1955) two-step flow of information model, "opinion-leaders," channeling information from the mainstream news media to the blogosphere at large. Put differently, while observers claim that citizen-produced weblogs force topics onto the mainstream news media agenda, the empirical research literature shows that the agenda-setting process runs in the exact opposite direction: from mainstream news media, through certain influential weblog writers, to the blogosphere at large.

While it is difficult to determine, in the absence of large-scale surveys, why so many weblog writers link to a small number of weblogs, it is certainly possible, as Mortensen and Walker (2002) speculate, that they do so to enhance their visibility and perceived credibility. Yet, while prevailing netiquette requires weblog writers to link back to those who link to them (see Mead, 2002), the highly skewed distribution of inter-weblog links shows that these influential weblog writers do not reciprocate to the same extent as the rest of the blogosphere.

The influence of mainstream news media on weblog coverage, whether through their direct impact on the blogosphere as a whole or via certain influential weblog writers, is likely strengthened by the fact that some of the most highly linked weblog writers are professional journalists rather than ordinary citizens, who, in addition to maintaining their private weblogs, work for mainstream news organizations. According to weblog counts such as *Blogdex, Blogstreet, Daypop, Technorati,* and *Truth Laid Bear,* some of the most highly linked weblog writers include Mickey Kaus (*Kaus Files*), Joshua Marshall (*Talking Points Memo*), and Andrew Sullivan (*Andrew Sullivan*), who write for such elite mainstream news organizations as *Newsweek* (Kaus), the *New York Times* (Marshall), and the *Sunday Times* in London (Sullivan). As employees of mainstream news organizations, these weblog writers might be even less likely than ordinary citizens to juxtapose the news reporting and commentary of an ideologically diverse range of sources for fear of upsetting their employers. Indeed, there are many examples of professional journalists who have been reprimanded, or even fired, for transgressing the separation of news from views on their private weblogs (see Olson, 2004).

Given the disproportionate amount of influence of a small number of weblog writers, it should come as little surprise that mainstream journalists do not, as is commonly assumed, read a variety of citizen-produced weblogs to gauge public opinion on given topics. In a survey of more than 140 journalists working for national and local U.S. news organizations, Drezner and Farrell (2004) found that, although the respondents collectively read more than 125 different weblogs, the 10 most read weblogs accounted for more than 50% of the weblogs mentioned. Among journalists working for elite mainstream news organizations, this skewness was even more pronounced; the 10 most read weblogs accounted for 75% of the weblogs mentioned. For all respondents, the weblogs maintained by Mickey Kaus, Joshua Marshall, and Andrew Sullivan were among the five most read weblogs. Considering that a small number of weblog writers wield a strong influence on the blogosphere as a whole, mainstream journalists only need to attend to the opinions of these weblog writers to obtain a relatively accurate impression of the distribution of opinions on any given topic. Again, since these influential weblog writers link to mainstream news organizations rather than to alternative news providers, and many of them are professional journalists themselves, mainstream journalists are more likely to encounter a narrow range of views that mirror their own than to encounter an ideologically diverse range of views.

HYPER-LOCAL COMMUNITY WEB SITES

The prior discussion shows that citizen-produced weblogs do not, as scholarly and journalistic observers speculate, further public journalism's democratic ideals. Despite their positioning outside the confines of mainstream news media, weblog writers follow their agendas, rely on them for news reporting and commentary on given topics, and, as a result, end up reproducing, as opposed to challenging, the views of their predominantly elite sources of information. Equally problematic, discourse in the blogosphere tends to be highly fragmented along ideological lines, with little, if any, genuine interaction among individuals of different political persuasions.

While much of the current speculation about a new public's journalism centers around citizen-produced weblogs, other venues for citizens to participate in news reporting exist, including so-called hyper-local community web sites. During the past couple of years, many local news organizations (primarily local newspapers), local civic organizations, and universities have created web sites for residents of specific neighborhoods to engage in their own news reporting (see Dube, 2007, for a listing of dozens of such web sites). Many of these community web sites have been supported financially by J-Lab: The Institute for Interactive Journalism, headed by Jan Schaffer, former Executive Director of the Pew Center for Civic Journalism, through its "New Voices" initiative (see the web site of "New Voices," http://www.j-newvoices.org).

Despite their growing popularity, very little empirical research has looked at the actual modes of operation and content of such community web sites. Indeed, aside from two surveys of citizen contributors to two university-led initiatives, the University of Missouri's *MyMissourian* (see Bentley, Hamman, Ibold, Littau, & Meyer, 2006) and the University of Wisconsin's *Madison Commons* (see Friedland et al., 2006), only one study has been conducted to date: Nip's (2006) brief ethnographic study of the *Northwest Voice*.

The *Northwest Voice*, launched in May 2004 by the *Bakersfield Californian*, a local newspaper, is a community web site which, as the name implies, serves the northwest neighborhood of Bakersfield, California. It is managed by a small staff consisting of a publisher, an editor, a designer, a sales and production manager, and a sales executive. Importantly, while the web site is officially run according to the editorial policy that all articles relevant to the neighborhood, unless libelous, will be published with minimal editing, in reality the editorial staff has instituted a sharp separation between its own contributions (approximately 20% of the articles) and those of local residents. While the staff has taken on responsibility for reporting on local public issues and events, residents are encouraged to contribute articles that, as Nip (2006, pp. 224–225) puts it, revolve around their "*private* [italics added] interests and concerns [as] parents, students and teachers." As such, Nip (2006, p. 225) notes, the *Northwest Voice* "does not seek to engage [residents] as citizens by giving them their voices on public issues." During the time frame of Nip's (2006) study (February 22–March 4, 2005), the staff reported on various local public issues and events while posting a call for residents to submit articles on such topics as upcoming academic achievement events, fundraising events for schools and clubs, open house nights, parent–teacher club meetings, sports events, and team tryouts. More broadly, the web site of the *Northwest Voice* is organized in terms of various decidedly apolitical content categories to which local residents are invited to contribute articles, including "cars," "celebrations," "contests," "dining out," "fitness," "gardening," "homes," "horses," "pets," "photos," "recipes," "outdoor life," "sports," and "travel" (see http://www.northwestvoice.com).

While it is obviously difficult to draw any generalizations on the basis of a single case study, my own informal review of many of the community web sites listed by Dube (2007) suggests that Nip's (2006) findings might indeed be more broadly representative. Like the *Northwest Voice*, many community web sites operate in terms of a journalistic division of labor whereby the staff takes on responsibility for reporting on local public issues and events while local residents are encouraged to contribute articles relating to their private interests and concerns. Indeed, many community web sites situate residents as individual producers and consumers of news concerned with its relevance to their personal, everyday lives rather than as members of larger, politically involved publics. For example, *Backfence.com*, a network of 10 community web sites in California, Maryland, and Virginia, describes itself as "a new way to find out what's going on in the world closest and most important to you: Your neighborhood." *Backfence.com* proceeds to outline the kinds of contributions that would be appropriate in the following way:

> What's happening with the new development down the street? Does anybody know a good house painter? Who won the T-ball championship? What's the best place in town to find good Thai food? Have your seen the photos from the church fundraiser? Who's going to be the new junior high school principal? Anybody got tips about good bike trails? When is the next PTA meeting? (see http://www.backfence.com)

Similarly, other community web sites describe themselves as spaces "where consumers can find everything necessary to navigate daily life in their town" (*American Town Network*, http://www.americantowns.com) or even as "a great way to learn about local businesses, with advertising that keeps you up to date on local services, restaurants, entertainment, shops, and savings offers" (*Blount County Voice*, http://www.blountcountyvoice.com). Indeed, there are prominent examples of community web sites that function more as outlets for promotional activities than as spaces for news reporting. In a review of *Your Hub*, a network of more than 100 local community web sites across six states, Grubisich (2006) found that the network "highlights content that's more PR than grassroots journalism." *Your Hub* serves as "a place where publicists…can be sure their releases will be published, with every product placement intact."

More generally, community web sites appear to conceive of their local communities as unified sites, bounded by shared values and goals, while failing to acknowledge that most contemporary communities are fragmented into multiple social groups with different, if not conflicting, interests. To take just a few examples, while the *New West Network*, a network of 10 community web sites across six states, describes its goal as "sharing common interests and hopes" (see http://www.newwest.net), *Backfence.com* describes its goal as "bringing together the community's collective knowledge" (see http://www.backfence.com). Similarly, while *Bluffton Today*, a community web site in Bluffton, South Carolina, describes its goal as "helping Bluffton come together as a community" (see http://www.bluffton.com), the *Northfield Cities Online*, a community web site in Northfield, Minnesota, describes its goal as "strengthening the fabric of community in the greater Northfield area" (see http://www.northfield.org).

Finally, most community web sites feature little actual interaction among users, despite ample opportunities to do so in the form of feedback to individual articles and more general discussion forums. Indeed, my own informal review suggests that George's (2005) observations of the lack of user interaction on *Backfence.com* might hold true for community web sites more generally: "Clicking through *Backfence.com*'s pages feels like frontier land—remote, often lonely, zoned for people, but not home to any." Thus, in contrast to the blogosphere, where citizens at least interact with those of similar political persuasions, community web sites have not managed to inspire much citizen interaction. While no research has explored why this might be the case, it is certainly possible that the sites' emphasis on local residents' private, as opposed to public, interests and concerns explains the lack of interaction. Simply put, most of the information posted can easily be accessed—and used—without requiring any actual interaction with others.

That said, there are several examples of community web sites that not only aim to involve citizens in news reporting and deliberation about local public issues and events but also acknowledge the fragmented nature of most contemporary communities. Coincidentally or not, many of these community web sites are led by veterans of the public journalism movement and supported financially by J-Lab: The Institute for Interactive Journalism. For example, Professor Lewis Friedland of the University of Wisconsin's School of Journalism and Mass Communication heads a community web site called the *Madison Commons*, which is aimed at providing residents of some of Madison's most impoverished, primarily minority neighborhoods with opportunities to report on and deliberate about political topics of concern to them. Similarly, Jeremy Iggers, ethics columnist at the *Minneapolis Star Tribune*, heads a community web site called the *Twin Cities Daily Planet*. Like the *Madison Commons*, the *Twin Cities Daily Planet* serves as a space for citizen-based news reporting and deliberation on political topics of concern to the racially and ethnically diverse populations of Minneapolis and St. Paul (see the web sites of the *Madison Commons*, http://www.madisoncommons.org, and the *Twin Cities Daily Planet*, http://www.tcplanet.net, for further details).

OHMYNEWS AND INDYMEDIA

Unlike local community web sites that, at best, aim to inspire citizen-based news reporting on topics of concern to relatively narrow, geographically based communities (e.g., the *Madison Commons* and the *Twin Cities Daily Planet*), other recent Internet-based initiatives such as the South Korean online newspaper *OhmyNews* and the global *Indymedia* network seek to engage citizens in news reporting on a much larger scale. One of the largest and most popular venues is *OhmyNews*, with approximately 2 million daily readers. Established in February 2000 by a well-known investigative journalist by the name of Yeon-Ho Oh, and led by a relatively small editorial and administrative staff of 60, *OhmyNews* relies in large part on more than 40,000 citizen reporters for its news reporting. Of the approximately 200 news stories published each day, about 150 are contributed by these citizen reporters after having been copyedited and fact-checked by the editorial staff; the remaining 50 articles are written by the site's staff reporters. In May 2004, *OhmyNews* launched an English-language version, called *OhmyNews International*, which relies on more than 800 citizen reporters from over 80 countries (see Cheon, 2004; Kim & Hamilton, 2006; Woo-Young, 2005).

Despite its much larger scale, *OhmyNews* operates in terms of the same problematic journalistic division of labor as that found on many local community web sites. As Kim and Hamilton (2006, pp. 545–546) put it, while its "staff reporters cover current, serious issues that need in-depth investigation [citizen-reporters contribute articles relating to] daily lives in their surroundings." Moreover, whether the result of the copyediting performed by the site's editorial staff, or the citizen reporters' own efforts to emulate the staff reporters or professional journalists more generally, most of the contributed articles are reported in the same, detached manner as that found in mainstream news media. Ironically, while *OhmyNews* was launched to offer a distinct alternative to conventional, mainstream news media in South Korea and abroad, the site's editorial policies mirror those of mainstream news organizations. On the "Frequently Asked Questions" section of *OhmyNews International*, would-be contributors are informed that some of the most common reasons for rejecting submitted articles include that they fail to conform to conventional "news article style," such as by neglecting "to answer 'when, where, who, what, how and why'" (see the web site of *OhmyNews International*, http://english.ohmynews.com).

In contrast to *OhmyNews*, *Indymedia* has emerged as an important site for genuinely alternative, citizen-based news reporting, providing counterinformation to that offered by mainstream news media on a wide range of topics. It was established in November 1999 by a diverse group of left-wing activists in conjunction with the anti-corporate globalization demonstrations in Seattle, Washington, against the meeting of the World Trade Organization. From a single chapter in Seattle in 1999, *Indymedia* has become a global network of more than 140 autonomously operated but interlinked chapters in 50 countries, with 500,000–2,000,000 daily readers. Aside from these individual chapters, *Indymedia* has a main web site, established in May 2000, that aggregates content from across the network. While *Indymedia* began as a grassroots response to corporate globalization, and the mainstream news media's perceived failure to address its social, political, and economic consequences, it has over time become a site for news reporting, deliberation, and action on a much wider range of social justice topics, including human rights abuses and environmental degradation. Indeed, *Indymedia* functions as a source of information for international wire services like the Associated Press and Reuters, who rely on it for news reporting about the demonstrations that the meetings of the major international organizations now commonly inspire (see Garcelon, 2006; Pickard, 2006; Stengrim, 2005).

Despite some local variation, the web sites of individual chapters generally follow the same format. The right column is devoted to an open news wire where would-be contributors can and do freely upload their own independent news reports, in the form of written text, photographs, and streaming audio and video footage, as well as news commentary and hyperlinks to other alternative news providers and social justice movements. The main column consists of a selection of items from the open news wire, referred to as "news features," chosen through a consensus-based process by the editorial collective of each individual chapter as well as a calendar of upcoming activist events. The left column is reserved for various kinds of organizational information as well as hyperlinks to all the other chapter web sites.

The democratic significance of the *Indymedia* network, as should be apparent, rests on several features. First, in contrast to citizen-produced weblogs, which tend to re-mediate the news reporting and commentary of mainstream news media, and hyper-local community web sites and *OhmyNews*, which tend to solicit citizen-based news reporting on topics of private, as opposed to public, concern, *Indymedia* is explicitly aimed at publishing alternative, citizen-based news reporting and commentary on political topics ignored by mainstream news media. And indeed, research shows that the articles posted on the open news wires of individual chapter web sites consist of first-hand, eyewitness reports as well as original news commentary and analysis. Moreover, in contrast to the detached writing style of *OhmyNews* postings, such reporting tends to be written from the standpoint of contributors' own personal, political engagement with given topics (see Brooten, 2004; Deuze, 2006; Jankowski & Jansen, 2003). As Deuze (2006, p. 65) puts it, *Indymedia* articles consist of "personal experiential accounts" rather than "professionalized detached observations." Jankowski and Jansen's (2003) research shows, moreover, that despite the autonomy of individual chapter web sites, contributors tend to link heavily to the news reporting, commentary, and mobilization efforts of other chapters. This facilitates a form of discourse that allows participants not only to appreciate the broader parameters and manifestations of given topics but also to coordinate their actions at local, national, regional, and even global levels.

Perhaps most impressively, despite *Indymedia*'s predominantly leftist politics, the network remains open to and respectful of participants from other, even opposing, political persuasions. In a textual analysis of 73 news features related to the war in Iraq posted on *Indymedia*'s main web site, Brooten (2005) found that not only were the contributions of many conservative, pro-war individuals included, their views were discussed in great detail and respectfully by the predominantly leftist participants. As Brooten (2005, p. 253) notes:

> The [*Indymedia*] network challenges the status quo in several ways, not least in its function as a forum for the collective exchange of, sorting through, and debating of information counter to the official [leftist] line. In the best IMC discussions, those who participate are treated with respect and held to the same standards, despite their political persuasions.

That said, the *Indymedia* network has over time instituted certain journalistic gate-keeping methods that resemble those applied by mainstream news organizations. When *Indymedia* was originally established, contributors could freely post items on the news wire of the main web site. However, as the volume of contributions began to increase dramatically, it was decided to abandon the open publishing policy. Following considerable internal debate, which included proposals to institute a selection system for entries based on how highly a group of readers ranked them, the Seattle collective, which remains the network's de facto center (Atton, 2005), decided that it would choose which items, among those submitted, would appear on the main news wire (Downing, 2002).

More generally, the Seattle collective reserves the right to remove from the network any contributions deemed unsuitable; these include items that comment on existing news reports rather than offer original reporting, false or libelous contributions, and hate speech (Atton, 2005). The Seattle collective's editorial oversight and journalistic gate-keeping was particularly pronounced during *Indymedia*'s coverage of the September 11 terrorist attacks where, in contrast to the usual practice of relying on an international network of citizen reporters, the collective commissioned contributions from a small number of prominent leftist intellectuals, primarily from the United States (Atton, 2003). Interestingly, *Indymedia*'s reliance on prominent leftist intellectuals for its coverage of the September 11 terrorist attacks parallel the practice of mainstream news media during times of war of carrying opinion pieces and letters to the editor from elite commentators rather than ordinary citizens (see Page, 1996). Although it may be an exaggeration to claim, as one observer does, that *Indymedia*'s implementation of editorial oversight and journalistic gate-keeping has rendered the network "a fairly standard newsroom operation" (Fisher, 2000, p. 47), it does show, as Atton (2005, p. 34) notes, "how even in avowedly non- or anti-hierarchical structures, hierarchies might still develop." Indeed, over time, "*Indymedia* might become professionalized, with greater reliance on de facto staff reporters and more stringent editing" (Meikle, 2003, p. 6).

CONCLUDING THOUGHTS

In his study of some of the news organizations most widely associated with the public journalism movement, Friedland (2003) cited a 1999 decision by the *Wichita Eagle*'s then-editor Rick Thames to decline an invitation by Wichita's superintendent of schools to help organize public deliberation about whether a new school bond was needed and, if yes, how the funds should be spent as a potential turning point in the practice of public journalism. Instead of partnering with the superintendent, the *Eagle* only committed itself to what Rick Thames referred to as public journalism "done at arm's length," by reporting on the public deliberations that did eventually take place.

There can be little doubt that Friedland's (2003) prediction has been right on the mark. While many news organizations continue to practice public journalism in the "classic" sense of both organizing and reporting back on public deliberations on given topics (see the web site of the *Public Journalism Network*, http://www.pjnet.org, for continuously updated information on such initiatives), there is growing evidence that news organizations have begun to relinquish some of their previous commitment to help form, as opposed to merely inform, the public. Indeed, at least at the present time, news organizations appear more concerned with improving their relationships with citizens as audiences than with ensuring that citizens, as members of larger publics, become more involved with politics. At the same time, and independently of the initiative of news organizations, citizens themselves are becoming increasingly more politically involved, whether individually, such as through the writing of politically–oriented weblogs or as participants in larger collectives, such as through involvement with the global *Indymedia* network.

While such citizen-based initiatives are noteworthy and should be applauded, they do not, I believe, relieve mainstream news organizations of their responsibility for trying to generate more politically-involved publics. As discussed throughout this book, under conditions of widespread social inequality, news organizations should help ensure that the concerns of the most marginalized social groups are articulated and heard to the same extent as those of dominant social groups. This implies, among other issues, that news organizations should help organize public deliberation, that focus on their particular concerns, advance those concerns through their reporting, and partner with political actors and institutions to ensure that those concerns are promoted in practice. While it is certainly possible that citizens themselves could accomplish such goals, there is evidence that this does not happen in practice. While the *Indymedia* network offers important discursive spaces for news reporting, deliberation, and action on behalf of marginalized voices and perspectives, the much larger interactional space represented by the political blogosphere continues to be dominated by societal elites.

To return to the example of the *Wichita Eagle*, it is certainly possible, although Friedland (2003) does not address this particular point, that the *Eagle*'s subsequent reporting on the school bond (it was passed) included a critical assessment of whether the funds were fairly distributed among Wichita's various schools districts. Nevertheless, by waiting for citizens themselves to organize public deliberation, the *Eagle* and other news organizations committed to a similar approach to public journalism would risk allowing social groups with the resources necessary to organize such deliberation in the first place to set their news agenda while ignoring those social groups arguably most in need of public attention.

BIBLIOGRAPHY

Ackerman, B., & Fishkin, J. (2004). *Deliberation day.* New Haven, CT: Yale University Press.

Ackland, R. (2005, June). *Mapping the U.S. political blogosphere: Are conservative bloggers more prominent?* Paper presented at the BlogTalk Convention, Sydney, Australia.

Adamic, L., & Glance, N. (2005, June). *The political blogosphere and the 2004 U.S. election: Divided they blog.* Paper presented at the BlogTalk Convention, Sydney, Australia.

Allan, S. (2002). Reweaving the Internet: Online news after September 11. In B. Zelizer & S. Allan (Eds.), *Journalism after September 11* (pp. 119–140). London: Routledge.

Amis, D. (2002, September 21). Web logs: Online naval gazing? *Netfreedom.* Retrieved February 1, 2007 from http://www.netfreedom.org.

Andersen, I., & Jaeger, B. (1999). Scenario workshops and consensus conferences: Towards more democratic decision-making. *Science and Public Policy, 26*(5), 331–340.

Anderson, R., Dardenne, R., & Killenberg, G. (1994). *The conversation of journalism: Communication, community, and news.* Westport, CT: Praeger.

Anderson, R., Dardenne, R., & Killenberg, G. (1997). The American newspaper as the public conversational commons. In J. Black (Ed.), *Mixed news: The public/civic/communitarian journalism debate* (pp. 96–115). Mahwah, NJ: Lawrence Erlbaum.

Andrews, P. (2003). Is blogging journalism? *Nieman Reports, 57*(3), 63–64.

Arant, D., & Meyer, P. (1998). Public journalism and traditional journalism: A shift in values? *Journal of Mass Media Ethics, 13*(4), 205–218.

Ash, S., & Lowe, C. (1984). The consensus development program: Theory, practice, and critique. *Knowledge: Creation, Diffusion, Utilization, 5*(4), 369–385.

Ashbee, E. (2003). The Lott resignation, blogging and American conservatism. *Political Quarterly, 74*(3), 361–370.

Associated Press Managing Editors, (2002). *Credibility in action.* New York: Author.

Associated Press Managing Editors, (2003). *2003 Update: Credibility in action.* New York: Author.

Atton, C. (2003). Reshaping social movement media for a new millennium. *Social Movement Studies, 2*(1), 3–15.

Atton, C. (2005). *An alternative Internet: Radical media, politics and creativity.* Edinburgh, Scotland: Edinburgh University Press.

Austin, L. (1997). Public journalism in the newsroom: Putting ideas into practice. In J. Rosen, D. Merritt, & L. Austin (Eds.), *Public journalism: Lessons from experience* (pp. 36–47). Dayton, OH: Kettering Foundation Press.

Baoill, A. (2004). Weblogs and the public sphere. In L. Gurak, S. Antonijevic, L. Johnson, C. Ratliff, & J. Reyman (Eds.), *Into the blogosphere: Rhetoric, community, and culture of weblogs.* Retrieved February 1, 2007 from http://blog.lib.umn.edu/blogosphere/weblogs_and_the_public_sphere.html.

Barabasi, A., & Albert, R. (1999). Scaling in random networks. *Science, 286,* 509–512.

Bare, J. (1998). A new strategy. In E. Lambeth, P. Meyer, & E. Thorson (Eds.), *Assessing public journalism* (pp. 83–108). Columbia, MO: University of Missouri Press.

Barney, R. (1996). Community journalism: Good intentions, questionable practice. *Journal of Mass Media Ethics, 11*(3), 140–151.

Barney, R. (1997). A dangerous drift? The sirens' call to collectivism. In J. Black (Ed.), *Mixed news: The public/civic/communitarian journalism debate* (pp. 72–90). Mahwah, NJ: Lawrence Erlbaum.

Barns, I. (1995). Manufacturing consensus? Reflections on the UK national consensus conference on plant biotechnology. *Science as Culture, 23*(5), 200–218.

Beckman, P. (2003). *Medierne som motesplats: Public journalism i svensk tappning* [*The media as a meeting place: A Swedish version of public journalism*]. Stockholm, Sweden: Sellin & Partner.

Becksmo, B., & Stjernfeldt, D. (2001). *Public journalism paa svenska dagstidningar* [*Public journalism at daily newspapers in Sweden*]. Sundsvall, Sweden: The Democracy Institute.

Bennett, W. (1990). Toward a theory of press-state relations in the United States. *Journal of Communication, 40*(2), 103–125.

Bennett, W. (2006). *News: The politics of illusion.* White Plains, NY: Longman.

Bennett, W., Gressett, L., & Haltom, W. (1985). Repairing the news: A case study of the news paradigm. *Journal of Communication, 35*(1), 50–68.

Bentley, C., Hamman, B., Ibold, H., Littau, J., & Meyer, H. (2006, August). *Sense of community as a driver for citizen journalism.* Paper presented at the Annual Convention of the Association for Education in Journalism and Mass Communication, San Francisco, CA.

Betz, H. (1994). *Radical right-wing populism in Western Europe.* New York: Macmillan.

Bilderbeek, R., & Andersen, I. (1994). *Involving citizens in sustainable development: Experiences from European scenario workshops in urban ecology.* Copenhagen, Denmark: Danish Board of Technology.

Bishop, R. (2001). News media, heal thyselves: Sourcing patterns in news stories about news media performance. *Journal of Communication Inquiry, 25*(1), 22–37.

Blazier, T., & Lemert, J. (2000). Public journalism and changes in content of the *Seattle Times. Newspaper Research Journal, 21*(3), 69–80.

Blomquist, D., & Zukin, C. (1997). *Does public journalism work? The Campaign Central experience.* Washington, DC: Pew Center for Civic Journalism.

Blood, R. (2002). Weblogs: A history and perspective. In J. Rodzvilla (Ed.), *We've got blogs: How weblogs are changing our culture* (pp. 7–16). Cambridge, MA: Perseus.

Bloom, J. (2003, August). *The blogosphere: How a once-humble medium came to drive elite media discourse and influence public policy.* Paper presented at the Annual Convention of the American Political Science Association, Philadelphia, PA.

Bowers, J., & Walker, G. (2003). Public journalism and voting participation in state-wide referendums: Results from a media partnership in Rochester, New York. In J. Harper & T. Yantek (Eds.), *Media, profit, and politics: Competing priorities in an open society* (pp. 109–121). Kent, OH: Kent State University Press.

Bowman, S., & Willis, C. (2003). *We the media: How audiences are shaping the future of news and information.* Reston, VA: American Press Institute.

Bratich, J. (2004). Trust no one (on the Internet): The CIA–Crack–Contra conspiracy theory and professional journalism. *Television & New Media, 5*(2), 209–239.

Braun, S. (2004). *Uden filter [Without filter].* Aarhus, Denmark: Center for Journalism and Continuing Education.

Brickman, A. (2005). *Evaluation of the APME credibility roundtables initiative.* New York: Associated Press Managing Editors.

Brooten, L. (2004). Digital deconstruction: *Indymedia* as a process of collective critique. In R. Berenger (Ed.), *Global media go to war: Role of news and entertainment media during the 2003 Iraq war* (pp. 265–279). Spokane, WA: Marquette Books.

Brooten, L. (2005). The power of public reporting: The Independent Media Center's challenge to corporate media. In L. Artz & Y. Kamalipour (Eds.), *Bring 'em on: Media and politics in the Iraqi war* (pp. 239–254). Lanham, MD: Rowman & Littlefield.

Brown, C., Thorson, E., & Fleming, K. (2006, August). *Taking action on credibility: Does APME's credibility roundtable project have measurable effects?* Paper presented at the Annual Convention of the Association for Education in Journalism and Mass Communication, San Francisco, CA.

Bruns, A. (2005). *Gatewatching: Collaborative online news production.* New York: Peter Lang.

Button, M., & Matson, K. (1999). Deliberative democracy in practice: Challenges and prospects for civic deliberation. *Polity, 31*(4), 609–637.

Bybee, C. (1999). Can democracy survive in the post-factual age?: A return to the Lippmann–Dewey debate about the politics of news. *Journalism & Communication Monographs, 1*(1), 29–66.

Byrd, J. (1995, February 5). Conversations with the community. *The Washington Post,* p. C6.

Calabrese, A. (2000). Political space and the trade in journalism news. In C. Sparks & J. Tulloch (Eds.), *Tabloid tales: Global debates over media standards* (pp. 43–61). Lanham, MD: Rowman & Littlefield.

Calamai, P. (1995, December 9). Self-muzzling undercuts public journalism. *The Ottawa Citizen,* p. B6.

Campaign Study Group. (2001). *Journalism interactive: New attitudes, tools, and techniques change journalism's landscape.* Washington, DC: Pew Center for Civic Journalism.

Canedy, D. (2000). The hurt between the lines. In *New York Times* Correspondent Staff (Eds.), *How race is lived in America: Pulling together, pulling apart* (pp. 171–188). New York: Henry Holt.

Cannon, C. (1993, November 1). Loans elude black business owners. *Akron Beacon Journal,* pp. A1, A8.

Cannon, C., Know, D., & Paynter, B. (1993, November 1). Road to economic parity. *Akron Beacon Journal,* pp. A1, A6–A8.

Carey, J. (1987). The press and public discourse. *The Center Magazine, 20,* 4–16.

Carey, J. (1993). The mass media and democracy: Between the modern and the postmodern. *Journal of International Affairs, 47*(1), 1–21.

Carey, J. (1995). The press, public opinion, and public discourse. In T. Glasser & C. Salmon (Eds.), *Public opinion and the communication of consent* (pp. 373–402). New York: Guilford.

Carey, J. (1997). Community, public, and journalism. In J. Black (Ed.), *Mixed news: The public/civic/communitarian journalism debate* (pp. 1–15). Mahwah, NJ: Lawrence Erlbaum.

Carroll, B. (2004). Culture clash: Journalism and the communal ethos of the blogosphere. In L. Gurak, S. Antonijevic, L. Johnson, C. Ratliff, & J. Reyman (Eds.), *Into the blogosphere: Rhetoric, community, and culture of weblogs.* Retrieved February 1, 2007 from http://blog.lib.umn.edu/blogosphere/culture_clash.html.

Chaffee, S., McDevitt, M., & Thorson, E. (1997, August). *Citizen response to civic journalism: Four case studies.* Paper presented at the Annual Convention of the Association for Education in Journalism and Mass Communication, Chicago, IL.

Chancellor, C. (1993, February 28). A separate, but equal, focus on our differences. *Akron Beacon Journal,* pp. A1, A6–A7.

Charity, A. (1995). *Doing public journalism.* New York: Guilford.

Charity, A. (1996). Public journalism for people. *National Civic Review, 85*(1), 7–13.

Chavez, M. (2005). *News agendas and community participation: A Mexican model for change.* Los Angeles: Center for Communication and Community, University of California.

Chen, R., Thorson, E., Yoon, D., & Ognianova, E. (2002, May). *General news, a civic journalism project, and indices of social capital.* Paper presented at the Annual Convention of the International Communication Association, Seoul, South Korea.

Cheon, Y. (2004). Internet newspapers as alternative media: The case of *OhmyNews* in South Korea. *Media Development, 5*(1), 28–32.

Choi, Y. (2004). Study examines daily public journalism at six newspapers. *Newspaper Research Journal, 25*(2), 12–27.

Christians, C. (1997). The common good and universal values. In J. Black (Ed.), *Mixed news: The public/civic/communitarian journalism debate* (pp. 18–33). Mahwah, NJ: Lawrence Erlbaum.

Christians, C. (1999). The common good as first principle. In T. Glasser (Ed.), *The idea of public journalism* (pp. 67–84). New York: Guilford.

Clinton, W. (1997). Remarks in a roundtable discussion on race in Akron. *Weekly Compilation of Presidential Documents, 33,* 1959.

Coe, K., Domke, D., Graham, E., John, S., & Pickard, V. (2004). No shades of gray: The binary discourse of George W. Bush and an echoing press. *Journal of Communication, 54*(2), 234–252.

Cohn, J. (1995). Should journalists do community service? *The American Prospect, 6*(22), 14–17.

Coleman, R. (1997). The intellectual antecedents of public journalism. *Journal of Communication Inquiry, 21*(1), 60–76.

Coleman, R. (2000a). The ethical context for public journalism: As an ethical foundation for public journalism, communitarian philosophy provides principles for practitioners to apply to real world problems. *Journal of Communication Inquiry 24*(1), 41–66.

Coleman, R. (2000b). Use of visual communication in public journalism. *Newspaper Research Journal, 21*(4), 17–37.

Coleman, R., & Wasike, B. (2004). Visual elements in public journalism newspapers in an election: A content analysis of the photographs and graphics in Campaign 2000. *Journal of Communication, 54*(3), 456–474.

Compton, J. (2000). Communicative politics and public journalism. *Journalism Studies, 1*(3), 449–467.

Cook, T. (1998). *Governing with the news: The news media as a political institution.* Chicago: University of Chicago Press.

Coote, A., & Lenagham, J. (1997). *Citizens juries: Theory into practice.* London: Institute for Public Policy Research.

Corrigan, D. (1996, March 18). Press seeks remedy for its failings. *St. Louis Post-Dispatch,* p. 15B.

Corrigan, D. (1999). *The public journalism movement in America: Evangelists in the newsroom.* Westport, CT: Praeger.

Craig, D. (1996). Communitarian journalism(s): Clearing conceptual landscapes. *Journal of Mass Media Ethics, 11*(2), 107–118.

Cronberg, T. (1995). Do marginal voices shape technology? In S. Joss & J. Durant (Eds.), *Public participation in science: The role of consensus conferences in Europe* (pp. 125–133). London: Science Museum.

Crosby, N., & Nethercut, D. (2005). Citizens juries: Creating a trustworthy voice of the people. In J. Gastil & P. Levine (Eds.), *The deliberative democracy handbook: Strategies for effective civic engagement in the 21st century* (pp. 111–119). San Francisco: Jossey-Bass.

Davis, C. (2005, August). *Are bloggers journalists or just very lonely pamphleteers?* Paper presented at the Annual Convention of the Association of Education in Journalism and Mass Communication, San Antonio, TX.

Delli Carpini, M. (2005). News from nowhere: Journalistic frames and the debate over public journalism. In K. Callaghan & F. Schnell (Eds.), *Framing American politics* (pp. 21–53). Pittsburgh, PA: University of Pittsburgh Press.

Delwiche, A. (2003, October). *Reconstructing the agenda in the world of participatory media*. Paper presented at the Annual Convention of the Association of Internet Researchers, Toronto, ON, Canada.

Dennis, E. (1995). Raising questions about civic or public journalism. *Editor & Publisher, 128*(30), 48–49.

Denton, F., & Thorson, E. (1997). *Civic journalism: Does it work?* Washington, DC: Pew Center for Civic Journalism.

Denton, F., & Thorson, E. (1998). Effects of a multimedia public journalism project on political knowledge and attitudes. In E. Lambeth, P. Meyer, & E. Thorson (Eds.), *Assessing public journalism* (pp. 143–157). Columbia, MO: University of Missouri Press.

Deuze, M. (2006). Participation, remediation, bricolage: Considering principal components of a digital culture. *The Information Society, 22*(2), 63–75.

Dewey, J. (1927). *The public and its problems*. New York: Swallow Press.

Dickson, T., Brandon, W., & Topping, E. (2001). Editors, educators agree on outcomes but not goals. *Newspaper Research Journal, 22*(4), 44–56.

Dickson, T., & Topping, E. (2001). Public trust, media responsibility and public journalism: US newspaper editors' and educators' attitudes about media credibility. *Asia Pacific Media Educator, 11*, 72–86.

Dinges, J. (2000). Public journalism and National Public Radio. In A. Eksterowicz & R. Roberts (Eds.), *Public journalism and political knowledge* (pp. 91–118). Lanham, MD: Rowman & Littlefield.

Dotson, J., & Allen, D. (1993, May 2). You're invited to help promote racial harmony. *Akron Beacon Journal*, pp. A1, A11.

Downing, J. (2002). Independent media centers: A multi-level, multi-media challenge to global neo-liberalism. In M. Raboy (Ed.), *Global media policy in the new millennium* (pp. 215–232). Luton, UK: University of Luton Press.

Drezner, D., & Farrell, H. (2004, September). *The power and politics of blogs*. Paper presented at the Annual Convention of the American Political Science Association, Chicago, IL.

Dube, J. (2007). The cyberjournalist list. *CyberJournalist.Net*. Retrieved from http://www.cyberjournalist.net/cyberjournalists.php February 1, 2007.

Dubuisson, D. (1995, October 15). Public journalism: Just another way of doing what we've always done. *News & Record*, p. F2.

Durant, J. (1995). An experiment in democracy. In S. Joss & J. Durant (Eds.), *Public participation in science: The role of consensus conferences in Europe* (pp. 75–80). London: Science Museum.

Dyer, B. (1993, December 29). The struggle for balance. *Akron Beacon Journal*, pp. A1, A6–A7.

Dzur, A. (2002). Public journalism and deliberative democracy. *Polity, 34*(3), 313–336.

Effron, S. (1997). The North Carolina experiment. *Columbia Journalism Review*, January-February, 12–14.

Einsiedel, E., & Eastlick, D. (2000). Consensus conferences as deliberative democracy: A communications perspective. *Science Communication, 21*(4), 323–343.

Einsiedel, E., Jelsoee, E., & Breck, T. (2001). Publics at the technology table: The consensus conference in Denmark, Canada, and Australia. *Public Understanding of Science, 10*(1), 83–98.

Eisner, J. (1994, October 16). Should journalists abandon their detachment to solve problems? *Philadelphia Inquirer,* p. E7.

Entman, R. (1993). Framing: Toward clarification of a fractured paradigm. *Journal of Communication, 43*(4), 51–58.

Esmark, A., & Kjaer, P. (2000). Den sidste mediepolitik og den politiske journalistik [The last media policy and political journalism]. In O. Pedersen, P. Kjaer, A. Esmark, M. Horst, & E. Carlsen (Eds.), *Politisk journalistik [Political journalism]* (pp. 25–59). Aarhus, Denmark: Ajour.

Evatt, D. (1999). Prologue to diverging patterns of election year coverage. In M. McCombs & A. Reynolds (Eds.), *The poll with a human face: The National Issues Convention experiment in political communication* (pp. 133–144). Mahwah, NJ: Lawrence Erlbaum.

Ewart, J. (2000). Public journalism and the news gender agenda. *Asia Pacific Media Educator, 9,* 119–131.

Ewart, J. (2002). Overlooked and underused: How Australia's first public journalism project treated women and indigenous people. *Australian Journalism Review, 24*(1), 61–81.

Ewart, J. (2003). Including women in the news: Does public journalism address the gender imbalance of the news sources used by journalists? *Australian Studies in Journalism, 12,* 213–228.

Ewart, J., & Massey, B. (2006). Exploring some of the factors that contribute to the use of ordinary people as news sources. *Australian Journalism Review, 28*(1), 103–124.

Fallows, J. (1996). *Breaking the news: How the media undermine American democracy.* New York: Vintage.

Fee, F. (2002, August). *Whose values are news values? What journalists and citizens want.* Paper presented at the Annual Convention of the Association for Education in Journalism and Mass Communication, Miami Beach, FL.

Fisher, M. (2000). Low-power to the people. *American Journalism Review,* October, 42–48.

Fishkin, J. (1991). *Democracy and deliberation: New directions for democratic reform.* New Haven, CT: Yale University Press.

Fishkin, J. (1995). *The voice of the people: Public opinion and democracy.* New Haven, CT: Yale University Press.

Fishkin, J., & Farrar, C. (2005). Deliberative polling: From experiment to community resource. In J. Gastil & P. Levine (Eds.), *The deliberative democracy handbook: Strategies for effective civic engagement in the 21st century* (pp. 68–79). San Francisco: Jossey-Bass.

Fixdal, J. (1997). Consensus conferences as extended peer groups. *Science & Social Policy, 24*(6), 366–376.

Ford, P. (1998). *Don't stop there: Five adventures in civic journalism.* Washington, DC: Pew Center for Civic Journalism.

Ford, P. (2001). *Delving into the divide: A study of race reporting in forty-five news-rooms.* Washington, DC: Pew Center for Civic Journalism.

Frank, T. (1998). Triangulation nation: Affirming mediocrity in a jaded age. *The Baffler, 11,* 3–12, 75–93.

Frankel, M. (1995, May 21). Fix-it journalism. *New York Times Magazine,* p. 28.

Fraser, N. (1990). Rethinking the public sphere: A contribution to the critique of actually existing democracy. *Social Text, 25/26,* 56–80.

Friedland, L. (2000). Public journalism and community change. In A. Eksterowicz & R. Roberts (Eds.), *Public journalism and political knowledge* (pp. 121–142). Lanham, MD: Rowman & Littlefield.

Friedland, L. (2003). *Public journalism: Past and future.* Dayton, OH: Kettering Foundation Press.

Friedland, L., & Nichols, S. (2002). *Measuring civic journalism's progress: A report across a decade of activity.* Washington, DC: Pew Center for Civic Journalism.

Friedland, L., Rojas, H., Long, C., Abril, E., Hildebrandt, V., Kim, N., et al. (2006). *Surveying citizen journalism: Describing emerging phenomena that posit a reno-vation of the public sphere.* Paper presented at the Annual Convention of the Association for Education in Journalism and Mass Communication, San Francisco, CA.

Friedland, L., Sotirovic, M., & Daily, K. (1998). Public journalism and social capi-tal: The case of Madison, Wisconsin. In E. Lambeth, P. Meyer, & E. Thorson (Eds.), *Assessing public journalism* (pp. 191–220). Columbia, MO: University of Missouri Press.

Gade, P., Abel, S., Antecol, M., Hsueh, H., Hume, J., Morris, J., et al. (1998). Jour-nalists' attitudes toward civic journalism media roles. *Newspaper Research Journal, 19*(4), 10–26.

Gallo, J. (2003). Weblog journalism: Between infiltration and integration. In L. Gurak, S. Antonijevic, L. Johnson, C. Ratliff, & J. Reyman (Eds.), *Into the blogosphere: Rhetoric, community, and culture of weblogs.* Retrieved February 1, 2007 from http://blog.lib.umn.edu/blogosphere/weblog_journalism.html.

Garcelon, M. (2006). The *Indymedia* experiment: The Internet as movement facili-tator against institutional control. *Convergence: The International Journal of Research into New Media Technologies, 12*(1), 55–82.

Gartner, M. (1998). Seeing through the gimmicks. In E. Lambeth, P. Meyer, & E. Thorson (Eds.), *Assessing public journalism* (pp. 226–231). Columbia, MO: University of Missouri Press.

George, L. (2005, November 30). *Backfence.com* seven months after launch. *Press-Think.* Retrieved February 1, 2007 from http://journalism.nyu.edu/pubzone/weblogs/pressthink/2005/11/30/lz_bcfc.html

German, W. (2000, April 21). Nurturing the infant of public journalism. *San Fran-cisco Chronicle,* p. A25.

Gillis, T., & Moore, R. (2004, October). *Engaging journalism: Community journal-ism and its effects on social interaction and citizen empowerment in Sub-Saharan Africa.* Paper presented at the Global Fusion Convention, St. Louis, MO.

Gillmor, D. (2004). *We the media: Grassroots journalism by the people, for the people.* Sebastopol, CA: O'Reilly Media.

Glaberson, W. (1994, October 3). A new press role: Solving problems. *New York Times*, p. D6.

Glaser, M. (2004, March 9). Papers' online units allow editorial boards to lift veil with video, blogs. *Online Journalism Review*. Retrieved February 1, 2007 from http://www.ojr.org.

Glasser, T. (1999). The idea of public journalism. In T. Glasser (Ed.), *The idea of public journalism* (pp. 3–18). New York: Guilford.

Glasser, T. (2000). The politics of public journalism. *Journalism Studies, 1*(4), 683–686.

Glasser, T., & Bowers, P. (1999). Justifying change and control: An application of discourse ethics to the role of mass media. In D. Demers & K. Viswanath (Eds.), *Mass media, social control, and social change: A macrosocial perspective* (pp. 399–418). Ames, IA: Iowa State University Press.

Glasser, T., & Craft, S. (1998). Public journalism and the search for democratic ideals. In T. Liebes & J. Curran (Eds.), *Media, ritual and identity* (pp. 203–218). London: Routledge.

Glasser, T., & Lee, F. (2002). Repositioning the newsroom: The American experience with public journalism. In R. Kuhn & E. Neveu (Eds.), *Political journalism: New challenges, new practices* (pp. 203–224). London: Routledge.

Goidel, R. (2000). If you report it, will they care? Political knowledge and public journalism. In A. Eksterowicz & R. Roberts (Eds.), *Public journalism and political knowledge* (pp. 143–168). Lanham, MD: Rowman & Littlefield.

Goodnight, G. (1981). The personal, technical, and public spheres of argument: A speculative inquiry into the art of public deliberation. *Journal of the American Forensic Association, 18*(2), 214–227.

Gorgura, H. (2004, October). *Warblogging networks: Online spheres of dissensus.* Paper presented at the Annual Convention of the Association of Internet Researchers, Toronto, ON, Canada.

Greenberg, P. (1996, November 18). Public journalism harms newspapers' credibility. *Post & Courier*, p. A9.

Greer, J., & Mensing, D. (2006). The evolution of online newspapers: A longitudinal content analysis, 1997–2003. In X. Li (Ed.), *Internet newspapers: The making of a mainstream medium* (pp. 13–32). Mahwah, NJ: Lawrence Erlbaum.

Grimes, C. (1999). *Whither the civic journalism bandwagon?* (Discussion Paper D-36). Joan Shorenstein Center on Press, Politics and Public Policy, John F. Kennedy School of Government, Harvard University, Boston, MA.

Grubisich, T. (2006, March 12). The sweet (and sour) smell of success at *Your Hub. Online Journalism Review*. Retrieved February 1, 2007 from http://www.ojr.org.

Grundahl, J. (1995). The Danish consensus conference model. In S. Joss & J. Durant (Eds.), *Public participation in science: The role of consensus conferences in Europe* (pp. 31–40). London: Science Museum.

Gunaratne, S. (1998). Old wine in a new bottle: Public journalism, developmental journalism, and social responsibility. In M. Roloff (Ed.), *Communication yearbook 21* (pp. 277–321). Thousand Oaks, CA: Sage.

Guston, D. (1999). Evaluating the first U.S. consensus conference: The impact of the citizens' panel on telecommunications and the future of democracy. *Science, Technology & Human Values, 24*(4), 451–482.

Habermas, J. (1989). *The structural transformation of the public sphere: An inquiry into a category of bourgeois society.* Cambridge, MA: MIT Press.

Habermas, J. (1990). *Moral consciousness and communicative action.* Cambridge, MA: MIT Press.

Habermas, J. (1993). *Justification and application: Remarks on discourse ethics.* Cambridge, MA: MIT Press.

Hackett, R., & Zhao, Y. (1998). *Sustaining democracy? Journalism and the politics of objectivity.* Toronto: Garamond Press.

Halavais, A. (2002a, October). *Blogs and the social weather.* Paper presented at the Annual Convention of the Association of Internet Researchers, Maastricht, The Netherlands.

Halavais, A. (2002b, October). *The web as news: September 11 and new sources of web news.* Paper presented at the Annual Convention of the Association of Internet Researchers, Maastricht, The Netherlands.

Halavais, A. (2004, January). *Tracking ideas in the blogosphere.* Paper presented at the 37th Hawaii International Conference on System Sciences, Island of Hawaii, HI.

Hamlett, P. (2002, July). *Enhancing public participation in participatory public policy analysis concerning technology: A report of two Danish-style consensus conferences.* Paper presented at the International Summer Academy on Technology Studies, Deutchlandsberg, Austria.

Hansen, M. (1999). Tag ved laere af public journalism [Learn from public journalism]. In L. Kabel (Ed.), *Nye nyheder: Om nyhedsjournalistik og nyhedsdaekning i dagblade, radio, TV og online [New news: On news journalism and news coverage in daily newspapers, radio, TV, and online]* (pp. 215–219). Aarhus, Denmark: Ajour.

Hardt, H. (1999). Reinventing the press for the age of commercial appeals: Writings on and about public journalism. In T. Glasser (Ed.), *The idea of public journalism* (pp. 197–209). New York: Guilford.

Hargittai, E., Gallo, J., & Kane, M. (2005, May). *Cross-ideological discussions among a group of conservative and liberal bloggers.* Paper presented at the Annual Convention of the International Communication Association, New York, NY.

Harper, C. (2005, May). *Blogging and journalistic practice.* Paper presented at the Media in Transition Convention, Massachusetts Institute of Technology, Boston, MA.

Harris, S., Outlaw, W., & Paynter, B. (1993, December 26). Prisoners of violence. *Akron Beacon Journal,* pp. A1, A5–A7.

Harwood, R. (1991). *Citizens and politics: A view from main street.* Dayton, OH: Kettering Foundation Press.

Hayward, J. (1996). *Elitism, populism and European politics.* Oxford, UK: Oxford University Press.

Heider, D., McCombs, M., & Poindexter, P. (2006). What the public expects of local news. *Journalism & Mass Communication Quarterly, 82*(4), 952–967.

Heikkila, H. (2000). How to make thin journalism strong? Experiences of a public journalism project in Finland. *Nordicom Review, 21*(2), 83–100.

Heikkila, H., & Kunelius, R. (1996). Public journalism and its problems: A theoretical perspective. *Javnost - The Public, 3*(3), 81–95.

Heinonen, A., & Luostarinen, H. (2005, October). *Media journalism and public's journalism.* Paper presented at the International Seminar on Journalism Education, University of Helsinki, Helsinki, Finland.

Hendriks, C. (2005). Consensus conferences and planning cells: Lay citizen deliberation. In J. Gastil & P. Levine (Eds.), *The deliberative democracy handbook: Strategies for effective civic engagement in the 21st century* (pp. 80–110). San Francisco: Jossey–Bass.

Henriksen, K. (2001). *Da lytterne fik ordet [When the listeners got their say].* Aarhus, Denmark: Center for Journalism and Continuing Education.

Himelboim, I., & Southwell, B. (2005, October). *Are blogs actually an alternative information source compared to traditional media? Linking patterns in news blogs.* Paper presented at the Annual Convention of the Association of Internet Researchers, Chicago, IL.

Hindman, E. (2005). Jayson Blair, the *New York Times*, and paradigm repair. *Journal of Communication, 55*(2), 225–241.

Hindman, M., Tsiotsiouliklis, K., & Johnson, J. (2003, August). *Googlearchy: How a few heavily-linked sites dominate politics online.* Paper presented at the Annual Convention of the American Political Science Association, Philadelphia, PA.

Hippocrates, C. (1999). Public journalism: The media's intellectual journey. *Media International Australia Incorporating Culture & Policy, 90*, 65–78.

Hjarvad, S. (2000). Proximity: The name of the ratings game. *Nordicom Review, 21*(2), 63–81.

Hodges, L. (1997). Ruminations about the communitarian debate. In J. Black (Ed.), *Mixed news: The public/civic/communitarian journalism debate* (pp. 38–49). Mahwah, NJ: Lawrence Erlbaum.

Holley, M., Kirksey, R., & Paynter, B. (1993, March 2). Reach for top, mind your place. *Akron Beacon Journal*, pp. A1–A7.

Hopkins, K., & Matheson, D. (2005). Blogging the New Zealand election: The impact of new media practices on the old game. *Political Science, 57*(2), 93–105.

Howley, K. (2003). A poverty of voices: Street papers as communicative democracy. *Journalism: Theory, Practice & Criticism, 4*(3), 273–292.

Hoyt, M. (1992). The Wichita experiment: What happens when a newspaper tries to connect readership and citizenship? *Columbia Journalism Review*, July/August, 43–47.

Hoyt, M. (1995). Are you now, or will you ever be, a civic journalist? *Columbia Journalism Review*, September/October, 27–33.

Hoyt, M. (1996). Can James Fallows practice what he preaches? *Columbia Journalism Review*, November/December, 27–30.

Huang, H. (2006, August). *Deliberative reporting, conflict frame, and civic cognitions.* Paper presented at the Annual Convention of the Association for Education in Journalism and Mass Communication, San Francisco, CA.

Hudspith, R., & Kim, M. (2002). Learning from a university co-sponsored regional consensus conference. *Bulletin of Science, Technology & Society, 22*(3), 232–238.

Hutchins Commission. (1947). *A free and responsible press.* Chicago: University of Chicago Press.

Iggers, J. (1998). *Good news, bad news: Journalism ethics and the public interest.* Boulder, CO: Westview Press.

Ito, T. (2005). Public journalism and journalism in Japan. *Keio Communication Review, 27*, 43–63.

Iyengar, S. (1991). *Is anyone responsible? How television frames political issues.* Chicago: University of Chicago Press.

Jacobs, J. (2003, August). *Communication overexposure: The rise of blogs as a product of cybervoyeurism.* Paper presented at the Annual Convention of the Australia–New Zealand Communication Association, Brisbane, Australia.

Jacoby, I. (1995). The consensus development program of the National Institutes of Health: Current practices and historical perspectives. *International Journal of Technology Assessment in Health Care, 1*(4), 420–432.

Jankowski, N., & Jansen, M. (2003, December). *Indymedia: Exploration of an alternative Internet-based source of movement news.* Paper presented at the Digital News, Social Change and Globalization Convention, Hong Kong Baptist University, Hong Kong.

Jeffres, L., Cutietta, C., Lee, J., & Sekerka, L. (1999). Differences of community newspaper goals and functions in large urban areas. *Newspaper Research Journal, 20*(3), 86–98.

Joergensen, L. (2002). *Samspil mellem borgere og medier [Interplay of citizens and media]. Journalisten [The Journalist], 19*, 19.

Joergensen, L. (2005). *Laeserne vil have velourjournalistik [The readers want velvet journalism]. Journalisten [The Journalist], 14*, 8.

Joergensen, T. (1995). Consensus conferences in the health sector. In S. Joss & J. Durant (Eds.), *Public participation in science: The role of consensus conferences in Europe* (pp. 17–29). London: Science Museum.

Johnson, T., & Kaye, B. (2004). Wag the blog: How reliance on traditional media and the Internet influence credibility online. *Journalism & Mass Communication Quarterly, 81*(3), 622–642.

Johnson-Cartee, K. (2004). *News narratives and news framing: Constructing political reality.* Lanham, MD: Rowman & Littlefield.

Joss, S. (1995). Evaluating consensus conferences: Necessity or luxury? In S. Joss & J. Durant (Eds.), *Public participation in science: The role of consensus conferences in Europe* (pp. 89–108). London: Science Museum.

Joss, S. (1998). Danish consensus conferences as a model of participatory technology assessment: An impact study of consensus conferences on Danish Parliament and Danish public debate. *Science and Public Policy, 25*(1), 2–22.

Joss, S. (2002). Participation in parliamentary technology assessment: From theory to practice. In N. Vig & H. Paschen (Eds.), *Parliaments and technology: The development of technology assessment in Europe* (pp. 325–362). Albany, NY: State University of New York Press.

Joss, S., & Durant, J. (1995). The U.K. national consensus conference on plant biotechnology. *Public Understanding of Science, 4*(2), 195–204.

Jurkowitz, M. (1996, May 27). The media's best-kept secret. *Boston Globe Magazine,* p. 17.

Jurkowitz, M. (2000, April 26). Civic journalism: Taking stock after a decade. *Boston Globe,* p. F1.

Kambsgaard, M. (2005, March 3). Seniorsagen rammer radioen [Senior citizens on the radio]. *DR Midt & Vest.* Retrieved February 1, 2007 from http://www.dr.dk/Regioner/Vest/Tema/Seniorjob.

Kambsgaard, M., & Stephansen, P. (2003). *En levende fremtid: Et public journalism projekt paa DR Midt & Vest [A living future: A public journalism project at DR Midt & Vest]*. Odense, Denmark: University of Southern Denmark.

Katz, E., & Lazarsfeld, E. (1955). *Personal influence: The part played by people in the flow of mass communications.* New York: Free Press.

Keeping a Vigil. (1993, December 26). *Akron Beacon Journal,* p. A6.

Kennamer, D., & South, J. (2002). Election coverage reflects civic journalism values. *Newspaper Research Journal, 23*(4), 34–45.

Kim, E., & Hamilton, J. (2006). Capitulation to capital? *OhmyNews* as alternative media. *Media, Culture & Society, 28*(4), 541–560.

Kirksey, R., Holley, M., & Paynter, B. (1993, March 1). Disparity between the races growing in almost all facets. *Akron Beacon Journal,* pp. A1–A2, A4.

Kirksey, R., Jenkins, C., & Paynter, B. (1993, August 22). Public education: Win few, lose many. *Akron Beacon Journal,* pp. A1, A12–A14.

Kluver, L. (1995). Consensus conferences at the Danish Board of Technology. In S. Joss & J. Durant (Eds.), *Public participation in science: The role of consensus conferences in Europe* (pp. 41–49). London: Science Museum.

Knox, D., Cannon, C., & Paynter, B. (1993, November 2). Stopped short of success. *Akron Beacon Journal,* pp. A1, A6–A8.

Kramer, S. (1997). *Civic journalism: Six case studies.* Washington, DC: Pew Center for Civic Journalism.

Krippendorff, K. (2003). *Content analysis: An introduction to its methodology.* Newbury Park, CA: Sage.

Kunelius, R. (2001). Conversation: A metaphor and a method for better journalism. *Journalism Studies, 2*(1), 31–54.

Kurpius, D. (2002). Sources and civic journalism: Changing patterns of reporting? *Journalism & Mass Communication Quarterly, 79*(4), 853–866.

Lambeth, E. (1998). Public journalism as a democratic practice. In E. Lambeth, P. Meyer, & E. Thorson (Eds.), *Assessing public journalism* (pp. 15–35). Columbia, MO: University of Missouri Press.

Lasica, J. (2002). Blogging as a form of journalism. In J. Rodzvilla (Ed.), *We've got blog: How weblogs are changing our culture* (pp. 173–170). Cambridge, MA: Perseus.

Lasica, J. (2003). Blogs and journalism need each other. *Nieman Reports, 57*(3), 70–74.

Lee, S. (2001). Public journalism and non-elite actors and sources. *Newspaper Research Journal, 22*(3), 92–95.

Lemert, J. (1981). *Does mass communication change public opinion after all?* Chicago: Nelson-Hall.

Levidow, L. (1998). Democratizing technology—Or technologizing democracy? Regulating agricultural biotechnology in Europe. *Technology in Society, 20*(2), 211–226.

Levine, P. (1998, October). *The press in a deliberative democracy: On public journalism and its critics.* Paper presented at the "Public Journalism: A Critical Forum" Conference, University of South Carolina, Columbia, SC.

Levine, P., Fung, A., & Gastil, J. (2005). Future directions for public deliberation. In J. Gastil & P. Levine (Eds.), *The deliberative democracy handbook: Strategies for effective civic engagement in the 21st century* (pp. 271–288). San Francisco: Jossey-Bass.

Lichtenberg, J. (1999). Beyond the public journalism controversy. In R. Fullinwider (Ed.), *Civil society, democracy, and civic renewal* (pp. 341–354). Lanham, MD: Rowman & Littlefield.

Lippmann, W. (1922). *Public opinion.* New York: Free Press.

Lippmann, W. (1925). *The phantom public.* New York: Harcourt Brace.

Loka Institute. (2005). *Danish style, citizen-based deliberative consensus conferences on science & technology policy worldwide.* Washington, DC: Author.

London, S. (2004). *Creating citizens through public deliberation: How civic organizations in ten countries are using deliberative dialogue to build and strengthen democracy.* Dayton, OH: Kettering Foundation.

Loomis, D. (1998, August). *Is public journalism cheap journalism? Putting public journalists' money where their mouths are.* Paper presented at the Annual Convention of the Association for Education in Journalism and Mass Communication, Baltimore, MD.

Loomis, D., & Meyer, P. (2000). Opinion without polls: Finding a link between corporate culture and public journalism. *International Journal of Public Opinion Research, 12*(3), 276–284.

Love, S. (1993, December 28). Both sides of the story. *Akron Beacon Journal,* pp. A1, A4–A5.

Lund, A., Jensen, K., & Marosi, K. (2001). *Danskernes syn paa medier og demokrati [Danes' views on media and democracy].* Odense, Denmark: University of Southern Denmark.

Maier, S., & Potter, D. (2001). Public journalism through the lens: How television broadcasters covered campaign '96. *Journal of Broadcasting & Electronic Media, 45*(2), 320–334.

Mancini, P. (1997). Toqueville revisited: The gap between citizens and politics. *Harvard International Journal of Press/Politics, 2*(1), 131–135.

Marris, C., & Joly, P. (1999). Between consensus and citizens: Public participation in technology assessments in France. *Science Studies, 12*(2), 2–32.

Martin, C. (2001). The limits of community in public journalism. In G. Shepherd & E. Rothenbuhler (Eds.), *Communication and community* (pp. 235–250). Mahwah, NJ: Lawrence Erlbaum.

Massey, B. (1998). Civic journalism and nonelite sourcing: Making routine newswork of community connectedness. *Journalism & Mass Communication Quarterly, 75*(2), 394–407.

Massey, B. (1999, August). *Civic journalism and gender diversity in news-story sourcing.* Paper presented at the Annual Convention of the Association for Education in Journalism and Mass Communication, New Orleans, LA.

Matheson, D. (2004). Weblogs and the epistemology of the news: Some trends in online journalism. *New Media & Society, 6*(4), 443–468.

Matheson, D., & Allan, S. (2003, November). *Weblogs and the war in Iraq: Journalism for a network society?* Paper presented at the Digital Dynamics Conference, Loughborough, U.K.

Mayer, I., de Vries, J., & Geurts, J. (1995). An evaluation of the effects of participation in a consensus conference. In S. Joss & J. Durant (Eds.), *Public participation in science: The role of consensus conferences in Europe* (pp. 109–124). London: Science Museum.

Mayer, I., & Geurts, J. (1998). Consensus conferences as participatory policy analysis: A methodological contribution to the social management of technology. In P. Wheale, R. Schomburg, & P. Glasner (Eds.), *The social management of genetic engineering* (pp. 279–301). Aldershot, UK: Ashgate.

McChesney, R. (1999). *Rich media, poor democracy: Communication politics in dubious times.* Urbana, IL: University of Illinois Press.

McCombs, M. (2005). A look at agenda-setting: Past, present and future. *Journalism Studies, 6*(4), 543–547.

McDevitt, M., Gassaway, B., & Perez, F. (2000, August). *The making and unmaking of civic journalists: Influences of classroom and newsroom socialization.* Paper presented at the Annual Convention of the Association for Education in Journalism and Mass Communication, Phoenix, AZ.

McDonald, J. (1999). Mechanisms for public participation in environmental policy development: Lessons from Australia's first consensus conference. *Environmental and Planning Law Journal, 16*(3), 258–266.

McEaney, M., Allen, L., & Paynter, B. (1993, May 2). Streets where we live. *Akron Beacon Journal,* pp. A1, A8–A10.

McGregor, J., Comrie, M., & Campbell, J. (1998). Public journalism and proportional representation: The New Zealand experiment. *Australian Journalism Review, 20*(1), 1–22.

McGregor, J., Comrie, M., & Fountaine, S. (1999). Beyond the feel-good factor: Measuring public journalism in the 1996 New Zealand election campaign. *Harvard International Journal of Press/Politics, 4*(1), 66–77.

McGregor, J., Fountaine, S., & Comrie, M. (2000). From contest to content: The impact of public journalism on New Zealand election campaign coverage. *Political Communication, 17*(1), 133–148.

McKay, E., & Dawson, P. (1999). *Evaluation report: Phase 1.* Canberra, Australia: P. J. Dawson & Associates.

McMillan, S., Guppy, M., Kunz, W., & Reis, R. (1998). Public journalism: What difference does it make to editorial content? In E. Lambeth, P. Meyer, & E. Thorson (Eds.), *Assessing public journalism* (pp. 178–190). Columbia, MO: University of Missouri Press.

Mead, R. (2002). You've got blog: How to put your business, your boyfriend, and your life online. In J. Rodzvilla (Ed), *You've got blog: How weblogs are changing our culture* (pp. 47–56). Cambridge, MA: Perseus.

Meikle, G. (2003). *Indymedia* and the new net news. *Media Development, 4*, 3–6.

Meraz, S. (2005, August). *2004 Conventions: Media bloggers, non-media bloggers, and their network connections.* Paper presented at the Annual Convention of the Association for Education in Journalism and Mass Communication, San Antonio, TX.

Merrill, J. (1997). Communitarianism's rhetorical war against enlightenment liberals. In J. Black (Ed.), *Mixed news: The public/civic/communitarian journalism debate* (pp. 54–65). Mahwah, NJ: Lawrence Erlbaum.

Merrill, J. (2000). Social stability and harmony: A new mission for the press? *Asian Journal of Communication, 10*(2), 33–52.

Merrill, J., Blevens, F., & Gade, P. (2002). *Twilight of press freedom: The rise of people's journalism.* Mahwah, NJ: Lawrence Erlbaum.

Merritt, D. (1988, November 13). A new political contract must restore meaning to election campaigns. *Wichita Eagle,* p. A15.

Merritt, D. (1998). *Public journalism and public life: Why telling the news is not enough.* Mahwah, NJ: Lawrence Erlbaum.

Messner, M., & Terilli, S. (2005, February). *Gates wide open: The impact of weblogs on the gatekeeping role of the traditional media in the 2004 presidential election.* Paper presented at the Mid-Winter Convention of the Association for Education in Journalism and Mass Communication, Kennesaw, GA.

Meyer, P. (1998). If it works, how will we know? In E. Lambeth, P. Meyer, & E. Thorson (Eds.), *Assessing public journalism* (pp. 251–283). Columbia, MO: University of Missouri Press.

Meyer, P., & Potter, D. (2000). Hidden value: Polls and public journalism. In P. Lavrakas & M. Traugott (Eds.), *Election polls, the news media, and democracy* (pp. 113–141). New York: Seven Bridges Press.

Miller, E. (1994). *The Charlotte project: Helping citizens take back democracy.* St. Petersburg, FL: Poynter Institute for Media Studies.

Moore, R., & Gillis, T. (2005). Transforming communities: Community journalism in Africa. *Transformations, 10.* Retrieved February 1, 2007 from http://transformations/cqu.edu.au/journal/issue_10/article_06.shtml.

Mortensen, T., & Walker, J. (2002). Blogging thoughts: Personal publication as an online research tool. In A. Morrison (Ed.), *Researching ICTs in context* (pp. 249–279). Oslo, Norway: Intermedia.

Moscowitz, L. (2002). Civic approach not so different from traditional model. *Newspaper Research Journal, 23*(4), 62–75.

Mwangi, S. (2001). International public journalism. *Kettering Foundations Connections, 12*(1), 23–27.

Mwangi, S. (2002). *A survey of international media and democracy projects.* Wilberforce, OH: Center for International Studies, Central State University.

Nichols, S. (2004, August). *Public journalism: Using new institutionalism to explore the rise and spread of the movement.* Paper presented at the Annual Convention of the Association for Education in Journalism and Mass Communication, Toronto, ON, Canada.

Nichols, S., Friedland, L., Rojas, H., Cho, J., & Shah, D. (2006). Examining the effects of public journalism on civil society from 1994 to 2002: Organizational factors, project features, story frames, and citizen engagement. *Journalism & Mass Communication Quarterly, 83*(1), 77–100.

Nip, J. (2006). Exploring the second phase of public journalism. *Journalism Studies, 7*(2), 212–236.

Nofziger, L. (2000, January 2). The limits and wishful thinking of do-good journalism. *The Washington Times,* p. B8.

Nord, D. (2001). *Communities of journalism: A history of American newspapers and their readers.* Urbana, IL: University of Illinois Press.

O'Brien, S. (1996). [Letter to the editor]. *American Journalism Review,* October, 8.

Olson, K. (2004, April). *Citizens or journalists? Legal and ethical rules governing journalists' personal weblogs.* Paper presented at the Fifth International Symposium on Online Journalism, University of Texas, Austin, TX.

Outing, S. (2005, August 24). Modernizing the editorial page. *Editor & Publisher Interactive.* Retrieved February 1, 2007 from http://www.editorandpublisher.com.

Outlaw, W., Harris, S., & Paynter, B. (1993, December 27). If he looks like a criminal. *Akron Beacon Journal,* pp. A1, A5.

Page, B. (1996). *Who deliberates? Mass media in modern democracy.* Chicago: University of Chicago Press.

Palser, B. (2005). Journalism's backseat drivers. *American Journalism Review,* August/September, 43–51.

Papacharissi, Z. (2004, October). *The blogger revolution? Audiences as media producers.* Paper presented at the Annual Convention of the Association of Internet Researchers, Toronto, ON, Canada.

Parisi, P. (1997). Toward a philosophy of framing: News narratives for public journalism. *Journalism & Mass Communication Quarterly, 74*(4), 673–686.

Parisi, P. (1998). *The New York Times* looks at one block in Harlem: Narratives of race in journalism. *Critical Studies in Mass Communication, 15*(3), 236–254.

Parkin, F., & Taggart, P. (2000). *Populism*. London: Open University Press.

Paterno, S. (1996). Whither Knight-Ridder? *American Journalism Review*, January/February, 19–27.

Patterson, T. (1993). *Out of order*. New York: Vintage.

Patterson, T. (1998). Political roles of the journalist. In D. Graber, D. McQuail, & P. Norris (Eds.), *The politics of news: The news of politics* (pp. 17–32). Washington, DC: CQ Press.

Pauly, J. (1999). Journalism and the sociology of public life. In T. Glasser (Ed.), *The idea of public journalism* (pp. 134–151). New York: Guilford.

Payne, R. (1999, August). *Following in their footsteps: A lesson in launching public journalism*. Paper presented at the Annual Convention of the Association for Education in Journalism and Mass Communication, New Orleans, LA.

Pein, C. (2005). Blog-gate. *Columbia Journalism Review*, January/February, 30–35.

Peirce, N. (1994, June 27). Civic (public) journalism: New genre is taking hold. *New Orleans Times-Picayune*, p. B5.

Perry, D. (2003). *The roots of civic journalism: Darwin, Dewey, and Mead*. Lanham, MD: University Press of America.

Perry, K. (2004, February 19). Civic journalism gains momentum in Japanese newsrooms. *Japan Media Review*. Retrieved February 1, 2007 from http://www.japanmediareview.com/japan/media1077241122.php.

Peters, J. (1999). Public journalism and democratic theory: Four challenges. In T. Glasser (Ed.), *The idea of public journalism* (pp. 99–117). New York: Guilford.

Petralia, L. (2004). Public journalism: Moving the youth agenda forward. *Asia Pacific Media Educator, 15*, 17–31.

Pew Research Center for the People and the Press (1999). *Audience interests, business pressures and journalists' values*. Washington, DC: Author.

Pew Research Center for the People and the Press (2000). *Self censorship: How often and why*. Washington, DC: Author.

Pew Research Center for the People and the Press (2004). *How journalists see journalists in 2004*. Washington, DC: Author.

Pickard, V. (2006). Assessing the radical democracy of *Indymedia*: Discursive, technical, and institutional constructions. *Critical Studies in Media Communication, 23*(1), 19–38.

Poindexter, P., Heider, D., & McCombs, M. (2006). Watchdog or good neighbor? The public's expectations of local news. *Harvard International Journal of Press/Politics, 11*(1), 77–88.

Potter, D., & Kurpius, D. (2000). Public journalism and television news. In A. Eksterowicz & R. Roberts (Eds.), *Public journalism and political knowledge* (pp. 77–90). Lanham, MD: Rowman & Littlefield.

Purdue, D. (1999). Experiments in the governance of biotechnology: A case study of the UK national consensus conference. *New Genetics & Society, 18*(1), 79–99.

Putnam, R. (1995). Bowling alone: America's declining social capital. *Journal of Democracy, 6*(1), 65–78.

Quinland, M., Bucco, G., & Berens, C. (2004). *APME credibility roundtables study.* Lincoln, NE: University of Nebraska.

Race: The Great Divide. (1993, February 28). *Akron Beacon Journal,* p. A1.

Raines, H. (1996, February 26). The Fallows fallacy. *The New York Times,* p. D14.

Rasmussen, S. (2001). *Brobygning mellem medieoeer [Bridge-building between media islands].* Aarhus, Denmark: Center for Journalism and Continuing Education.

Redden, G. (2003). Read the whole thing: Journalism, weblogs and the remediation of the war in Iraq. *Media International Incorporating Culture and Policy, 109,* 153–166.

Redden, G., Caldwell, N., & Nguyen, A. (2003). Warblogging as critical social practice. *Southern Review, 36*(2), 68–79.

Reese, S., Gandy, O., & Grant, A. (Eds.) (2001). *Framing public life: Perspectives on media and our understanding of the social world.* Mahwah, NJ: Lawrence Erlbaum.

Reese, S., Rutigliano, L., Hyun, K., & Jaekwan, J. (2005, August). *Mapping the political blogosphere: Citizen-based media in the global news arena.* Paper presented at the Annual Convention of the Association for Education in Journalism and Mass Communication, San Antonio, TX.

Revah, S. (1996). Moving on. *American Journalism Review,* October, 8.

Reynolds, A. (1997, August). *The 1996 presidential campaign, civic journalism and local TV news: Does doing civic journalism make any difference?* Paper presented at the Annual Convention of the Association for Education in Journalism and Mass Communication, Chicago, IL.

Reynolds, A. (1999). Local television coverage of the NIC. In M. McCombs & A. Reynolds (Eds.), *The poll with a human face: The National Issues Convention experiment in political communication* (pp. 113–131). Mahwah, NJ: Lawrence Erlbaum.

Reynolds, G. (2004). The blogs of war. *National Interest, 75,* 59–74.

Reynolds, R. (2005, May). *Agenda-setting the Internet: Political news blogs and newspaper coverage of the 2004 U.S. Democratic presidential candidates.* Paper presented at the Annual Convention of the International Communication Association, New York, NY.

Rhodenbaugh, C. (1998, August). *Missing the link: Citizen-based journalism intent rather than election coverage content affects public trust in media.* Paper presented at the Annual Convention of the Association for Education in Journalism and Mass Communication, Baltimore, MD.

Richards, I. (2000). Public journalism and ethics. *Media International Australia Incorporating Culture and Policy, 95,* 171–182.

Riede, P. (1995, August). *Public journalism and the constraints on news content: A case study of "The People Project."* Paper presented at the Annual Convention of the Association for Education in Journalism and Mass Communication, Washington, DC.

Roberts, M., Wanta, W., & Dzwo, T. (2002). Agenda setting and issue salience online. *Communication Research, 29*(4), 452–465.

Romano, A. (2001). Inculcating public journalism philosophies into newsroom culture. *Australian Journalism Review, 23*(2), 43–62.

Romano, A., & Hippocrates, C. (2001). Putting the public back into journalism. In S. Tapsall & C. Varley (Eds.), *Journalism theories in practice* (pp. 166–184). Melbourne, Australia: Oxford University Press.

Roselle, L. (2003). Local coverage of the 2000 election in North Carolina. *American Behavioral Scientist, 46*(5), 600–616.

Rosen, J. (1991). Making journalism more public. *Communication, 12*(2), 267–284.

Rosen, J. (1994). Making journalism more public: On the political responsibilities of the media intellectual. *Critical Studies in Mass Communication, 11*(3), 363–388.

Rosen, J. (1995). Foreword. In A. Charity (Ed.), *Doing public journalism* (pp. v–vi). New York: Guilford.

Rosen, J. (1996). *Getting the connections right: Public journalism and the troubles in the press.* New York: Twentieth Century Fund Press.

Rosen, J. (1997). Public journalism as a democratic art. In J. Rosen, D. Merritt, & L. Austin (Eds.), *Public journalism: Lessons from experience* (pp. 3–34). Dayton, OH: Kettering Foundation Press.

Rosen, J. (1998). Imagining public journalism. In E. Lambeth, P. Meyer, & E. Thorson (Eds.), *Assessing public journalism* (pp. 46–56). Columbia, MO: University of Missouri Press.

Rosen, J. (1999a). *What are journalists for?* New Haven, CT: Yale University Press.

Rosen, J. (1999b). The action of the idea: Public journalism in built form. In T. Glasser (Ed.), *The idea of public journalism* (pp. 21–48). New York: Guilford.

Rosen, J. (2000). Questions and answers about public journalism. *Journalism Studies, 1*(4), 679–683.

Rosenberry, J. (2005). Few papers use online techniques to improve public communication. *Newspaper Research Journal, 26*(4), 61–73.

Rosendal, P. (2001). *Den skaeve skole: Et forsoeg paa borgerorienteret lokal journalistik* [*The uneven school: An experiment in citizen–oriented local journalism*]. Aarhus, Denmark: Center for Journalism and Continuing Education.

Rosendal, P., & Bro, P. (1998, January 19). Hvid og sort skole i et hus [White and black school under one roof]. *Jyllands-Posten Koebenhavn*, p. A1.

Rosenfeld, H. (1995, October 1). We regret to report that civic journalism is a bad idea. *Times Union*, p. E5.

Rothenburg, M. (2003, October). *Weblogs and the semantic web.* Paper presented at the Annual Convention of the Association of Internet Researchers, Toronto, ON, Canada.

Roush, J. (2003, August). *Elite and non-elite sourcing in civic and traditional journalism news projects.* Paper presented at the Annual Convention of the Association for Education in Journalism and Mass Communication, Kansas City, KS.

Rowe, G., & Frewer, L. (2005). A typology of public engagement methods. *Science, Technology & Human Values, 30*(2), 251–290.

Ruggiero, L., & Craft, J. (2001). An objective measure of the influence of public journalism: Framing a yardstick for connections sought by a new journalistic paradigm—A pilot study. *Southwestern Mass Communication Journal, 16*(2), 36–47.

Ruggiero, T. (2004). Paradigm repair and changing journalistic perceptions of the Internet as an objective news source. *Convergence: The International Journal of Research into New Media Technologies, 10*(4), 92–106.

Rutigliano, L. (2004, April). *When the audience is the producer: The art of the collaborative weblog.* Paper presented at the Fifth International Symposium on Online Journalism, University of Texas, Austin, TX.

Ruusunoksa, L. (2005a, September). *Developing a more participatory approach to local reporting: The civic reporter at Ita-Hame.* Paper presented at the conference on "Problems of the News Media: Focuses, Methodologies and Innovations in Journalism Research," Department of Journalism and Mass Communication, University of Tampere, Tampere, Finland.

Ruusunoksa, L. (2005b, August). *Public journalism at a Finnish regional newspaper: Redefining the roles of the journalist and the reader.* Paper presented at the Annual Convention of the Nordic Association of Media and Communication Research, Aalborg, Denmark.

Ruusunoksa, L. (2006, May). *Public journalism and public sphere(s): Citizen–oriented public sphere in a national, regional, and local context.* Paper presented at the Public Sphere(s) and Their Boundaries Convention, University of Tampere, Tampere, Finland.

Ryan, M. (2001). Journalistic ethics, objectivity, existential journalism, standpoint epistemology, and public journalism. *Journal of Mass Media Ethics, 16*(1), 3–22.

Ryfe, D. (2002). The practice of deliberative democracy: A study of 16 deliberative organizations. *Political Communication, 19*(3), 359–377.

Schroll, C. (1999). Theorizing the flip side of civic journalism: Democratic citizenship and ethical readership. *Communication Theory, 9*(3), 321–345.

Schudson, M. (1978). *Discovering the news: A social history of American newspapers.* New York: Basic Books.

Schudson, M. (1999). What public journalism knows about journalism but doesn't know about the public. In T. Glasser (Ed.), *The idea of public journalism* (pp. 118–133). New York: Guilford.

Securing Your Home. (1993, December 26). *Akron Beacon Journal,* p. A6.

Shaw, D. (1999). The press as player. *Columbia Journalism Review,* November/December, 73–75.

Shepard, A. (1994). The gospel of public journalism. *American Journalism Review,* September, 28–34.

Shepard, A. (2000). You! Read this. *American Journalism Review,* November, 44–52.

Shirky, C. (2003, February 8). Power laws, weblogs, and inequality. *Clay Shirky's writings about the Internet.* Retrieved February 1, 2007 from http://www.shirky.com/writings/powerlaw_weblog.html.

Siebert, F., Peterson, T., & Schramm, W. (1956). *Four theories of the press*. Urbana, IL: University of Illinois Press.

Simmons, H. (1999). How public journalism set the agenda for a public safety complex. *Newspaper Research Journal, 20*(4), 82–90.

Singer, J. (2005). The political j-blogger: Normalizing a new media form to fit old norms and practices. *Journalism: Theory, Practice & Criticism, 6*(2), 173–198.

Sirianni, C., & Friedland, L. (2001). *Civic innovation in America: Community empowerment, public policy and the movement for civic renewal*. Berkeley, CA: University of California Press.

Skube, M. (1999, December 5). Civic journalism ideal is lofty, but not very realistic. *Atlanta Journal and Constitution*, p. 12L.

Smith, H., & Wales, C. (2000). Citizens juries and deliberative democracy. *Political Studies, 48*(1), 51–65.

Smolkin, R. (2004). The expanding blogosphere. *American Journalism Review*, June/July, 38–43.

Snow, T. (1996, September 12). Comment: Can journalists become priests? *Detroit News*, p. A13.

Soellinge, J. (1999). Danish newspapers: Structure and developments. *Nordicom Review, 20*(1), 31–76.

Soendergaard, U. (2005). *Berlingskes redningsplan: Taettere paa laeserne [Berlingske's rescue plan: Closer to the readers]*. Aarhus, Denmark: Center for Journalism and Continuing Education.

Stein, M. (1994). In praise of public journalism. *Editor & Publisher, 127*(48), *15*, 45.

Stempel, G., & Culbertson, H. (1984). The prominence and dominance of news sources in newspaper medical coverage. *Journalism Quarterly, 61*(3), 671–676.

Stengrim, L. (2005). Negotiating postmodern democracy, political activism, and knowledge production: *Indymedia*'s grassroots and e-savvy answer to media oligopoly. *Communication and Critical/Cultural Studies, 2*(4), 281–304.

Stepp, C. (1996). Public journalism: Balancing the scales. *American Journalism Review*, May, 38–40.

Technorati (2007, February 1). Currently tracking 52 million blogs. *Technorati*. Retrieved February 1, 2007 from http://www.technorati.com.

Tew, C. (2006, August). *The popularization of the Baghdad blogger: A case study of the authentication of a warblogger and social affiliation between bloggers and journalists*. Paper presented at the Annual Convention of the Association for Education in Journalism and Mass Communication, San Francisco, CA.

The Focus Groups. (1993, February 28). *Akron Beacon Journal*, p. A6.

Thompson, J. (1995). *The media and modernity: A social theory of the media*. Stanford, CA: Stanford University Press.

Thorson, E., Friedland, L., & Anderson, P. (1997). *Civic lessons*. Washington, DC: Pew Center for Civic Journalism.

Thorson, E., Ognianova, E., Coyle, J., & Lambeth, E. (1998). Audience impact of a multimedia civic journalism project in a small Midwestern community. In E. Lambeth, P. Meyer, & E. Thorson (Eds.), *Assessing public journalism* (pp. 158–177). Columbia, MO: University of Missouri Press.

Thorson, E., Shim, J., & Yoon, D. (2002, August). *Crime and violence in Charlotte, NC: The impact of a civic journalism project on knowledge, mental elaboration and civic behaviors.* Paper presented at the Annual Convention of the Association for Education in Journalism and Mass Communication, Miami Beach, FL.

Toft, J. (1996). Denmark: Seeking a broad-based consensus on gene technology. *Science & Public Policy, 23*(3), 171–174.

Tracey, M. (2003, December 13). Civic journalism double-edged; Movement may be good for bottom line but is it good for public or the media? *Rocky Mountain News*, p. 14C.

Venables, D. (2001). *City Voice*: A community newspaper does public journalism. *Australian Journalism Review, 23*(2), 21–41.

Vercelotti, T. (2001, September). *Something to talk about: The effects of civic journalism on political discourse and engagement.* Paper presented at the Annual Convention of the American Political Science Association, San Francisco, CA.

Verykoukis, A. (1998, August). *A journalism less ordinary? The inspirational tone of public journalism.* Paper presented at the Annual Convention of the Association for Education in Journalism and Mass Communication, Baltimore, MD.

Villano, D. (1996). Has Knight-Ridder's flagship gone adrift? Trouble at the Miami Herald. *Columbia Journalism Review*, January/February, 29–33.

Voakes, P. (1999). Civic duties: Newspaper journalists' views on public journalism. *Journalism & Mass Communication Quarterly, 76*(4), 756–774.

Waddell, L. (1997). In the beginning there was Columbus. In J. Black (Ed.), *Mixed news: The public/civic/communitarian journalism debate* (pp. 94–95). Mahwah, NJ: Lawrence Erlbaum.

Wall, M. (2004, August). *Blogs of war: The changing nature of news in the 21st century.* Paper presented at the Annual Convention of the Association for Education in Journalism and Mass Communication, Toronto, ON, Canada.

Wall, M. (2005). Blogs of war: Weblogs as news. *Journalism: Theory, Practice & Criticism, 6*(2), 153–172.

Wall, M. (2006). Blogging Gulf War II. *Journalism Studies, 7*(1), 111–126.

Wallsten, K. (2005, September). *Political blogs and the bloggers who blog them: Is the political blogosphere an echo chamber?* Paper presented at the Annual Convention of the Political Science Association, Washington, DC.

Ward, H. (1996). Doing public journalism. *Editor & Publisher, 129*(7), 23.

Warhover, T. (2000). Public journalism and the press: The Virginian-Pilot experience. In A Eksterowicz & R. Roberts (Eds.), *Public journalism and political knowledge* (pp. 43–60). Lanham, MD: Rowman & Littlefield.

Weaver, D., Beam, R., Brownlee, B., Voakes, P., & Wilhoit, G. (2006). *The American journalist in the 21st century: U.S. news people at the dawn of the 21st century.* Mahwah, NJ: Lawrence Erlbaum.

Weaver, D., & Wilhoit, G. (1996). *The American journalist in the 1990s: U.S. news people at the end of an era.* Mahwah, NJ: Lawrence Erlbaum.

Welsh, P. (2005, February). *Revolutionary vanguard or echo chamber? Political blogs and the mainstream media.* Paper presented at the Annual Convention of the International Network for Social Network Analysis, Redondo Beach, CA.

Whelan, D. (2003). In a fog about blogs. *American Demographics, 25*(6), 22–23.

Willey, K. (2003). Readers glimpse an editorial board's thinking. *Nieman Reports, 57*(3), 88–90.

Witt, L. (2004a). Is public journalism morphing into the public's journalism? *National Civic Review, 93*(3), 49–57.

Witt, L. (2004b, Winter). Do we need a name change? *Civic Journalism Interest Group News,* Winter, 3.

Woo-Young, C. (2005). Online civic participation and political empowerment: Online media and public opinion formation in Korea. *Media, Culture & Society, 27*(6), 925–935.

Wright, C. (2003). Parking Lott: The role of weblogs in the fall of senator Trent Lott. *Gnovis, 2.* Retrieved February 1, 2007 from http://gnovis.georgetown.edu/article.cfm?articleID=25.

Yankelovitch, D. (1991). *Coming to public judgment: Making democracy work in a complex world.* Syracuse, NY: Syracuse University Press.

Yardley, J. (1996, September 30). Public journalism: Bad news. *The Washington Post,* p. C2.

Ye, X., & Li, X. (2006). Internet newspapers' public forum and user involvement. In X. Li (Ed.), *Internet newspapers: The making of a mainstream medium* (pp. 243–259). Mahwah, NJ: Lawrence Erlbaum.

Zang, B. (1995, August). *Missing voices in the civic/public journalism debate: I never thought a newspaper could ask what if and other citizen-reader observations.* Paper presented at the Annual Convention of the Association for Education in Journalism and Mass Communication, Washington, DC.

Zelizer, B. (1992). CNN, the Gulf War, and journalistic practice. *Journal of Communication, 42*(1), 66–81.

Zelizer, B. (1999). Making the neighborhood work: The improbabilities of public journalism. In T. Glasser (Ed.), *The idea of public journalism* (pp. 152–172). New York: Guilford.

INDEX